# THE CHAMBERLIN READER:
The Education and Writings of Harry D. Chamberlin
1907-1942

Edited and with Commentary by Warren C. Matha

Xenophon Press

# THE CHAMBERLIN READER:
## The Education and Writings of Harry D. Chamberlin
## 1907-1942
### Brigadier General of Cavalry
### The United States Army

Editing and Commentary by Warren C. Matha,
Author of *General Chamberlin: America's Equestrian Genius*

Copyright © 2020 by Warren C. Matha

All rights reserved. No part of this work may be reproduced or transmitted in any form or by any means, electronic or mechanical, including photocopying, or by any information storage or retrieval system except by written permission from the publisher.

Photos of the Inter-Allied Games of 1919 and the practice sessions related to those games are private photos taken for an officer of the United States Army that reside in the editor's personal photo collection.
The Mounted Service School texts, *Saumur Notes on Equitation* and *The Manual of Equitation of the French Army for 1912* are publications of the French Army translated into English by the United States Army and reside in the public domain.
The West Point text books *Elements of Hippology* by F.C. Marshall and *Horses, Saddles, and Bridles* by General William H. Carter reside in the public domain.
The booklet *École d'application de Cavalerie* is a publication of the French Army and resides in the public domain.
All re-prints of Chamberlin articles and photos from *The Cavalry Journal* and *Riding and Schooling Horses* [Xenophon 2020] are with permission from the publisher, The U.S. Cavalry and Armor Association. The reprints of other Chamberlin articles and monographs reside in the public domain since they were printed originally at U.S. Government expense, in *The Rasp*, or as U.S. Army training materials.
The quotations from *Breaking and Riding with Military Commentaries* by James Fillis (aka *Principles of Dressage and Equitation*) are re-printed with the permission of Xenophon Press.
Photos supplied by the United States Equestrian Team Foundation are re-printed with the Foundation's permission. All photos of the Olympic Games of 1932 are reproduced with the permission of the U.S. Olympic Committee. Other photos reside in the public domain as photos of the U.S. Army, the Italian Army, and the French Army. The CRTC Marching Schedule is a U.S. Army document. The photo of William Steinkraus on Bold Minstrel at Hickstead, we reproduce with the permission of the copyright holder *L'Année Hippique*/Jean Bridel.

Published by Xenophon Press LLC
7518 Bayside Road, Franktown Virginia 23413
XenophonPress@gmail.com

ISBN: 9781948717267

Front Cover Photo "Major Harry D. Chamberlin on Pleasant Smile jumps an obstacle on the 1932 Olympic Three-Day Event's cross-country course. The course extends 22 ½ miles of steep hills, deep gullies, and 49 obstacles. Chamberlin lost his hat in a fall at previous jump." Photo courtesy of Lydia Moore and US Olympic Committee.
Back Cover Photo "Lt. Col. Harry D. Chamberlin on High Hat in the mid-1930's rides Pariani Borsarelli model 320 saddle." Photo courtesy of Lydia Moore nee Chamberlin

***Figure 1.*** *Major Harry Dwight Chamberlin prepares for the 1932 Olympics on his prized jumper Tanbark as they surmount a 5'3" jump. Chamberlin displays uncanny abilities as a horseman and genius as a theorist. Photo courtesy of Ms. Lydia Moore.*

# Contents

Introduction: Thirty-four Years of Education, Riding, and Writing ............ 1

1. The West Point Years, Horsemanship 1907–1910 ................................... 7

   Checklist for Hoof Care and Pre-purchase: Never touch a healthy frog! The sole takes care of itself! Always trot them barefoot on concrete!" In the commanding officer's discretion, horses may go barefoot when in garrison.

   Conformation Study: "The long-distance weight carrier sound after 2500 miles of continuous march."

2. The Mounted Service School 1915–1917 ............................................. 16

   *Saumur Notes on Equitation*: "The French cavalry's guide to horse training."

   Except from *The Manual of Equitation of the French Army for 1912* (FEM)

   James Fillis, *Principles of Dressage and Equitation* [Xenophon Press 2017] On the Rider's Use of the Hands: "giving and taking."

3. The Inter-Allied Games of 1919:
   A Turning Point in the American Jumping Style .................................. 77

   The Practice Sessions: "the old ways meet the new."

   The Games: "In jumping, the Italians steal the show and astound the Americans."

4. The Evolving American Jumping Style 1920–1922 ............................... 94

   *Observations on Riding and Training Jumpers* by Major Harry D. Chamberlin (*The Rasp 1922*)

   The Early Evolution of the American Jumping Style in Photos.

5. The French Cavalry School for Advanced Riding
   at Saumur, France 1922–1923 ............................................................. 115

   *École d'Application de Cavalerie* a Booklet Published at Saumur (1923)

6. The Italian Cavalry School for Advanced Riding
   at Tor di Quinto, Italy 1923–1924 ........................................................ 141

   Photos of the Riders at Tor di Quinto.

*The Italian Cavalry School at Tor di Quinto* by Major Harry D. Chamberlin (*The Cavalry Journal 1924*)

Major Chamberlin's comments regarding the Italian Method.

7. The Olympic Games of 1932 .................................................................. 150

    The Three-Day Event in Photos: Team Gold for America.

    *The Prix des Nations* Jumping Competition in Photos: Individual Silver for Chamberlin.

8. Chamberlin Writings in Periodicals, Letters, and Manuals 1934–1941 .. 163

    *The Modern Seat: A Discussion of the Differences Between the Seats of Various Countries (The Cavalry Journal 1934)*

    Letter to Col. Albert Phillips on Saddle Design. (1935)

    *The Conformation of Three-Day Event Horses* (*The Cavalry Journal* 1937)

    *High School for Horses* (*The Cavalry Journal* 1937)

    *Cavalry Training* (*The Cavalry Journal* 1940)

    *Crossing Rivers* (*The Cavalry Journal* 1941)

    *Horsemanship and Horsemastership 1942 Edition.* The Cavalry School, Ft. Riley Kansas, 1942. Writings, editorial supervision, and photographs by Brigadier-General Harry D. Chamberlin prepared in late 1941. Excerpt: "The Military Seat."

    *Breaking, Training, and Reclaiming Cavalry Horses*—Four simple exercises to break, train and reclaim cavalry horses, polo ponies, hunters, jumpers, eventers, hacks, and off-the-track Thoroughbreds. (Monograph 1941)

9. The American Military Riding Style ..................................................... 231

    The Military Seat aka "The Chamberlin-Military Seat" in Photos (1942)

    The American Jumping Style According to Chamberlin in Photos (1942)

    The U.S. Cavalry's Endurance Riding Protocol (1942) "30 miles a day indefinitely; 100 miles in 24 hours and be prepared for combat the next day."

    The U.S. Cavalry's Method to Negotiate a Steep Slide. "There is no exception to the rule that the body must be inclined forward *at all times*…"—Chamberlin.

    The Olympic Gold Medalist William Steinkraus rides Bold Minstrel and demonstrates the teachings of the Cavalry Replacement Training Center.

10. The End of the Trail .............................................................................. 243

    Chamberlin as soldier, author, trainer, teacher, theorist, and horseman.

# TABLE OF PHOTOS

Figure 1: *Chamberlin on Tanbark* .... v
Figure 2: *"...a good head, neck, shoulder* ........................... 13
Figure 3: *Deadwood* ....................... 14
Figure 4: *Deadwood from the front* .. 15
Figure 5. *Deadwood from the back* .. 15
Figure 6. *A French officer* ............... 77
Figure 7: *At the practice sessions* .... 78
Figure 8: *Another French officer* ..... 78
Figure 9: *Another French officer applies the "close seat"* ............... 79
Figure 10: *An American officer applies the "close seat"* ............... 79
Figure 11: *This Italian officer* ........ 80
Figure 12: *Another view of the French Cavalry's "close seat* ...... 80
Figure 13: *Another French Officer* .. 81
Figure 14: *Another Italian officer* ... 81
Figure 15: *Another photo of a French officer in* ..................... 82
Figure 16: *A Belgian officer* ........... 82
Figure 17: *A Belgian officer* ........... 83
Figure 18: *This officer with stirrup irons "home"* ................. 83
Figure 19: *Notice the tension on the reins* ............................. 84
Figure 20: *This French officer keeps the close seat* ..................... 84
Figure 21: *The rider's position over burdens the horse's hindquarters* ... 85
Figure 22: *Another French example*. 85
Figure 23: *Feet forward* ................. 86
Figure 24: *A Belgian officer* ........... 86
Figure 25: *Another example of the French 'close seat* ....................... 87
Figure 26: *Another variation with the upper body more forward* ........... 87
Figure 27: *French officer with his heels up* ..................... 88
Figure 28: *This Italian officers displays the method of Federico Caprilli* .. 88
Figure 29: *Italy's Major Ubertalli and Major Caffaratti* ..................... 89
Figure 30: *Ubertalli and Caffaratti clear another* ............................. 89
Figure 31: *Two other Italian officers, Captain Aluisi and Major Antonelli* ....................... 90
Figure 32: *Two more riders display the Italian jumping style* ................ 90
Figure 33: *Two French officers show their style* ................................. 91
Figure 34: *A Belgian officer* ........... 92
Figure 35: *Another officer surmounts* ............................... 92
Figure 36: *This French officer struggles* ..................................... 95
Figure 37: *Major Ubertalli achieves a personal triumph* ..................... 95
Figure 38: *Correct Position at Top of Jump* .................................... 97
Figure 39: *Wrong Position at Top of Jump* .................................... 98
Figure 40: *Wrong Position at Top of Jump* ................................... 100
Figure 41: *Correct Position at Top of Jump* ................................... 101
Figure 42: *Correct Position On Landing* .................................. 103
Figure 43: *Wrong Position On Landing* .................................. 107
Figure 44: *Adna R. Chaffee, Jr.* ... 108
Figure 45: *Captain Innis Palmer Swift* .......................... 109

Figure 46: *The French style 1912*.. 110
Figure 47: *The style 1914*............ 110
Figure 48: *The style 1920*............ 111
Figure 49: *This photo was taken in 1920*................... 111
Figure 50: *The style 1923*............ 112
Figure 51: *No rider weight on the horse's loins* ............. 112
Figure 52: *The Italian influence 1923* ..................... 112
Figure 53: *Horse and rider beginning to descend* .............. 113
Figure 54: *Good position* ............ 113
Figure 55: *"The rider's body should be inclined more forward*............. 113
Figure 56: *The rider has lost contact* ..................... 114
Figure 57: *The rider stays with his horse* ................... 114
Figure 58: *Saumur The Main Building*................. 118
Figure 59: *Saumur School of Cavalry Applications* ........................... 118
Figure 60: *Saumur Introduction*.. 119
Figure 61: *Saumur Introduction*.. 119
Figure 62: *Saumur Introduction*.. 120
Figure 63: *Saumur Introduction*.. 120
Figure 64: *Saumur Campaign Honors* .................. 121
Figure 65: *Saumur The Commandant*.......................... 121
Figure 66: *Saumur The Headquarters*......................... 122
Figure 67: *Saumur The Town*...... 122
Figure 68: *Saumur Equitation*..... 123
Figure 69: *Saumur The Hall of Honor*................................ 123
Figure 70: *Saumur A ride along the promenade*....................... 124

Figure 71: *Saumur Combat Exercises* ................................. 124
Figure 72: *Saumur The Hospital*.. 125
Figure 73: *Saumur Surgery for Horses* ................................... 125
Figure 74: *Saumur Hoof Care* ..... 126
Figure 75: *Saumur Grooming and Stable Call*............................ 126
Figure 76: *Saumur The Flying Fox* 127
Figure 77: *Saumur The Museum of the Horse* ............................... 127
Figure 78: *Saumur The Charge of Richefeu*............................. 128
Figure 79: *Saumur The Chief of Equitation*.......................... 128
Figure 80: *Saumur d'Ecuyer*........ 129
Figure 81: *Saumur d'Ecuyer*........ 129
Figure 82: *Saumur au Piaffer* ..... 130
Figure 83: *Saumur Jumping Obstacles*.............................. 130
Figure 84: *Saumur Commandant Watel*............... 131
Figure 85: *Saumur Jumping cross country*................................... 131
Figure 86: *Saumur A military jumping course* ...................... 132
Figure 87: *Saumur A steeplechase*. 132
Figure 88: *Saumur Polo*.............. 133
Figure 89: *Saumur High School* .. 133
Figure 90: *Saumur at Liberty* ...... 134
Figure 91: *Saumur at Liberty* ...... 134
Figure 92: *Saumur A beauty of a horse*................................. 135
Figure 93: *Saumur an Angelo-Arab*..................... 135
Figure 94: *Saumur Sabre Instruction*..................... 136
Figure 95: *Saumur Physical Exercise* ..................... 136

Figure 96: *Saumur More Exercise*. 137
Figure 97: *Saumur Cross Country Riding*.................... 137
Figure 98: *Saumur Swimming Rivers*.................... 138
Figure 99: *Saumur A Combat Vehicle*.................... 138
Figure 100: *Saumur Military Maneuvers*.................... 139
Figure 101: *Saumur Digging In*.. 139
Figure 102: *Saumur Combat Vehicle*.................... 140
Figure 103: *Saumur Outdoor Work*.................... 140
Figure 104: *Saumur The Horse*... 140
Figure 105: *An Instructor at Tor di Qunito* .................... 141
Figure 106: *Descending slides*...... 142
Figure 107: *Riders remain forward* 142
Figure 108: *An Italian officer*...... 143
Figure 109: *Major Ubertalli* ........ 143
Figure 110: *Ubertalli's triumph* ... 143
Figure 111: *Captain Argo* ........... 150
Figure 112: *Lt. Co. Kido*............. 151
Figure 113: *Lt. Schummelketel*..... 151
Figure 114: *Captain Yamamoto*... 152
Figure 115: *Mortanges of Holland*. 152
Figure 116: *Mortanges on Marcroix*.................... 153
Figure 117: *Mortanges on Marcroix*.................... 153
Figure 118: *Lt. von Rosen of Sweden*.................... 154
Figure 119: *Lt. van Lennep of Holland*.................... 154
Figure 120: *Major Chamberlin*.... 155
Figure 121: *Lt. van Lennep* ........ 155
Figure 122: *Major Chamberlin*.... 156
Figure 123: *Lt. Thompson*........... 156

Figure 124: *Captain Hallberg* ..... 157
Figure 125: *Baron Nishi* ............. 158
Figure 126: *Hallberg on Kornett*.. 158
Figure 127: *A most difficult course*.159
Figure 128: *Lt. Francke of Sweden* 159
Figure 129: *Baron Nishi* ............. 160
Figure 130: *Chamberlin on Show Girl*.................... 160
Figure 131: *Bradford on Joe Aleshire*.................... 161
Figure 132: *Captain Hallberg takes a tumble*.................... 161
Figure 133: *Chamberlin and Show Girl* .................... 162
Figure *134*: *Chamberlin-Military Seat*.................... 231
Figure 135: *Snaffle Bridle* ........... 232
Figure 136: *Lt. Thompson*........... 232
Figure 137: *Chamberlin with short stirrups* .................... 233
Figure 138: *Chamberlin up* ......... 234
Figure 139: *Chamberlin up* ......... 234
Figure 140: *Chamberlin up* ......... 235
Figure 141: *Chamberlin up* ......... 235
Figure 142: *Lower legs correct*...... 236
Figure 143: *Chamberlin on Tanbark*.................... 236
Figure 144: *Lt. Wofford up* ......... 237
Figure 145: *Chamberlin on Tanbark* .................... 237
Figure 146: *CRTC Long Distance Riding Protocol*.................... 238
Figure 147: *Breakneck Canyon*.... 240
Figure 148: *Proper seat to negotiate a slide*.................... 240
Figure 149 *William Steinkraus on Bold Minstrel*.................... 242
Figure 150: *Brig. Gen. Chamberlin*.................... 245

# TABLE OF ILLUSTRATIONS

Diagram of the Rider's Base of Support ....................................................... 198

Image of the Horse Soldier ........................................................................... 211

1st  Rein Effect:  Right Opening Rein ......................................................... 226

2nd  Rein Effect: Right Rein of Direct Opposition ...................................... 227

3rd  Rein Effect: Right Bearing Rein or Neck Rein .................................... 228

4th  Rein Effect: Right Rein of Indirect
Opposition in Front of the Withers ....................................................... 229

5th  Rein Effect: Right Rein of Indirect Opposition
in Rear of the Withers ........................................................................... 230

# Introduction

By
Warren C. Matha, Editor
Thirty-four Years of Education Riding, and Writing
1907–1941

Those who have read *General Chamberlin: America's Equestrian Genius* [Xenophon Press 2020] know that Brigadier General Harry D. Chamberlin, to this day, garners international acclaim as a great theorist, author, teacher, trainer, and horseman. He begins writing about horsemanship in the 1920's and continues writing on the subject until November of 1941. The influence on American horsemanship of General Chamberlin's theories and writings remains second to none. The influence on international horsemanship of his theories and writings in eventing and jumping remains second only to that of Federico Caprilli.

Three of the most renown American horsemen of the last fifty years recognize Chamberlin's genius and his contributions to educated riding:

James Wofford—Olympic silver medalist, renown author and eventing coach. Mr. Wofford has had at least one student on every U.S. Olympic, World Championship, or Pan Am team since 1978. He writes: "Chamberlin is to horsemanship as Mozart is to music," and "not a day goes by without my quoting from one of Chamberlin's works, or applying his methods. We are the beneficiaries of Col. Chamberlin's genius, and horses around the world live far more comfortable and productive lives because of his work" [1]

George H. Morris—Olympic team silver medalist, the father of hunt seat equitation, president of the United States Show Jumping Hall of Fame, world-renown author and teacher. His students won medals in the Olympic

---

[1] Wofford, James, Forward to *General Chamberlin: America's Equestrian Genius*, Warren Matha, Xenophon Press 2020

Games of 1984, 1992, 1996, and 2004. He writes of Chamberlin: "this one man is the founding father of equestrian sport in the United States." [2]

William Steinkraus—The first American to win an Olympic individual gold medal, the winner of more than 500 awards in national and international competition. Mr. Steinkraus, a graduate of Ft. Riley's Cavalry Replacement Training Center, studied Chamberlin's works intensely. He rode for the United States Equestrian Team for 22 years. He served as chairman of the International Equestrian Federation's World Cup jumping committee for 10 years. He writes of Chamberlin: "So often, I think I have come up with an idea of my own, only to find it clearly stated in one of his books."[3]

In *The Chamberlin Reader*, you will find Chamberlin's difficult to locate writings on jumping obstacles; evaluating horses and their conformation; re-training off-the-track Thoroughbreds, polo ponies, and cavalry horses; developing the rider's seat; riding cross country; and training riders in methods that helped William Steinkraus win Olympic gold in 1968.

In addition, you will find excerpts from texts on horsemanship that Chamberlin studies as a student at West Point. You also will find the full text that Chamberlin studies as a student in the basic and the advanced horsemanship courses at the U.S. Cavalry's Mounted Service School at Ft. Riley. Each offers learning valuable to this day.

The equestrian history enthusiast will find: Never before published photos of the Inter-Allied Games of 1919 at which the Italian jumping performance causes Chamberlin and other American officers to question French jumping principles; a rare booklet that describes the curriculum, personnel, and facilities of the French Cavalry School at Saumur published in the year Chamberlin attends the school; photos of the Italian Cavalry's advanced school at Tor di Quinto where Chamberlin studies Caprilli's revolutionary jumping style, astounds his teachers, and assesses the Italian method; photos of the 1932 Olympic Games where the United States wins the gold team medal in Eventing and where Chamberlin wins the individual silver medal in Stadium Jumping; and finally, photos of the Chamberlin inspired riding methods taught at the U.S. Army's Cavalry School and its Cavalry Replacement Training Center both located at Ft. Riley.

In words and photos, *The Chamberlin Reader* describes the milestones in Chamberlin's career as he creates the foundation for what George H. Morris calls "The American Jumping Style" and establishes what James Wofford calls "a whole new system" for training horses and riders. You will find equestrian

---

2   Matha, Warren, *Chamberlin: America's Equestrian Genius*, Xenophon Press, 2020.
3   Ibid.

history preserved, the origins and methods of Chamberlin's system revealed, and the story of how American riding evolved. Above all, you will gain valuable insights into the art and science of riding and training horses.

In "The West Point Years, Horsemanship 1907–1910," we include principles that West Point teaches to Chamberlin as a cadet. Most of this information comes from the two main text books that West Point of that era uses to teach horsemanship and equine science to all West Point cadets during Chamberlin's time at the military academy: *Elements of Hippology* by F. C. Marshall and *Horses, Saddles, and Bridles* by General William H. Carter. We discuss hoof care, the pre-purchase examination; and finally, the confirmation of a solid, weight carrying horse suitable for long distance riding. With the passing of the U.S. Cavalry, much of this learning has been lost to present day riders.

In "The Mounted Service School 1915–1917," we include the school text *Saumur Notes* in a slightly abridged and edited form to ease reading by the modern reader. *Saumur Notes* forms the foundation of the curriculum on training horses at the Mounted Service School when Chamberlin attends. We include select passages from *The Manual of Equitation of the French Army for 1912* which also serves as a text for the Mounted Service School. In addition, we include selected passages from the school's textbook *Breaking and Riding with Military Commentaries* by James Fillis (also published under the title *Principles of Dressage and Equitation*) [Xenophon Press 2017] which Chamberlin devours while at the school. He highly recommends the passages that we reproduce: The Fillis discussion of the rider's hands.

In "The Inter-Allied Games of 1919: The Turning Point," we display privately taken and (we believe) previously unpublished photographs of the practice sessions prior to the Games and of the jumping competitions in which the Italian team triumphs. The Italian jumping performance inspires a turning point in American riding theory and makes a distinct impression on Chamberlin.

In "The Evolving American Jumping Style 1919–1923," we include a 1922 article on obstacle jumping that Chamberlin publishes in *The Rasp*—the official yearbook of The Cavalry School at Ft. Riley. In addition, we display photos from *The Rasp* that demonstrate how the Italian performance at the Inter-Allied Games of 1919 influences the evolving American riding theory and practice even before then Major H.D. Chamberlin and Major W.W. West attend the Italian advanced cavalry school at Tor di Qunito.

In "The French Cavalry School for Advanced Riding at Saumur, France 1922–1923," we reproduce a rare booklet from the editor's collection that the French Cavalry School for Advanced Riding at Saumur publishes in the year that Chamberlin attends that school. The booklet: *École d'application de Cavalerie, Saumur, France* offers photos that describe the school's facilities, senior personnel, and theories of equitation.

In "The Italian Cavalry School for Advanced Riding at Tor di Quinto, Italy 1923–1924," we present photos of the instructors who teach and the obstacles that Tor di Quinto presents to its students. Thereafter, we include Chamberlin's 1924 *Cavalry Journal* article in which he describes the school, its methods, and its theory. He evaluates the Italian methods of riding and horse training. He makes his recommendations regarding the Italian methods to the Chief of Cavalry at Ft. Riley. We also include Chamberlin's comments regarding the Italian method that he writes in a later unpublished manuscript.

In "The Olympic Games of 1932," we include photos from the Three-Day Event and the *Prix des Nations* competition at those Olympic Games. The Americans win the team gold medal in the Three-Day Event. Chamberlin student, Lt. Thomson wins the individual silver medal in that event. Chamberlin competes in both the Three-Day and the *Prix des Nations*. He wins a team gold medal for the Three-Day and the individual silver medal in the *Prix des Nations*.

In "Chamberlin Writings in Periodicals, Letters, and Manuals 1934–1941," we re-print what we believe to be all but two of the articles that Chamberlin writes between 1934 and 1941. Chamberlin's articles span the horizon of equestrian thought: he discusses the confirmation of a show jumper as well as a Three-Day eventer. He discusses other topics from dressage to crossing rivers; from the riding seat of the Italians to the riding seats of the Swedes, the Germans, the French, the Americans, and others; from training cavalrymen to training all manner of horses.

One article in *Country Life Magazine* entitled *The Modern Jumping Seat* that Chamberlin writes in 1941, we read but were not able to reproduce. We were unable to secure copyright permission. The article merely restates for *Country Life Magazine* readers the concepts Chamberlin explains in articles reprinted here. Also, Chamberlin writes a two-installment photo essay on the proper seat for hacking, hunting, and show jumping for the *Chicago Tribune*. The *Tribune* headlines the essay under the title *The World's Best Rider Demonstrates Correct Technique*. The essay appears in two installments; the first on May 31 and the second installment on June 7, 1936. Unfortunately, the management of the *Chicago Tribune* refused to grant us permission to reproduce those installments for this book.

We include in this chapter an excerpt from the U.S. Cavalry's *Field Manual 25–5, Animal Transport, Horsemanship and Horsemastership 1942 Edition.* Chamberlin supervises the manual's revision, contributes concepts and writings, and appears in photos to demonstrate various aspects of "The Military Seat" also known as the "Chamberlin-Military Seat."[4] The manual also reveals Chamberlin's and the U.S. Cavalry's method of jumping obstacles—which forms the foundation for what Mr. George H. Morris calls the "American Jumping Style."

In this section, you also will find Chamberlin's final written discussion regarding horse training in his November 1941 monograph *Breaking, Training, and Reclaiming Cavalry Horses.* As commander of the 1st Brigade, 2nd Cavalry Division, Chamberlin explains four simple exercises to break, train and reclaim cavalry horses, polo ponies, hunters, jumpers, eventers, hacks and former race horses. Chamberlin applies these methods as the first steps to train his hot-as-they-come, off-the-track Thoroughbred, Pleasant Smile, and to transition the horse from horse racing to Olympic level eventing.

In "The American Military Riding Style," you will find photos of Chamberlin and his student Lt. Earl Thomson, the two-time Eventing Olympic individual silver-medalist. Both riders demonstrate the Chamberlin-Military Seat. In other photos, Chamberlin demonstrates the jumping style that he develops. You will also find the U.S. Cavalry's long-distance riding protocol which will be of interest to endurance and other long distance riders.

We show photos of Chamberlin's recommended manner to descend steep slides and to negotiate drop jumps. Chamberlin recommends that the rider keep the upper body forward from the hips in all such circumstances. Hopefully, this will interest those eventers—even at the Olympic level—who persist in leaning back behind the vertical as they descend steep banks, slides, drop jumps, and similar obstacles. These riders throw their weight back over the horse's hindquarters as opposed to forward over the forehand where Chamberlin argues that such weight belongs.

Those who have read the Chamberlin biography's chapters regarding The Cavalry School at Ft. Riley and The Cavalry Replacement Training Center (The CRTC), also at Ft. Riley, know that Brigadier General Harry Chamberlin, Captain Paul Kendal of the Cavalry School's Advanced Equitation program, and Sergeant William H. Offill of the CRTC would not take kindly to a rider who leans behind the vertical when descending a slide or taking a drop jump into water. Without question, each of these horseman would

---

4  *Historical and Pictorial Review, 1st Training Regiment, Cavalry Replacement Training Center, Fort Riley, Kansas of The United States Army,* The Army and Navy Publishing Company, 1941.

order such riders to study the photo of the CRTC graduate and Olympic gold medalist, William Steinkraus on Bold Minstrel at Hickstead to see how he descends an almost vertical bank.

In "The End of the Trail," we summarize Chamberlin's place in the history of equestrian sport and in the history of the U.S. Cavalry. With the passing of the Cavalry and General Chamberlin some of the knowledge that you will find in these pages vanished from our contemporary repertoire and discourse. Hopefully, this volume will expand the resources available to those interested in Brigadier General Harry D. Chamberlin's riding and training concepts, in the origins of those concepts, and in the history and evolution of educated riding.

—Warren C. Matha, Editor.

# Chapter 1

# West Point Horsemanship 1907–1910

**Concepts That Offer Value to This Day**

**Checklist for Hoof Care and Pre-purchase**

Of particular interest to the modern equestrian might be the West Point teachings regarding horseshoeing and the pre-purchase examination of the horse. Colonel Marshall and General Carter offer the following rules:
- Remove all shoes at the end of a month's wear.
- After shoes are removed, the horse should, if practicable, be left barefoot for twenty-four to forty-eight hours.
- The horseshoer should lower the wall to the level of the sole with the pincers, never with a knife.
- The shoer must leave the sole alone and never pair out or trim the sole.
- The sole and frog grow in the direction of their own thickness, and surplus growth scales off, unassisted. The frog, like the sole, requires only to be let alone. The frog, if healthy, is not to be pared or even trimmed. The bars are not to be cut away.
- Do not burn out a seat for the shoe with a hot shoe.
- Clenches should not be rasped after being turned down. A slight groove is then made on the underside of the clenches in the horn and the clenches are bent into the groove with a hammer. Except to make this groove for the clenches, the rasp should not be used on the outside wall of the foot.
- When leaving a horse in garrison barefoot, the farrier should "round the hoof wall" to prevent chipping and cracking.

- Regarding the hoof's role in a pre-purchase examination: *the purchaser must watch how sound the horse appears as he is trotted on a hard surface with the shoes taken off.*
- All horses undergoing a purchase examination should be examined unshod. [5]

*Warren C. Matha, Editor:* For the U.S. Cavalry's Remount Service purchaser, watching a horse trot back and forth without shoes on a concrete surface offers a clear indication of whether the anterior areas of the hoof are well developed. A horse who spends its entire life in shoes often fails to develop these anterior areas. In essence, an eight-year-old horse may have the anterior hoof structure of a two-year-old or a horse even younger. Many horses go lame when trotted without shoes over concrete or another hard surface: a clear indication that the structures deep within the hoof have not developed adequately. For this reason, the Remount Service purchaser examines only unshod horses.

At Ft. Riley's Mounted Service School, officers and non-commissioned officers study the recommendation of James Fillis in *Principles of Dressage and Equitation* aka *Breaking and Riding with Military Commentaries* [Xenophon Press 2017] that horses should remain barefoot when working on soft ground—the ground on which most modern dressage horses and show jumpers work. In army parlance, soft ground would equate to "in garrison." The term "on campaign" means cross country riding over all manner of rough terrain. In the world of James Fillis, the farrier applies shoes only to prepare the horse for campaigning.

In the U.S. Cavalry world of General Chamberlin, if a horse remains "in garrison," then at the discretion of the officer in command, the horse may remain unshod. If the horse in garrison remains unshod, then the farrier periodically trims the hoof wall carefully to within an eighth of an inch of the sole plane. He then rounds the edge of the hoof wall off so that it does not chip. Regardless of whether the horse remains shod or unshod, under no circumstances does the farrier trim the healthy frog, pare down or otherwise touch the sole or rasp the outer surface of the hoof wall. When the horse remains unshod, these practices enable the sole, frog, bars, heels, and the internal structures of the hoof to develop as nature intended. The sole naturally exfoliates. The frog expands and grows large. The hoof flexes

---

5   Marshall, F.C. *Elements of Hippology,* Prepared for the Dept. of Tactics, United States Military Academy, Hudson Press, 1906; Carter, General William H., *Horses, Saddles, and Bridles,* Lord Baltimore Press, The Friedenwald Company, 1906.

and the anterior structures deep inside the hoof grow strong. Shoes inhibit this natural development. The practice of continuous shoeing hardens and inhibits the growth of frogs; contracts heels, creates tender hooves, and renders horses lame.

The *Army Drill Regulations for Cavalry, 1916* at page 378 states:

"In garrison, at the discretion of the colonel or commanding officer in charge, the horses may be left unshod."

At Ft. Bliss, the editor's father served in the 1st Cavalry Division. The division remained horse-mounted during the early days of World War II. He became friends with a number of stable sergeants—men with up to 30 or more years of service in the U.S. Cavalry. These old soldiers were highly experienced professionals. They knew how to care for the 12,000 horses then stationed at Ft. Bliss. The sergeants kept barefoot those horses periodically rotated out of active service for short periods or put on sick call. Those horses remained barefoot, especially over the winter months and until they returned to active campaigning.

The Army Remount Service and the stable sergeants at Ft. Bliss understood that constant or continuous shoeing degrades the quality and functionality of the hoof over time. Leaving the hoof unshod at least half of the time restores soundness. If properly conditioned to harsh terrain, then the hoof can remain unshod even for most campaigning. This remains sound advice today.

The U.S. Cavalry experienced instances where barefoot horses were kept on harsh terrain during the fall and winter months before re-entering service. When they returned to service in the spring, these horses marched as far as 900 miles barefoot all the way without problems. For one such example, see *The Journal of the United States Cavalry Association, Vol. II, 1889*, pages 410-411 for a detailed discussion. Only toward the end of the ride, did horses show tenderness due to a radical change in footing. One need only to observe the wild horses on the plains of northern Nevada to see horses so well-conditioned that they traverse all manner of harsh terrain without shoes.

Of course, the realities of domestic horse keeping, absent the appropriate terrain, inhibit this conditioning. The future development of long-wearing, flexible alternatives to metal shoes might offer, however, a workable compromise where conditioning on harsh terrain proves unfeasible. Until then, for the long-term health of horse and hoof, one should condition the horse to go barefoot as much as feasible—especially, as Fillis recommends, if that horse works on soft ground.

# The Conformation of the Horse and Standards for Purchase:

The instructors at West Point consider the study of equine conformation and temperament to be two of the most important aspects of horsemanship. They give the subject exhaustive treatment both in the classroom and also in the stable where cadets examine actual horses that demonstrate the characteristics that the academy teaches.

The army teaches that different conformations offer different strengths depending on the class of work the rider intends. For example, a "chunky" pony-like horse offers the best service in mountainous terrain. The fundamental question the cadet must ask: "Does the horse possess sufficient mobility to execute tactical maneuvers at varying degrees of speed and the ability to stand hard service while carrying great weight?"

Beyond that first question: Cadets must recognize lameness and diseases of the hoof with particular attention to "pointing a toe" of the foreleg as a symptom of founder. They focus on defects that should disqualify a horse from purchase and how to ameliorate such defects for a horse already in service. They examine in great detail: pegged splints and those very close to the knees, ring bones, side bones, and sit-fasts. *The Army teaches that all horses undergoing a purchase examination should be examined unshod.*

The cadets examine closely the relative merits and demerits of various attributes of the head, neck, back shoulder, ribs, chest, the stomach, loins, croup, tail, fore and hind legs with particular attention to the knees, hocks, pasterns, and cannon bones. They learn to examine the horse in motion to observe if the horse moves at all gaits in a regular, free, and natural fashion; to recognize irregularities as a sign of lameness, however subtle, of potential future weakness when on campaign. Cadets learn a detailed, 15 step protocol for examining horses for soundness.

Important characteristics: a gentle disposition; regular and easy gaits, without stumbling, interfering or over-reaching; courage without being nervous or fidgety.

Grounds to reject a horse outright: cribbing, kicking, showing the whites of an eye when there exists no reason to be frightened; pointing a toe of the foreleg; weaving, pawing, wind sucking, biting.

Size: about 15-hands to 15-hands and 3 inches high at the withers, and weighing from 950 to 1100 pounds. In the ideal, the horse should enjoy 8 ½ inches or more of bone under the knee; 9 ½ inches or more of bone under the hock. The full circumference at the girth should measure approximately 6'4".

Fitness: F.C. Marshall makes the following important statement that all modern horse owners should learn:

"It is a surprising fact that most purchasers want to buy a fat horse… Horses in this fat, smooth condition cannot be put to hard work at once; they are more subject to inflammatory diseases than when properly hardened to their work, and, more than all, the fat covers up defects of conformation that would be apparent in working condition." [6]

Marshall devotes 12 pages of description to the pre-purchase inspection. In *Elements of Hippology* on page 224, he summarizes:
- "Well-bred horses that may be predicted as capable of giving good service have about the following conformation:
- Head small, clear-cut, and well set on a long, slender neck.
- Shoulders sloping well forward, muscular, and long.
- Front leg well-muscled above the knee, cannon shorter than legbone, and both upright and straight, ankle sloping forward, long and elastic; fetlock, ankle, and pastern, smooth, firm, and small.
- Feet small, sound, and with well-developed frogs. Barrel deep, long, and well-ribbed up, about equal in size at girth and middle, and sloping gradually from the middle towards the sheath.
- Withers reasonably prominent and well-muscled.
- Back flat, well-muscled, and free from saddle-marks.
- Coupling short and strong.
- Croup slightly convex, viewed from side and rear. There should be considerable length from loin to tail, and not much curvature.
- Tail well set on, and, when the animal is in motion, carried away from the body. The hair should be fine and silky.
- Thighs prominent and muscular and well filled up, when viewed from behind. measured from hip to hock, the thigh should be long.
- Hocks clean-cut, not puffy, wide from the side, large and well bent. The point of the hock should not be noticeably prominent. Both

---

6   Marshall, F.C. *Elements of Hippology*, Dept. of Tactics, United States Military Academy, Hudson Press, 1906.

hocks, viewed from behind, should be parallel and straight under the horse's body.
- The cannon-bone should be flat and broad.
- Pasterns and feet as in front legs."[7]

The cadet studies the strengths and weaknesses of every aspect of confirmation. High withers, low withers; long back, short back; long neck, short neck and so on. In *Horses, Saddles, and Bridles*, General Carter writes:

"Horses with very high withers, while pleasant to ride, are unsuited for hard service with packed saddles. High, thin withers are usually accompanied by flat muscles about and in rear of the shoulder blade, where the front end of the side bars of military saddles are intended to rest; this flatness allows the saddle to slip unduly forward, which is very objectionable…Horses with low withers, not well defined or outlined, are not suited for heavy, packed saddles, because such a formation permits the saddle to slip forward… Short, straight backs are the strongest for weight carriers, but a certain amount of length is essential both for speed and jumping; moreover a horse with a very short back is apt to overreach."

To learn "excellent" confirmation, the cadets also study photos of a horse named "Deadwood." General Carter comments that "Deadwood" is fat and age 13 in the photos but displays the confirmation of a confirmed weight carrier.

The Army Remount Service acquires Deadwood at age five. After eight years of service, he carries his rider for a low estimate of 2,500 miles *on one continuous march* in 1887. He then performs well in garrison and in field service. At the time of Carter's writing in 1902, the horse continues to serve solidly in the Philippine Islands. He remains sound throughout.

Using this horse to judge the appropriate relative dimensions of body parts, Carter advises cadets to "size up" the horse's head and then use multiples of the head's length to determine the appropriate conformation of the neck, withers, shoulders, back, ribs, chest and so on down to the hoof.

---

7   Ibid.

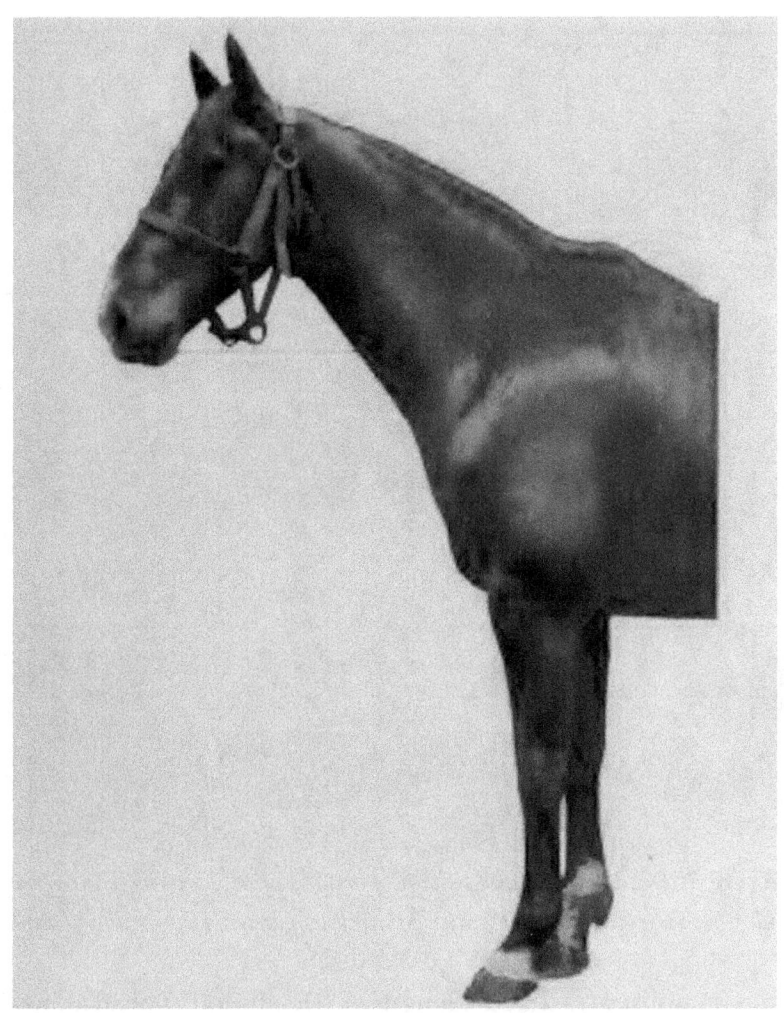

*Figure 2.* Carter: "…a good head, neck, shoulder, and forelegs with proper elevation of the withers." Photo from Horses, Saddles, and Bridles *by Carter 1906 Public Domain.*

***Figure 3.*** *Deadwood displays the proportions of an ideal weight carrier. Photo from* Horses, Saddles, and Bridles *by Carter. 1906 Public Domain.*

Carter demonstrates that the length of "Deadwood's" head almost exactly equals the distance:
1. from the top of the withers to the point of the shoulder;
2. from the lowest point of the back to the abdomen;
3. from the point of the stifle to the point of the hock;
4. from the point of the hock to the lower line of the hoof;
5. from the shoulder blade to the point of the haunch.

Two and one-half times the head gives:
1. the height of the withers above the ground;
2. the height of the top of the croup above the ground; and
3. very nearly the length from point of the shoulder to point of buttock.

***Figure 4.*** *Deadwood from the front. Notice the straight line formed by the large bone through the knee and through the cannon bone. Photo from* Horses, Saddles, and Bridles *by Carter 1906. Public Domain.*

***Figure 5.*** *Deadwood from the back. The thighs should be deep, well developed but spaced to prevent friction. Photo from* Horses, Saddles, and Bridles *by Carter 1906, public domain.*

# Chapter 2

# The Mounted Service School

### Texts that Chamberlin studies in 1915-1917
### that offer value today

The following texts form the theoretical basis of training at the Mounted Service School when Chamberlin attends the school:

*Notes on Equitation and Horse Training in Answer to the Examination Questions at the School of Application for Cavalry at Saumur, France;* (*Saumur Notes on Equitation* or *Saumur Notes* for short) is published by the French Cavalry School at Saumur and is translated into English by the Mounted Service School;

*Riding and Breaking Horses with Military Commentaries* by James Fillis; (also published under the title: *Principles of Dressage and Equitation*). [Xenophon Press 2017]

*The Manual of Equitation of the French Army for 1912* published by the French Army and translated into English;

*Elements of Hippology* by Colonel F. C. Marshall.

In "*Saumur Notes*" the French Cavalry at Saumur discusses basic "questions" or principles regarding the training of the horse. These Saumur teachings remain valuable to this day. *Saumur Notes* constitutes one of the early foundations of Chamberlin's horse training theory. The Cavalry Board firmly believes that to be an expert rider, one needs to know how to train a horse. The more the general rider knows about the process of horse training, the better rider that person will become—even if not interested in training a horse. *Saumur Notes* offers you the opportunity to review, first hand, one of the foundation documents in Chamberlin's equestrian education. As you will note when reading Chamberlin's books, he remains selective regarding the theories he adopts from the French, the Italians, the Germans, the Poles, as well as his own U.S. Cavalry.

As the biography *General Chamberlin: America's Equestrian Genius* [Xenophon Press 2020] reveals, Chamberlin and other American officers modify French theory in a variety of ways. The American concepts continue to develop and undergo refinement as American cavalrymen visit other schools across Europe. Ultimately, Chamberlin decides that select concepts of French dressage apply to the training of all horses. His book *Training Hunters, Jumpers, and Hacks* [Xenophon Press 2019] demonstrates his conviction. In 1915, *Saumur Notes* offers Chamberlin his first truly in-depth discussion of how the French at Saumur train a horse.

Section I of *Saumur Notes* devotes considerable time to the history and evolution of French equitation. Section II deals with horse training. Our abridgment omits most of those items strictly applicable to the military horseman of the nineteenth and early twentieth centuries such as feeding protocols, inducing sweats to shed fat, applying "purges with laxative effect," as well as medical advice that may prove obsolete. For the most part, we confine the editing to re-writing a few clauses in the translation in less cumbersome language and in a style that is both simple and direct. The objective: to make the manual easier to read.

—Warren C. Matha, Editor

**Notes on Equitation and Horse Training
in answer to the
Examination Questions
at the
School of Application for Cavalry
at
Saumur, France**

**Mounted Service School
Originally Translated from the French
and Abridged for the United States Cavalry Service
by Captain George H. Cameron,
Assistant Commandant, Mounted Service School,
Fort Riley, Kansas
1909**

**Edited and abridged for the modern reader by Warren C. Matha
2020**

"Saumur Notes"

# I
# History

The history of equitation reaches back to remotest antiquity. The horse has always been used in combat, and here we find the origin or, more properly speaking, the cause of the equestrian art. If man had utilized the horse merely to cover long distances or to bear burdens, sufficient training for the purpose would have been an easy matter. But when he decided to fight from the horse's back, he was obliged to develop a complete and logical system of steps in training and handling.

**Antiquity.**—We will not concern ourselves with the manner in which the Greeks, Gauls, and Romans rode. Covering this long period, only the works of Xenophon need be cited; they are especially worthy of mention because they include all the fundamental principles of equitation, and even in our day may be consulted to advantage. It should also be stated that prior to the fifth century a covering stretched over the horse's back was the only form of saddle. The Orientals made slaves bend their backs to serve as mounting blocks, and the Romans made use of stones called "stades," which were set along the roads for the same purpose. It was not until the end of the fifth century that the saddle-tree was invented, and later stirrups were added. This invention materially modified methods of equitation and permitted the rider to remain longer in the saddle without becoming fatigued.

**Middle ages.**—During the long period that constitutes the middle ages, two customs contributed largely to progress in equitation. These two fashions were chivalry and tournaments. All the youths of the French nobility, eager to rise to the dignity of knighthood, received an education in which the first essential was to learn how to ride. Equitation, it is true, was very limited. The lancer's deep saddle, required to resist an adversary's shock, led to a very constrained seat. Methods of controlling the horse were neither accurate nor progressive; the legs held straight and far out from the horse could be closed only by jerks; the overloaded horses necessarily lacked suppleness. Equitation was simply an exhibition of brute strength, but it was well adapted to the form of combat and to the breed of horses then existing.

During this period of the middle ages we find no works on equitation. The horsemen of that period were certainly not writers and, moreover, equitation with them was a business rather than an art.

**Italian schools.**—The lack of authors and of historical documents brings us up to the time of Pignatelli, an Italian nobleman, who, in the sixteenth century, founded at Naples the first school of equitation that ever existed. His example was promptly followed in Italy, and other schools were founded, one at Ferrare by Caesar Fiaschi and one at Naples by Frederick Grison. Their system consisted in exaggerated supplings, exacted in a brutal manner. They obtained results, however, and horses trained in these schools were certainly well in hand, but training was very long and not always successful. All the horses of Italy, especially those of Naples, had a reputation for viciousness, which was probably due simply to the exceptional severity of the horsemen.

**French schools—Sixteenth century.**—The principles of the Italian school were brought to France at the end of the sixteenth century by La Broue and de Pluvinel, pupils of Pignatelli. The nobility eagerly took up the theoretical study of an art that seemed new to them; competition took the place of tourneys, and at the death of Henry II the latter disappeared entirely.

De Pluvinel, who was successively first equerry to Henry III and director of the royal stables under Henry IV, founded the first academies in France.

Equitation as taught in these academies was still slow and restricted. The seat in the high saddle was always straight and stiff. Immoderate use was made of the spur and switch, and the methods of training were based principally on the use of the cavesson and of the posts.

**Seventeenth century.**—In the seventeenth century, the principal riding masters were Solleysel (1617–1680), who published the *Parfait Maréchal* and translated the works of Newcastle; Du Plessis; de la Vallée; Vendeuil, who was de la Guérinière's teacher; and Gaspard Saunier (1663–1746), who wrote *Treatise on the Complete Knowledge of Horses, The True Principles of Cavalry*, and *The Art of Cavalry*. In England, the Marquis of Newcastle is worthy of mention.

Equitation was still about the same, but they began to work outside the riding hall. Solleysel took up conditioning and published *A Method of Preparing Horses to Cover Extraordinary Distances*.

Gaspard Saunier insists on the necessity of working horses out of doors. He tells us that the best horses of the Versailles school, when put on the road in the campaign of 1691, had great difficulty in becoming accustomed to this new work, and that "they stumbled and seemed to have scarcely enough strength to stand up."

**Eighteenth century.**—It was not until the eighteenth century that the French school was really and definitely founded, and the honor of establishing it is due to M. de la Guérinière. He was the first to conceive the idea of the natural seat. He had the pommel and cantle of the manège saddle cut down and taught that the rider should seek a firm seat in the balance and uprightness of his position. His instruction in equitation was reasonable and natural; he greatly simplified methods of training, and the system that he published may still be consulted with advantage.

Following the riding masters of the eighteenth century, we advance step by step. The Versailles school became celebrated the world over. It was a real academy, which, after laying down the principles of French equitation, sought to maintain these principles and prove their superiority.

Among the numerous riding masters of the eighteenth century should be mentioned La Guérinière, who published *Ecole de Cavalerie* [Xenophon Press, 2015] and the *Elements of Cavalry* (he died in 1751); De Nestier; De Salvert; De Lubersac, who trained his horses by riding them eighteen months at a walk; De Montfaucon De Rogles, who, in his *Treatise on Equitation*, gives some useful information on work with the longe; De Neuilly; Bourgelat, founder of veterinary schools; Du Paty De Clam, who published numerous works and was a writer rather than a riding master; D'Auvergne, head riding master at the military school in Paris; Mottin de la Balme, pupil of d'Auvergne, who wrote *Essays on Equitation;* De Bohan, who published a *Critical Review of the French Army* (he thought that equitation should proscribe all artificial gaits); de Boideffre, a pupil of d'Auvergne, who wrote *Principles of Equitation and of Cavalry*; de la Bigne, and D'Abzac.

**Military schools.**—It is important to note that progress in equitation was due not solely to instruction received at the Versailles school, but also to the reforms in cavalry tactics introduced by Fredrick the Great. The necessity of having squadrons able to maneuver proved to the King of Prussia that equitation should be the basis of the instruction of the trooper. He built riding halls in all cavalry garrisons and caused the principles of the equestrian art to be taught.

The example of the Germans was followed by the French cavalry. At the end of Louis XV's reign, the Duke of Choiseul, minister of war, had the King sign a decree, in 1764, creating five cavalry schools—at Douai, Metz, Besancon, La Fleche, and Cambrai. A central school at Paris was to receive the best pupils from the elementary schools after they had passed through a fixed period of instruction. This decree of 1764 was never completely carried out.

In 1770, regimental riding schools were established in nearly all cavalry garrisons. Among these schools the most celebrated were those at St. Germain, Versailles, and Saumur. The one at Saumur, which had been organized in 1763 by the regiment of carbineers, was transformed in 1771 into a cavalry school to which every colonel was directed to send four officers and four noncommissioned officers annually.

**Period from 1789 to 1815.**—The Revolution suppressed all cavalry schools. However, in 1798, the school at Versailles was re-established and took the name of National School of Instruction for Mounted Troops. In this new school, the instructors did not attempt equitation, but simply endeavored to teach the horse to carry his rider and to travel at marching gaits.

In 1799, two new schools were created, one at Luneville and one at Angers, having the same object and the same organization. The Versailles school was the only one left in 1808, when an imperial decree replaced it by the school of St. Germain, intended to complete the instruction of cavalry second lieutenants after the course at St. Cyr.

**Restoration.**—Upon the return to power of the Bourbons, the Versailles riding school was re-established and placed under the direction of M. d'Abzac, who was assisted by Messrs. De Goursac and Charrette de Boisfoucaud.

The most noted riding masters of that school were the Viscount O'Hegarty, de Vendière, de Millange, and de Vaugiro. The Versailles school lasted until 1830.

In 1814, the Restoration suppressed the school at St. Germain and founded a new one at Saumur. The latter was abolished in 1822, following

General Berton's conspiracy, and the decree of 1823 established a school of application for cavalry at Versailles.

The Riding School of the Pages, under the direction of O'Hegarty, formed a branch of the Versailles school. But this new organization lasted only a year and on November 11, 1824, the cavalry school was definitely established at Saumur.

**Contemporary equitation.**—We now come to contemporary equitation, for a long time divided into two schools; a new school, that of Baucher, and the d'Aure school, which continued the methods taught at Versailles.

**Baucher.**—Little is known of Baucher's antecedents. At the age of 15, he set out for Italy with one of his uncles, who was an instructor of riding schools. He returned to France a few years later and located in Paris. First, he gave lessons in a small riding academy in the Rue Montmartre; then, he went into a circus in order to popularize his methods. The minister of war had his system tested in the army on two different occasions; one trial was at Saumur. The Baucher system, however, was never officially adopted in the cavalry.

Baucher's methods were entirely different from those taught at the Versailles school. Much more complicated than the Count d'Aure's method, it marked in a way a return to the suppling of the early riding masters. The formula that Baucher often repeated was this: "Destroy the instinctive forces and replace them by transmitted forces." To carry out this program it was necessary to begin with a series of supplings: "Flexions of the jaw; flexions of the neck, lateral flexions and mobilizing the hind quarters about the shoulders; swinging the fore quarters about the haunches; combination of the play of both extremities or backing."

All this preliminary work was done in place and resulted in the "gather" (*Le ramener*); later by the use of so-called "attacks" and "collecting effects," he arrived at the "assemble" (*Le rassembler*). These first lessons were supplemented by a few movements at the walk, trot, and gallop, and were supposed to complete the training of a horse in two months.

As for high school, this was Baucher's triumph. He was an admirable riding master and could make his horses execute the most complicated steps. In one of this works, he mentions 16 new riding-school movements which he had added to the repertory of former riding masters.

Baucher wrote several works on equitation. The principal ones are a *Dictionary of Equitation* and a *Method of Equitation Based on New Principles.*

**D'Aure.**—The Count d'Aure, a former pupil of the St. Cyr school, graduated there as a second lieutenant of infantry. He subsequently went into the guard corps and was thus enabled to enter the riding school at Versailles under the direction of the Viscount d'Abzac.

In 1830, he resigned, but, although he gave up the profession of arms, he retained his fondness for equitation, and his brilliant success in that direction let to his being appointed in 1847 to the post of head riding master of the school at Saumur.

His equitation is far from being complicated and studied; it is instinctive, bold, and brilliant. The Count d'Aure was an improviser who, at the first glance, knew how to secure good results from the most difficult horses. Like all true horseman, he rode equally well in the riding hall and in the open; and while he encouraged hunting and racing, he could excel all others at the head of a riding-school exhibition. He directed his efforts particularly to the making of bold and energetic horsemen and always preached the movement to the front: "Push up to the bit," was the excellent precept that he continually repeated to his pupils. Count d'Aure wrote two works on equitation, one in 1830 and one in 1853, and during the eight years from 1847 to 1855 was head riding master of the cavalry school.

# II

## Horse Training

**Definition and Object of Horse Training.** The term horse training means a series of exercises that render the horse obedient, while preserving and developing his inherent qualities. Its object is not, therefore, to simply master and control the instincts of the animal; it must also subject him to a muscular training, that, by suppling, will strengthen all parts of the body. As a result, his gaits will be perceptibly developed by the very harmony of his movements and by the exact distribution of his weight produced under the influence of the aids.

**Circumstances Affecting Duration of Training.** The length and value of the service that a horse can render, depend, in great measure, upon the manner in which he has been trained. A colt should be called upon for only such exercise or work as is reasonable, considering his age, strength and ability. To exact anything beyond his capabilities is to set up resistance and to inevitably bring on injuries and early condemnation.

The breeding of a horse (Thoroughbred or underbred), the nature of his feed and the amount of work he has been equal to in the hand of his breeder, are considerations that will allow us to fix upon the date, more or less distant, when he should be fit for service. Training, when once begun, must be regulated by these same considerations. It is self-evident that a horse kept on grass until he is four years old needs more nursing than the pure-bred horse that is raised almost from birth on oats.

It is also obvious that conditions of training will differ widely according to the skill of the person in charge. An expert horseman will finish the work more satisfactorily and more quickly, and his composure and experience will enable him to mount without trouble a younger horse, because, in his hands there will be none of those struggles that produce blemished animals.

Finally, the time required for training will vary according to the object to be attained. Many long months are often necessary to work a young horse up to high school exercises, whereas, occasionally, a few weeks will be sufficient to produce a horse free at the three gaits and galloping with either lead.

**Three Periods of Training.** The training of a young horse may be divided into three periods: Preliminary work; Work in the snaffle bridle; Work in the double bridle.

**Preliminary Work.** In this first period, students learn to gentle the horse. They teach the horse to allow himself to be saddled and mounted, to go straight ahead at the walk and trot, to turn to the right and to the left. In the preliminary period, students and horses learn to work on the longe. Students longe their remounts extensively in a number of short periods.

**Work in the snaffle bridle.** In the second period, the student learns to teach the remount to understand thoroughly the effects of the rider's legs. Next, he teaches the remount to obey the simple effects of the snaffle. At the end of this period, the student should understand how to teach and the remount should understand how to work at the three gaits on a straight line, the circle and on the diagonal (the "three lines"); how to take the gallop with either lead, and how to work on two tracks at the walk and at the trot. (Work on "two tracks" occurs when the forelegs and the hind legs follow different tracks.) In this second period, the student trainer would continue or begin work outside the round pen or riding hall and into the countryside.

**Work in the double bridle.** In this third period, the method divides the work into two parts:

a. The student repeats with the double bridle all work previously done with the snaffle. The student completes the remount's understanding of the upper aids. The student confirms the remount's work at the gallop and finally, teaches the change of lead. At this stage, ordinary training for a trooper's horse stops;

b. The student learns to prepare the remount for high-school work; to develop the remount's obedience through a system of exercises that increases suppleness and strength. The student learns to teach and the horse learns to cadence the gaits and to become light, or, more precisely speaking, balanced.

## III
## Preliminary Work. Exercise by leading.

**How to Lead:** Initially, students exercise the remount by leading the horse on foot. Later, the students will lead the young horse beside kind old horses. The student should alternate leading the horse on both the near and the off sides to avoid a "false set of the neck." To accustom the remount to equipment, the students saddle the horses during the leading period. They put on the saddle without stirrups or stirrup straps and tighten the girth only slightly.

**How to Care for the young horse:** After exercise, students rub the remount's legs and massage the tendons. After hard work, the student washes down the remount's legs with water; then, he dries and wraps the fetlocks and the lower half of the cannon bones with flannel. He leaves the wraps on for five to six hours (but not longer). Instructors make sure that the fastening tapes remains "somewhat loose." Wrapping, the student learns, helps prevent wind puffs and swellings by helping circulation and retaining heat. Before and after each training session, the student officer grooms the horse in accordance with military procedures.

**How to Longe:** After leading the remount on foot for a time, the student learns how to work the horse on the longe. Three principles must dominate this work:

1. The student must control the horse with the longe and not with the whip. The only function of the whip is to move the horse forward.
2. The student should change the length of the longe frequently. The horse should alternately stretch himself on a large circle and bend himself on a small circle.
3. The student should change the gaits frequently; bring the horse to a walk from time to time to avoid stiffness of gait that results from prolonged work.

The student uses work on the longe for the following purposes:
1. To exercise the young horse without injury and without fatigue to the horse's joints.
2. To give first lessons to horses that are difficult to manage.
3. To work with horses that hold back or fight.
4. To work horses with one shoulder more developed that the other.
5. To work horses that will not work equally well on either hand.
6. To work horses that bend themselves with difficulty.
7. To give horses experienced with the longing process lessons in jumping on the longe; provided, however, the student must not put a horse to a jump until the horse remains thoroughly manageable with cavesson and longe.

The student should hold the longe line in the left hand, the longe whip in the right hand and place his body adjacent to the remount's shoulder. He remains opposite the remount's shoulder during the entire longing session. He learns to point the whip to the croup and to extend the longe to the remount's head thus forming a "V" from student to horse.

The student works the horse on the longe at the walk, trot and canter. The objective: to teach the horse to move in a straight, calm and forward manner. Instructors enforce the principle that one longes the remount to train him but not to exhaust him. The student learns to control the horse with the longe line *not* with the whip. He uses the whip only to move the horse forward if "clucking" or a voice command fails. He varies the length of the longe with frequent changes from a large to a small circle and back again. He varies the gaits frequently and brings the horse down to a walk often.

## IV

**How to Saddle the first time:** To accustom the young horse to his equipment, the student should saddle the horse during the period in which the horse is exercised by leading, should remove stirrups and stirrup straps, and should only slightly tighten the girth. The student should readjust the girth during exercise. The student should work nervous horses on the longe for a while to quiet them before placing the saddle on the back. After the student's remount becomes accustomed to the saddle, the student replaces the stirrups and allows them to hang down on each side during several leading and longe lessons.

**How to Mount the first time.** The student officer gives the mounting lesson after working the horse for some time or at the end of his work session. In preparation, an assistant faces the horse. The student approaches the horse's head, caresses him on the forehead, on the eyes, the neck, and the haunches. He slaps the saddle, pulls the stirrups out and lets them drop back; he then grasps the reins, leaving them very long.

At first, the student gets into the saddle as skillfully as possible without any attempt to mount by the numbers, and especially without being in any way exacting. Students give the mounting lesson on the off side as well as on the near side. They repeat the lesson on both sides daily until the horse learns to stand absolutely quiet.

If, during the lesson, the horse backs or moves away, the student should return to the horse's head, lead him forward a step or two with the snaffle reins, and gently begins the lesson anew.

After seating himself in the saddle, the student should use his right hand to assist in engaging the off side stirrup. If the student feels for that stirrup with the toe, he might frighten the horse by touching him unintentionally with the leg or the stirrup.

**Restless Horses.** An assistant should stand squarely in front of the horse and not on the off side. The assistant's business is to simply caress the animal's head without holding the reins. With horses that are hard to mount, the student should use the cavesson with the longe line held by an experienced and skillful person. The student should give mounting lessons on the off side as well as on the near side. The student should repeat the lesson each day until the horse stands absolutely quiet. The individual lesion, however should not be prolonged since the horse will have a greater tendency to become restless the more the student holds him in one place.

# V

**How to teach the horse to move forward and straight.** The Necessity of Using the Trot at the Beginning of a Lesson. After warming up the horse at the walk, to teach the horse to move forward and straight, students begin with the trot. They teach bending movements at the walk and then, once the horse understands a movement, they confirm it at the trot. As de la Guérinière points out, several advantages arise by using the trot to begin "straight and forward" work:

1. It starts the horses going straight ahead and brings them in hand; busy at the trot, they have less idea of resisting.
2. It expends the surplus vigor (takes the edge off) of young horses, and they become quieter and more attentive.
3. This gait must be considered as the best of suppling exercises.

In his book on equitation, de la Guérinière writes a chapter entitled "The necessity of the trot and the utility of the walk." In this chapter, he writes:

"By the trot, the most natural of the gaits, a horse is made light on the hand without spoiling his mouth, and his legs are stretched without straining them, because in this action, which is the highest of all natural gaits, the weight of the horse is borne equally by two legs, one front and one hind; as a result, the two others are easily raised, sustained in the air, and stretched to the front, thus giving a first stage of suppling to all parts of the body. The trot, therefore, without controversy, is the foundation of all lessons to make a horse obedient and clever."

**Resistance of Young Horses.** Under no circumstances should the student punish the horse in these first lessons. It often happens that when a horse frets, it occurs only due to timidity or high spirits or ignorance.

# VI

**Importance of the Straight-Ahead Movement.** French equitation, above everything else, stresses the point that the horse must go straight ahead freely. With this object in view, this lesson remains the first of all lessons. From the beginning of horse training, the student must accustom the horse to yield to the action of both legs and to move forward, straight and calm.

**How to accustom the horse to go straight ahead under the action of the legs.** For the student officers and the remounts, the lesson of the leg remains the most important lesson. Good reasons exist to return to it often during the whole training period. From the first occasion forward, students observe the following rules:
1. Never keep the lower leg glued to the horse's flank, but use repeated taps with the calves.
2. Tap the horse near the girth and do not reach too far back.
3. Begin by giving the lesson when passing from the walk to the trot; next when lengthening the trot; and finally, when passing from the halt to the trot.

4. Anticipate and assist the action of the legs by clucking with the tongue; if the remount fails heed the legs and to move forward instantly, then the use of light taps with the whip.

These rules especially apply to riding hall lessons. In outside work on a road, young horses naturally go straight ahead. They follow older horses who might ride ahead.

**How and when to expect Lightness.** A horse achieves lightness when he obeys easily and promptly the indications of the rider. This goes beyond a question merely of flexibility of jaw and suppleness of neck, but rather of balance. The degree of lightness corresponds, more or less, to finished balance. In the first lesson, the student should harbor no anxiety about lightness, however, since lightness will result naturally from training. A horse that the rider's legs cannot control easily or who is not well suppled in the shoulders, or who does not know how to employ properly his haunches cannot be light.

**How to apply the principle of constant tension on the reins.** Although the instructor, during the first weeks of training, does not concern himself with the lightness of the horse, he urges the students to keep a constant light tension (feel) on the reins. At first, the student must do the work—that is, must tighten the reins—but later the horse itself, having become accustomed to the pressure of the bit and having always the idea of going straight ahead, will keep, of its own accord, the reins taut.

One must distinguish between pulling on the reins and keeping a constant tension on the reins, an important distinction. A hand too rigidly fixed, with fingers too firmly clasped, will oppose the free play of the neck and will be contrary to the principle just stated. In the leg lesson, when the rider's leg urges the horse straight ahead, therefore, the rider's hand must not oppose the stretching of the neck; on the contrary, the fingers should be slightly opened up so that nothing clashes with the animal's intention to obey the aids.

# VII

**How to Halt a Young Horse.** To halt, lean back slightly. Pull on the reins with gradually increasing force to slow and then to stop the forward movement. When the student pulls on the reins, the horse should neither raise nor lower its head. The horse's muzzle should remain to the front. The whole mass of the neck should flow back towards the withers. In other words, under the action of the reins, the horse should neither throw his nose up in the air nor bring it down against his chest and thus close up on the rider's hand. This latter fault, the rider should avoid at all costs. It is more difficult to raise the muzzle than to lower it. Any horse that, at the beginning of training, withdraws for neck control, becomes especially difficult to train.

**Should Halts be Frequent?** With a horse inclined to fret, the student should not halt frequently. So too, with a horse with its hind legs set under and thus liable to sit down on its haunches. On the contrary, with a horse whose conformation throws its weight on his shoulders, then frequent halts will prove beneficial as a suppling exercise for the horse with a high, powerful croup that makes him difficult to slow up. Training remains nothing more than the quest for balance.

**The Change of Direction.** The Aids to Use. To change direction to the right, open gently the right rein by carrying the wrist to the front and right. Do not move the elbow. Do not twist the hand. The rider must produce the effect of the opening rein laterally and with as little possible action from front to rear. The opening rein induces the haunches to move and furnishes, therefore, a preliminary means to accustom the horse to yield to the pressure of one leg. To change direction to the right, therefore, the rider uses the right rein and the right leg. When the rider uses the leg and rein on the same side of the horse as aids, they are lateral aids, also lateral effects and lateral equitation. (*The Cavalry Board*).

# VIII

**Outdoor Work.** Conditioning remains integral to the education of the young horse. Conditioning and training run together. The horse acquires, at the same time, habits of work and of obedience. To condition a horse, one does not need a jockey seat and a sand race track. Riding hall work and outdoor exercise generally provide sufficient conditioning.

**When to Begin.** Begin outside work as early as possible. Take the horse outside as soon as it knows how to go straight ahead and knows how to turn to the right and the left. Outdoor rides, intelligently conducted, "put horses into the bridle" and improve their carriage. Moreover, outdoor riding remains a good way to quiet the horse as troopers remain less exacting on the road than on the riding hall track. (To put a young horse into his bridle is to make him take hold of his bit and bear on it properly wherever he moves forward under the impulse of both legs. He thus produces a proper tension on the reins. If a horse fails to bear on the bit and to tighten the reins when the rider's legs urge him forward, then he is said to be "*behind the bit.*" *(The Cavalry Board.)*

**Combination of Riding Hall and Outside Work.** Combine outside work with the lessons in the riding hall. One need not blindly follow a set schedule. To alternate outside and riding hall work offers great advantages, especially if one takes at least two outdoor rides each week. The officer in charge of training must base his scheduling decision on the deportment, conformation, and the general condition of the horse. The rider should take outside frequently the horse in poor condition, or that frets, or that throws too much weight upon the hind quarters. The rider should keep in the riding hall for most of his work the horse that throws his weight on the forehand or that proves clumsy.

**Choice of Ground.** If possible, the trainer should select soft ground. Hard ground fatigues the fetlock joints and may injure the lower legs. On hard ground, the horse may develop wind puffs and splints. Heavy ground (like deep sand) may harm the hocks and cause spavins to appear.

When the trainer has completed the horse's training, he may obtain good results by riding the horse with loose reins over bad roads. This forces the horse to take the initiative as the loose reins allow him complete freedom of the head and this easily enables him to get out of difficulty even on very bad ground.

**Gaits.** In outdoor rides alternate between walk and trot. Gradually increase at each outing the amount of trot. Towards the end of the training period, lengthen the distances at the trot. Always introduce intervals of at least ten minutes at the walk to allow the horse to resume his normal breathing. Do not use the gallop except on very good ground. If you have available only bad or fair footing, then do not gallop. By rigidly enforcing a schedule, regardless of conditions, the inevitable result will be injury to the horse. In any case, galloping should not begin outside until the rider is sure of his ability to make his horse lead off freely with either foot. He can then work his mount equally on both sides. He can avoid those struggles that put a horse in the air during the whole ride.

**Sweats.** (*Ed. Note: omitted as obsolete.*)

**Purges.** (*Ed. Note: omitted as obsolete*)

**Condition of the Legs.** Over-exertion of the legs manifests itself in splints, wind puff, spavins, and in the swelling and stiffening of the fetlock joints. In case the fetlocks swell or wind puffs appear, avoid work on hard ground, cut down the work, hand rub the legs, and apply flannel bandages. For splints, follow veterinary recommendations as soon as the injury appears. For bog spavins, stop work in the riding hall and all collected work at the gallop: exercise quietly on the road.

**Appetite and Condition of the Horse.** Give a young horse substantial nourishment to resist the fatigues of training and also because the horse is still growing when he begins training at age four. *{Ed. Note: the feeding suggestions are obsolete and have been omitted.}*

**Results.** In conclusion: if you alternate outdoor work with riding hall work in the proper ratio, the young horse at the end of training:
1. has lost surplus fat;
2. has acquired muscle;
3. has strengthened his joints and tendons;
4. has developed his wind.

In short, after a length of time which varies with age, breeding, and disposition, the horse achieves a physical condition to undergo, without injury, the hardships of his destined service.

# IX

**Second Leg Lesson or First Suppling of the Haunches.** We have already given the horse the first leg lesson—the lesson in moving straight to the front—by drilling him to yield to the action of the legs. We will now teach him to yield to the effect of one leg and thus carry the haunches to the right or left. This second lesson, necessitates the crossing of the hind legs and gives mobility to the hind quarters. It remains a most useful exercise to supple the horse.

The best way to give the horse this second lesson is to use half turns on the forehand in reverse. Half turns on the forehand are nothing more or less than abouts on the forehand made while marching. For example, marching on the right hand, leave the track on the diagonal (oblique) and return to the track by a half turn to the left signaled by a very pronounced action of the left leg and the left rein. This strongly marked lateral effect carries the horse's haunches to the right. The horse, *while still gaining ground,* yields to the effect of the left leg and the left rein and thus describes a half turn. One executes the same movement while marching on the left hand and the horse eventually swings the haunches easily about the forehand, without halting, without striking the fetlocks, and without dancing. (And without either an increase of decrease in cadence.)

We specified half turns reversed, but the rider may use abouts, full turns; and later, serpentines.

**About on the Forehand.** The trooper may also give the second lesson by means of the about on the forehand. It would be wise, however, not to insist on this movement and to use it only when absolutely necessary. The great drawback to abouts on the forehand is the frequent halting of a young horse and of holding him in place by action of the legs. This lesson used repeatedly at the beginning of training will eventually check any movement straight to the front that has been already obtained.

Major Dutilh, although he explains in detail the system of abouts on the forehand, himself points out the danger of using them. He says: "Caution riders that abouts on the forehand have the disadvantage of rendering horses unresponsive to the action of the legs." In order to counteract this tendency, which promptly lead up to resistance, it is urged that the horse be pushed straight ahead at a trot after each one of these pivotings."

In spite of these drawbacks, the abouts on the forehand can be employed advantageously in certain cases. In fact, they should be used with horses that are too hot-headed, with those that bulge on the hand, and with those that are slow to learn.

**Suppling of the Haunches Continued.** If the preceding lessons have produced mobility of the croup by lateral effects, and if the horse yields readily to the action of the leg and the rein on the same side while marching on an arc, then it is time to exact the same obedience while marching on a straight line or following the track, that is to say, to start the horse on the movement called "haunches in." This movement, which continues the suppling of the croup, has the further advantage of confirming obedience to the legs.

**How to teach the Haunches In.** Marching on the right hand, the rider indicates opposition with the left rein and closes, at the same time, the left leg. If the horse yields and swings the croup inside of the track by even one step, while still gaining ground to the front, then straighten him again at once with the right rein and the right leg; repeat this swinging of the haunches several times, but in the first lessons, do not insist. Gradually lengthen the time before straightening.

Haunches in offers a suppling exercise for the hind quarters; it makes the spinal column pliable and accustoms the hind legs to stepping across each other. It also makes the haunches quick to obey and constitutes an excellent preparation for two-track work and for the gallop lead.

**The Difference Between Haunches in and Two-Track Work.** The movement of swinging the haunches in must not be confused with two-track work. The latter is a regular movement to be taken up after the completion of the suppling of the forehand as well as that of the haunches; in this movement the horse, placed or held correctly in a position from head to croup, is oblique to his path rather than curved to it. The former, on the contrary, is merely an exercise with the object of making the haunches supple and easily controlled.

**How to apply Dismounted Work.** Before beginning mounted work on the haunches, it is sometimes useful to pave the way by dismounted work with the whip; such work may be advantageously combined with longing. There are two principal movements:

1. To move the horse to the front with the whip. The horse being on the track and on the left hand, seize the reins about six inches from the bit with the left hand, pull them forward and at the same time strike light taps with the whip behind the girth where the leg is usually applied.

    If the horse moves forward, let him walk a few steps, make much of him, and then halt him.

    If he stands still, gradually increase the force of the whip taps until he moves.

    If the horse backs away, hold him tight with the hand on the reins and continue the use of the whip behind the girth until he moves forward; then caress him and halt him.

2. To swing the haunches. The trooper standing on the left of the horse seizes the reins with the left hand and applies light taps with the whip behind the girth until the horse moves the haunches from left to right. The left hand prevents the horse from getting away to the front and by opposing the forehand to the haunches, assists the action of the whip in moving the hind quarters.

    In this movement, the forehand should move and the fore legs should cross, but on an arc of very small radius. The student should consider dismounted work as of only secondary importance. It will offer great benefit with some horses and remain practically useless with others. In any case, dismounted lessons should always be very brief.

# X

**How to Supple the Forehand.** The hind quarters having been drilled by the foregoing work, the student must promptly train the forehand in order that both ends of the horse shall achieve harmony in mobility and suppleness.

**How to perform the Shoulder-in.** "Shoulder-in" provides the starting point in forehand suppling; this exercise furnishes the means of bending the forehand and spinal column and of training the fore legs to cross each other easily. De la Guérinière says: "This lesson produces so many good results at once, that I consider it the first and the last to be given to the horse."

The student obtains "Shoulder-in" in the following manner:

Marching on the right hand, the student opens the right rein as in changing direction to the right, and presses the left rein upon the neck.

He closes his right leg to push the mass from right to left and slips his left leg behind the girth to restrict as much as possible the swinging of the haunches.

The left rein offers indispensable support to keep the proper balance of the shoulders, that is to prevent the weight of the right shoulder from plunging heavily upon the left shoulder. The two reins must hold the horse's head firmly between them; otherwise, the exercise would become a lateral flexion of the neck and would do more harm than good.

The student should not over strain the bending of the horse's body. For example, the rider achieves a perfect position if, when traveling on the right hand, the left front foot and the right hind foot make tracks on a line obviously parallel to the riding hall wall.

The difference between "shoulder-in" and "two-track" work is similar to the difference between "haunches in" and "two track" work. In the "shoulder-in," if the trooper eases the hands slightly, the horse, being bent and not obliqued, will quit the track and start to make a circle. In "haunches out on two tracks," if the trooper eases the hands, then the horse, being traversed and not bent, quits the track and moves off at an oblique.

**How to achieve the About on the Haunches.** The about on the haunches consists of causing the forehand to describe a half circle around the haunches. It presents a difficult movement and, customary methods of instruction to the contrary notwithstanding, the student should take it up only after the horse completes the exercises of "haunches in" and "shoulder-in."

The student will find first part of the movement easy, but the last part difficult. Take for instance the right about. The student begins the movement like a change of direction to the right. He holds the haunches firmly with his left leg. In the remainder of the exercise, the student controls the horse with the left rein and the left leg. The student applies the left rein, at first, as a bearing rein that, assisted by the right rein, swings the forehand on its path; thereafter, the left rein shifts to create diagonal traction, pulling the mass back upon the right hock and thus holding the haunches stationary. The horse executes the about on the haunches on its inside hind leg with the outside hind leg gaining ground around it.

**How to apply the Lateral Effect and the Diagonal Effect.** The movements that have been already executed with the rein and the leg on the same side, suffice to show the difference between the lateral effect and the diagonal effect. It is easy to see that the former is the means and that the latter is the end in view. With young horses the right rein comes to the assistance of the right leg—lateral effect. With trained horses the rein places or controls the forehand while the leg controls the haunches—diagonal effect.

# XI

**How to work on Two Tracks.** Two track work consists in making the forelegs cross each other and the hind legs cross each other, gaining ground to the front or without gaining ground to the front; the horse is set (placed) to the flank toward which he is marching.

**1. How to work "On the Track."** Haunches in. When the student has suppled sufficiently both the forehand and the haunches, the student should change the movement of *"haunches in"* to *"haunches in on two tracks."* That is to say, that as the horse gradually becomes more obedient to the leg, the lateral effect should gradually make way for the diagonal effect. In other words, when the horse yields readily to the left leg, for instance, it is useless to continue the left rein in opposition, and we accordingly attain the full and regular movement in which the forehand is set in the direction of march.

**Haunches out.** After the horse has mastered the preceding movement, he should be taught haunches out on "two tracks." The principles are the same; but this latter lesson is much to be preferred, because the horse executes it without being guided by the wall or by routine; he merely obeys the reins and legs. In this movement the horse must not be allowed to hang back or to get behind the bit.

To keep him well into the reins, the two-track lesson must frequently be terminated by moving out either on a half turn in reverse or on an oblique to change hands. Two track movements with the haunches in or out are very fatiguing to the young horse and one should not prolong the movement beyond a few steps. To persist unduly in these movements would make a horse refuse; he would strike his fetlocks while stepping across and would sooner or later resist in order to escape the pain that these repeated blows cause.

**2. How to work On the Diagonal of the Hall.** Advantage of this exercise:

The student should repeat movements of the haunches on the diagonal of the hall (while changing hands) and in half turns. Two track work on the diagonal of the hall makes a perfect lesson. It avoids any tendency to slacken the gait, and the horse takes to this exercise more willingly than to that on the track because it proves easier and offers less chance of striking the fetlocks in cross stepping.

In two track work, do not persist in a movement poorly begun or poorly executed. If the horse frets, dances, or backs, then put him on a straight line again, quiet him, and return to the two-track lesson.

**3. How to work on a Circle.** The rider executes two-track work on a circle on the same principles. The following remarks apply:

(a) Haunches *out* on two-tracks on a circle puts the horse into his bridle and upon his forehand. He supports himself to a great extent on the fore legs and lightens the hind quarters which, having a longer route to travel, derive more benefit. The rider should use this movement for horses that hang back, or that have too much weight on the hind quarters.

(b) Haunches *in* on two tracks on a circle produces effects diametrically opposite. The rider should use the movement as a special exercise to supple the forehand of horses that put too much weight on the shoulders.

**Two Track Work at a Slow Trot.** The rider should repeat all two-track exercises at a slow trot. Such work, with the haunches set diagonally, develops rapid progress in young horses.

**Is it Advantageous to Prolong the First Part of Training?** *Prolonging the first part of training on the snaffle bit provides a distinct advantage.* So long as the young horse remains unsteady and wobbly, so long as there remains a danger of encountering resistance, it proves better to leave him on the snaffle.

With this bit, struggles are less frequent. Those that are unavoidable are less harmful. In addition, on the days of bad humor by the horse or by the rider, less chance exists of ruining the work accomplished in preceding lesson.

Moreover, the young horse nearly always needs to have his neck raised, strengthened, and set. If he has no breeding and the curb bit is used too soon, he has a tendency to bring the muzzle down against the chest or to bear heavily on the hand. If, on the contrary, he has class and energy and is put on the curb bit before he thoroughly understands the leg aids, he will struggle against the hand, use his strength in fighting the bit, and subsequently, it will take much time to quiet him and to smooth out his gaits.

**How and when to teach Bending Lessons on the Snaffle.** It remains better to take up bending lessons on the snaffle too late rather than too soon. As long as the horse is not well up in the reins, there exists no opportunity to begin. When he bears properly on the bit, and not before, he should be taught to yield the jaw and to place the head to the right or left.

In preliminary bending lessons, to draw the head to the right the rider pulls gently and slowly upon the right rein and holds the left rein steady to regulate the amount of displacement of the head as well as to prevent, as far as possible, any bending of the neck; the head alone should be turned to the right. The movement will be well executed *if* the head, held high rather than low, remains vertical; *if* the jaw is flexible; and *if* the displacement of the head to the right or left does not pass outside of the vertical planes parallel to the axis of the horse and passing through the points of the shoulders.

During these bending lessons, *invariably practiced while the animal moves*, the rider must use his legs to keep up a steady gait and to prevent slowing up. Once the horse maintains a gait, then the rider must release the leg aid immediately.

**When to Ease the Hand on the Snaffle.** The rider should ease the hand after bending lessons. This provides a rest for the horse after a somewhat fatiguing exercise, and a relief to the hind quarters; this exercise also provides a means to extend and lower the horse's head and to accustom him to keep in touch with his bit.

When the easing of the hand is done well, the horse, after yielding the jaw, should extend his neck little by little and answer to the bending lesson even after his head is down. These bendings at the end of the reins give most excellent results.

The easing of the hand should be most carefully distinguished from the movement when the horse bores savagely against the hand. The habit of boring or diving is easily acquired if the rider releases his hand suddenly instead of keeping a constant tension on the reins and gradually following the horse's head.

## XIII

**How and when Should the Gallop Be Exacted in the First Part of Horse Training?** Almost invariably, the rider should begin the gallop lesson early.... But a fixed rule cannot be laid down with horses and especially in this matter; the time to take up first work at a gallop depends upon the conformation of the horse, his condition, his leg development, and the kind of ground available. It would be stupidity to gallop frequently on a colt that drags his legs and is disunited at a trot and that has difficulty in holding up the part essential to training.

On the other hand, it is proper to gallop repeatedly on a vigorous horse that has been worked before purchase, on the horse with good strong legs, and particularly after the horse has been thoroughly confirmed in the correct trot.

This is a matter of common sense and experience. A horseman will promptly decide at what moment he can profitably begin gallop work with the horse he rides or with the squad he instructs.

**How to introduce The Gallop by Increase of Gait. Utility of Work on a Circle.** Passing from the walk to the gallop remains a test of advanced training; it remains entirely out of place at this stage. The rider must take up the gallop only by increasing the gait from the trot. Moreover, it is essential that the horse shall work equally well on both sides and since, on the circle, the horse is set to lead on the inside leg, we have an opportunity to insure the gallop lead on either foot.

Increasing the gait from a trot on a circle furnishes therefore the means of fulfilling the two essential conditions just cited.

The aids to be used are both legs and the outside rein. The two legs, by steadily forcing an increased gait, push the horse into the gallop. A slight tension on the outside rein prevents the horse from swinging the haunches out and consequently precludes a false lead or a disunited gallop. The circle is the best means to give the gallop lesson when drilling a squad of rather large numbers.

Besides the advantages already mentioned, troopers may work without interfering with each other, in spite of differences in speed which manifests itself in the gallop of young horses. But if a limited number of troopers work in the hall, then it is possible to secure the lead on the desired foot by increasing the gait from the trot at the corner or when the rider completes a flank movement, or comes to the end of a movement to change hands.

The rider must attain the gallop at the moment the horse begins the change of direction; for if the horse does not relinquish the trot until he completes the change of direction, then his haunches can easily swing out and the rider loses a favorable opportunity.

## XIV

**Backing.** How to Execute a Move Backward. The rider may give the first lesson in backing dismounted and in the following manner:

Being on the left side, with the reins in the left hand and the whip in the right, the rider stimulates the hind quarters by a touch with the whip and takes advantage of this mobility to exact one or two steps backward. The rider should make the horse move to the front again immediately by leading him forward with the left hand, and, if necessary, by touching him lightly with the whip.

To give this same lesson mounted, the rider begins by closing the legs as in moving to the front and then moves the horse backward by leaning back slightly and by pulling on the reins with gradually increasing force. Here we see a striking example of the principle of starting everything with the movement to the front. *The action of the legs before the action of the hands* stands as a fundamental idea that the instructor must inculcate into the mind of every trooper.

In backing, the legs are used first to produce the movement to the front and the hand is used next to transform the forward impulse into a backward movement. After a few steps backward, start the horse forward again, halt him and caress him. If a horse refuses to obey, then the rider dismounts, takes the horse by the reins, and causes him to execute the movement as in dismounted work.

If the horse braces himself on his hind legs when the rider's hand acts to make the horse move backward, then the rider moves him forward a step or two or makes the horse swing his haunches slightly, and the rider takes advantage of this mobility to force him backward. This movement is well executed when the horse moves backward step by step and voluntarily moves to the front again as soon as the trooper releases the hand.

If, instead of backing slowly and step by step, the horse hurries the move backward and is about to come down upon his haunches, then the trooper promptly stops all actions of his hands. (The trooper probably has lost all action of the hand because in this faulty movement, the horse invariably is behind the bit.) The trooper corrects the horse, therefore, by attacking him vigorously with the legs or with the spurs to push him forward again.

**When and When Not to "Back" as an Exercise.** Backing provides a suppling exercise for the back as well as for the haunches. It offers an indispensable movement for the saddle horse. Yet, the rider should not abuse it, particularly in the early stages of training, as the horse eventually will develop resistance. Moreover, it is not suitable for all horses indiscriminately. The rider should use it especially for those horses that have difficulty in bringing the hind legs under or that have too much weight on the forehand.

**Individual Work.** (At will.) Nearly all instructors have the bad habit of grouping young horses too much. The greater part of a drill is devoted to work with fixed distances. This gives horses the idea of sticking in ranks. We have already said that it is better to work without regard to distances. And from the very beginning, it is also essential to execute all movements in both directions and at will. If, in addition, we give a few outdoor rides in pairs, then the young horses will become quiet, free movers. The remainder of the training exercises will be that much easier.

**How to judge the Condition of the Horse at the End of the Work in the Snaffle Bridle.** At the end of instruction in the snaffle bridle, the horse should be willing on the road and tranquil in the riding hall. He executes correctly the movement of haunches in, shoulder-in and two track work at a walk and at a slow trot. He takes up the gallop easily on either foot by increasing the gait from the trot. He has found his balance while moving freely to the front, a double condition which he satisfactorily fulfills if he keeps the reins taut without ever bearing on the hand.

His gaits are clean; he can lengthen the walk without jigging and the trot without becoming disunited; his wind has been developed and he can keep up a lengthened gallop for several minutes. When this entire program has been carried out and especially when the horse begins to pull on the hand, it is time to take up the double bridle.

# XV

**Instruction in the Double Bridle.** The instructor's first care must be to the manner in which the horses are bitted. He should select a mild curb bit; one with large cannons, a low port (and thus only slightly restricts the tongue's freedom), and short branches. He should place the bit in the horse's mouth high rather than low. He should leave the curb chain long to facilitate, at first, a swinging motion of the bit. When horses bear freely on the curb bit and when they submit to this new mouthpiece just as they formerly received the effects of the snaffle, the instructor may lower the curb bit to its proper place and tighten the curb chain to its customary tension.

If the horse has a sensitive mouth, it is well to replace (for a time) the ordinary curb by a broken curb. (A curb bit with a snaffle mouthpiece.) The broken curb bit provides a more severe feeling than the snaffle but remains milder than the curb bit. This also enables the horse to become accustomed to the curb chain. The instructor should keep the broken curb bit for a certain length of time. The instructor may resume using that bit later if, during the course of training, the horse tends to get behind the bit.

**Successive Steps to Accustom the Young Horse to the Curb Bit.** The first lessons in the double bridle should commence with the snaffle bit. When the horse settles down and remains well in hand, his rider may apply the curb. The instructor should never, however, repeat never, use the curb bit to give Bending Lessons in the early stages of work on the curb. For these lesson, you must wait until the horse fearlessly accepts contact with the curb bit and tightens the curb reins as he does with the snaffle reins. This procedure sometimes produces mouths with little feeling, but we guarantee that it is less difficult to supple a part that presents stiffness than to make a part firm where all resistance is lacking.

To attain this bearing on the bit, the trooper should follow this schedule:
1. Ride the horse with the reins in both hands. Place the snaffle rein outside and under the little finger. (See Question XXV)
2. At first, during work at a walk and later during work at a trot, ride the horse with the curb rein alone. You may hold the reins in one hand or in both hands.
3. Finally, adopt the ordinary method of holding the reins.

With each of these different methods of holding the reins, the trooper must make the horse repeat the simple movements with which the horse is familiar. Moreover, the trooper frequently should put the horse back on the snaffle alone and ride the horse at extended gaits to restore the confidence that the horse may have lost when the trooper introduced him to lessons on the curb.

During this period of preparation, the trooper's legs play an important role. It is essential that the curb bit should produce upon the horse no slowing or backing effort. The forward movement that the trooper's legs urge on the horse should overcome any tendency for the horse to move in the other direction which might result from the first use of the curb bit.

**Bending Lessons.** As stated previously, the trooper must not begin bending lessons until the horse has become thoroughly accustomed to his new bit and fearlessly accepts the contact of both bit and chain. Before setting forth a schedule of bendings, let us cite the following principles related to bending:

1. Never slacken the gait during a bending lesson. The hand does not pull the horse back. The legs push the horse forward until he encounters the bit when a bending results.
2. Bendings with the snaffle bit should be performed with only one rein at a time. Since the trooper will use both snaffle reins to raise the head and to support the horse, he will not use both reins at the same time to exact bending.
3. It is just the reverse with the curb bit the reins of which are rarely separate in their action. The trooper should use both reins and rarely use them separately. As his main objective, the trooper seeks to attain a light feel on both reins acting together.
4. Do not bend the neck (laterally). Setting the head involves the upper part of the neck. That is generally good enough.
5. Frequently follow up the bendings by easing the hand. As soon as the horse extends his neck to the full extent, exact another bending with the head down.

The trooper should execute Bending lessons with the double bridle in accord with the following schedule:

1. With the snaffle bit: Flex the jaw using one rein. Set the head to the right and then to the left (as in a change of direction).
2. With both snaffle and curb bits: Use both right reins to execute a lateral flexion. (XII)
   - Use both left reins to execute a lateral flexion.
   - Use both right reins to set the head.
   - Use both left reins to set the head.

3. *With the curb bit:* Use one curb rein to flex the jaw.
   - Use both curb reins to flex the jaw (Direct flexion).
   - The most important bendings are:
     1. Setting the head by using on snaffle rein.
     2. Executing a direct flexion of the jaw by using both curb reins.

**Dismounted Bending Lessons.** Dismounted bending lessons should be the exception. *(Ed. Note: since Chamberlin advises against attempting Bending lessons while dismounted, we omit the discussion of the process.)*

## Definitions

**In hand.**—The horse is in hand after he has completed and fully understands the bending lessons and when he yields willingly to the effects of the bit.

**Lightness.**—Lightness is the correct balance of the horse that obeys promptly and easily all impulses given him by his rider.

**The set (Le placer)**—is the operation that places the center of gravity in the position required for the execution of any desired movement.—St. Phalle.

**The gather (Le ramener).**—To gather is nothing more or less than to set the forehand. When the horse carries his head and neck well up, the face approaching the vertical and the jaw flexible he is said to be in the position of the gather (or is gathered).

**The assemble (Le rassembler).**—The assemble consists of the gather perfected by bringing the hind legs under. The set of the forehand combines with the set of the hind quarters. *

> *The horse can be gathered at a halt although he should be *taught* the correct carriage of the head and neck at a walk, in which case there will be no chance of backing.
>
> On the other hand, the assemble, the highest form of collection, can be obtained only when the horse is in motion; the horse is assembled in the half halt to be sure, but this position can be held only for a moment before the horse moves again.
>
> Saint-Phalle says: "The *set,* as will be seen, is inseparable from the *in hand* and the *assemble.*"
>
> For instance, in the half halt, the horse is assembled; he is also in hand, ready for any indication of the bit and his is set for movement in any direction. (*The Cavalry Board*).

# XVI

**Easing the Hand on the Curb Bit.** We have discussed previously the easing of the hand on the snaffle bit. The suppling exercise is the same when made on the curb bit but in this case, it should be followed by raising the head.

Once the horse loosens the jaw, the trooper must loosen his fingers and continue his leg action to push the horse gently in pursuit of his bit. From the very beginning of training, the horse has grown accustomed to lean lightly on the bit. He therefore, extends his neck and lowers his head to recover this customary support.

The extension of the neck will be sufficient and will be well executed when the horse, without increasing or decreasing the gait, extends his nose downward and forward to the level of his knees and keeps his jaw flexible.

The rider raises the head by carrying his hands forward and by pulling upward on the reins with the legs still active to prevent any slowing of the gait.

These suppling exercises, the rider should repeat at the walk, the trot, and the gallop as well as on the three lines: straight, the circle, and the diagonal.

Easing the hand is an exercise suitable for horses too high in front, with a high neck, that is either upside down or ewe-necked, and for those with weak hind quarters, predisposed to injuries. It should be used very sparingly with horses that are high behind, especially if the withers are low and sunken, the shoulders straight, the neck thin and the head large.

**How to "Give and Take" on the Reins.** The Action of the Fingers on the Reins. As the horse should always be in close touch with the hand of the rider, the expression *"give and take"* has a certain significance which should be clearly stated.

*Take* does not mean drawing the hand back and *give* does not mean carrying the reins forward and releasing the reins.

Assuming the permanent contact which should exist between the horse's mouth and the rider's hand, *take* means to fix the wrist and tighten the fingers at the moment of halting or of half halting. *Give* means to relax the wrist and loosen the fingers without losing touch with the horse's mouth; if the horse has been well trained touch will not be lost because the horse himself will feel for his rider's hand.

Any slowing of gait should therefore be the result of the action of the fingers on the reins. If this action proves insufficient, then the rider must reinforce it by carrying the upper part of the body backward; *(Ed. Note: the concept of leaning the body backward, Chamberlin ultimately rejects when riding a trained horse.)* Any movement of the elbows should be avoided, however, as this remains the unfailing symptom of the unskilled horseman.

**Why one must return often to the lesson of going straight ahead.** All these bending lessons made on the bit, these halts and half halts, only too often result in slowing the horse and in diminishing any desire to go ahead that he may have acquired. (This is commonly called "steam," and is manifested by a proper voluntary tightening of the reins. The horse with "no steam" is voluntarily behind the bit. (*The Cavalry Board.*)

It is therefore necessary to resume frequently the first lesson of the legs—the lesson of moving straight ahead. The horse should be attacked vigorously with the calves, being careful to fully loosen the fingers, so that he shall have complete liberty to escape to the front.

**How to apply the Lesson with the spurs.**—With horses that hold back, that are too cold (phlegmatic), or that do not respond to the legs the spurs should be used. The lesson with the spurs does not occur at any fixed period, but is given when the occasion presents itself. If the horse is behind the legs* put him at a trot in order to have him securely in motion (not liable to stop), and then let him feel the spurs by vigorous and repeated action until he leaps to the front.

*See Question XXVIII.

Here it is particularly important to pay attention to the hand; you must not contradict with the hand what you demand with the legs, but must let the reins slip as much as is necessary to enable the horse to extend himself freely. With certain horses it is sometimes prudent to grasp the pommel of the saddle when giving the spur lesson. The rider is then more certain of not contradicting himself and the lesson thus administered is sure to be profitable in the training of the animal.

# XVII

**How to Work at the Trot.** Rising to the Trot. The rider should always rise to the trot unless the slowness of the gait renders it impossible or at any rate difficult.

To rise to the trot, the rider inclines the upper body forward and takes a firm grip with the knees in order to avoid throwing his whole weight into the stirrups and in order to have the lower legs perfectly free. (*Ed. Note: Chamberlin later recommends that while posting, the rider support his weight on the inner thighs, the knees, and the calves with weight sinking into the rider's depressed heels. The rider's calves "...are constantly closed against the horse's sides," writes Chamberlin in* Riding and Schooling Horses.*)* He then allows himself to be raised by the thrust of one diagonal pair of legs, the right for example (i.e. right hind and left fore). He avoids the thrust produced by the planting of the left diagonal pair and drops back into the saddle just as the right diagonal pair is replanted, the thrust of which raises him again.

The rider thus avoids every other thrust, tires himself less, and tires his horse less.

**Necessity of Frequently Alternating the Diagonal Pair from Which the Rise Is Made.** But unless he is careful, he gradually acquires the habit of always rising from the same pair, or as it is commonly expressed, of trotting on the same shoulder, and this habit has serious drawbacks.

1. The pair from which the rider rises becomes much more fatigued than the other because it raises and thrusts forward the weight of both horse and rider; whereas the other pair, which acts while the rider is in the air has only the weight of the horse to thrust forward.
2. If the rider is rising from the right diagonal pair, the left diagonal pair acts while he is in the air and thrusts the weight of the horse further in its own direction than is possible for the right diagonal pair on account of its additional burden. After a certain length of time, there results a disagreeable irregularity in the gait since one shoulder gains more ground than the other.

The results explained in the second remark above offer practical application: If the rider discovers that his horse trots unevenly and advances one shoulder more than the other, he should rise on the shoulder that gains less ground.

The rider also may use these results to correct the fault of a horse always leading with the same foot at a gallop. Suppose, for instance, a horse that always gallops on the right foot. To lead with the right foot, the horse sets the right shoulder in advance of the left. If the rider persists, therefore, for a certain length of time, in rising from the left diagonal pair, then he will push the left shoulder further forward than the right and the horse will be in a position at a trot that will induce him to lead with the left foot at a gallop.

From the preceding explanations, it remains evident that the rider should know how to trot his horse on either shoulder and to change shoulders without changing gait if he wishes to develop the animal's efficiency equally and have the horse always perfectly straight.

The only exception arises when the legs of one diagonal pair have been injured and the rider can save them by rising to the trot from the other diagonal pair.

**How to Lengthen and Shorten the Gait at a Walk and Trot.** The rider must lengthen and shorten the gaits gradually and by the steady use of the aids. When the horse lowers his head and extends his neck, it assists in producing a lengthened gait. When the horse raises the head and curves the crest, it favors a shortened gait.

In all changes of gait, the rider must accommodate his seat to the horse's movements. The lengthening of the trot should be moderate and of short duration. By demanding more than the horse is equal to, the rider will cause an irregular gait to develop. This will prove difficult to correct later.

# XVIII

**How and why to Work at the Slow Trot.** The slow trot especially gives excellent results in the last stages of training. Suppling exercises for the haunches, the shoulder and the jaw, when executed at this gait, produce rapid progress in the horse. They increase his strength and his suppleness by forcing him to acquire and preserve his balance.

**Small Circles.** Small circles lower the horse's croup; the horse necessarily brings the inside hock under and the horse develops the outside shoulder because it travels a greater distance. Moreover, this work on a restricted circle enables the rider to set a horse that experiences difficulty in bending the body. The work also aids in breaking up the contraction of the horse that pulls too hard on the hand.

The rider rarely should use small circles with horses that hang back since on the circle they especially are prone to get behind the bit. Nor should the rider use turns too much with young horses who suffer from blemished or worn out hocks. As for the aids the rider should use, it depends upon whether the horse has a tendency to let the haunches swing out or the reverse—to let them drag inside. When the haunches swing out, the rider should predominate with his inside rein and outside leg. When the haunches drag inside, then the rider should emphasize the inside rein and the *inside* leg.

**Serpentines.** Serpentines produce about the same results as small circles but, in addition, they accustom the horse to pass from one set (position) to the other, easily and *while advancing*.

**Two-Track Work.** Two track work at a slow trot on the diagonal of the hall offers another method to supple the hindquarters and to bring them under; it is an excellent preliminary to the gallop lead.

**Halts, Half-Halts, and Backing.** When the horse moves freely and begins to achieve balance and regularity in both gaits, the walk and the trot, we must take up the elements of the assemble, which is the gather perfected by bringing the hind legs under.

We begin with numerous halts, *the action of the legs always preceding the action of the hand,* and by this means alone, we gradually bring the hind legs towards the center. If, at the moment of halting, the horse contracts and endeavors to bore on the rider's hand, then the rider must keep up his action and exact a step or two backward in order to overcome all resistance. The rider must promptly move the horse to the front again to avoid the animal from sitting down on the haunches.

The rider makes half-halts according to the same principles, but the opposition of the hand remains less marked than in halts. If the horse proves obedient, then loosen the fingers and extend the horse. If, on the contrary, the horse resists the half-halt, then keep up the action of the aids to the halt or even resort to backing.

# XIX
# Work at The Gallop

**How to Progressively Perfect the Gallop Lead on Either Foot.**
**1. How to Take up the Gallop by increasing the gait from the Trot.** In the early stages of training, the rider should exact the gallop by increasing the gait from the trot. If the rider repeats this lesson every day, then he will accustom the horse to some extent to the gallop and he will cause the horse to take up the gait readily to the right and to the left, on the circle or at the corner, without the necessity of prolonged pushing from the trot.

**2. How Take up the Gallop from the Slow Trot by Lateral Effect.** We now reach the second step. A somewhat restricted circular movement should assist this new lesson. and the rider will exact a gallop only at the end of a circle or at the corner. If the rider requires the same leads on a circle of greater radius, or at the end of a diagonal, or at the end of a half turn, or of the diagonal, or of the change of hands, then the execution will be slightly more difficult.

**3. How to Take up the Gallop from the Slow Trot by Diagonal Effect.** The series of leads made by lateral effect on small circles, circles, and at the end of oblique lines, we will again exact by diagonal effect and we thus gradually reach the gallop lead on a straight line, being careful to always divide the movement into two parts: first, the set; and then, the impulse that produces the gallop. Thus, for the gallop lead with the right foot:

    a. Collect the horse to the right and pull diagonally on the right rein in order to restrain the left shoulder and to free the right shoulder; carry the body to the rear, throwing more weight on the left buttock: close the left leg to make the haunches yield to the right and to bring the right hind leg in advance.

    b. The horse having been set in this manner, close the right leg in order to add its effect to that of the left leg and to thus obtain, by the action of both legs, the forward impulse necessary to bring about the gallop.

**4. How to Take up the Gallop from the Walk.** A horse that takes the gallop readily from the slow trot will also take the gallop without difficulty from the walk. The procedure is the same; that is, first set the horse and then push him into the gallop.

With horses that hesitate or fret, this last lesson should be subdivided by passing through the trot; that is to say, the horse will be set for the gallop while at a walk, from this set he will be urged into the trot and from the trot into the gallop. Little by little this intermediate trot will diminish in duration until the horse takes the gallop immediately from the walk.

In this progressive method of obtaining the gallop lead on either foot, we began by increasing the gait from the trot and finished by taking the gallop from the walk because we are convinced that taking the gallop is easier in proportion to the speed of advancing.

In our opinion, taking the gallop from the walk is the most difficult exercise and if insisted upon too early will result in horses that back or stand and resist. Our method appears, perhaps, rather long, but it has the advantage of producing horses that act smoothly, that take the gallop without fretting, and without losing touch with the rider's hand.

# XX

**Where Should the Training of the Troop Horse Stop?** The training of the troop horse should stop after the gallop lead has been included. It is useless, or rather impossible, to proceed further with the material available. A horse for the ranks, that goes straight and free at all gaits, that is easily handled in any direction, and that takes the gallop lead readily on either foot, is in condition to satisfy all demands imposed in the service. But this elementary education is not sufficient to meet the requirements of an officer, who should always have a perfectly trained horse. It is therefore important to point out, what movements will perfect and complete the animal's schooling. *(Ed. Note: Chamberlin will advocate training Troop horses up to and including the flying change of lead.)*

**Why practice The False Gallop aka "Counter Canter."** Galloping false provides a means to lower the croup, to balance the horse. and to hold him in his gallop. There exist no special instructions about leading with the outside foot. The only difficulty is if the horse becomes disunited as he passes the corners. To avoid this, the rider's inside leg must strongly support the haunches and the outside rein (supporting rein) must hold the horse in order to free the shoulder on that side and to keep it in the lead. In making a change of direction when galloping false, the rider should lower (ease) slightly his hands so that the movements of the hind quarters will not be hampered and checked. (It is also important to forcibly keep up the gait. If allowed to slow up, the horse will almost certainly escape from the aids and change the lead. (*The Cavalry Board.*)

**Why to Alternate the Gallop at Short Intervals.** The gallop leads comprise all the essential principles of training: setting the head, the neck, the shoulders, and the haunches, bringing the hind legs under and moving to the front. This very complexity shows their importance. It will be readily understood, therefore, that gallop leads, alternated at short intervals, will rapidly perfect the young horse's training and, moreover, that this practice offers the best method to pave the way to teach the change of lead.

**How to teach the Change of Lead.** The change of lead is nothing more than exacting the gallop lead when the horse proceeds at the gallop. It is the most difficult of leads and must not be attempted until the horse is thoroughly confirmed in the gallop lead from the trot and walk. The rider must not attempt it until the horse is thoroughly confirmed in the gallop lead from the trot and the walk. If the lesson of change of lead is given too soon or if the rider is too exacting at first, then the horse will slow up and become uncertain in gait. The horse will learn the trick of holding back and especially of galloping disunited. Hence, all the benefit of the preceding lessons will be lost.

To bring the horse up to the change of lead, gradually decrease the intervals between the alternate leads exacted from the slow trot. The set of the horse must be changed before he returns to the trot. Thus, for instance, if the horse is galloping right, set him with the left diagonal effect (right leg and left supporting rein). The change of set causes the horse to balance himself and brings him down to the trot (where he feels steadier) but, if the lower aids continue to force the gait the horse will take the gallop with the left lead.

This is the analysis of the change of lead. Little by little the length of time of the intermediate trot is diminished until the change of lead in the air is obtained.

The rider can give the lesson of the change of lead on the riding hall tack or on a circle. At first, it remains advantageous to lead off with the outside foot and then attempt the change of lead to the inside foot. This plan especially applies to work on a circle.

In all of this work, the thing the rider must avoid is the desire to progress too rapidly. If the horse resists, then you must not be bull-headed. You must begin again and take up the analytical parts of the movement by going back to the simple gallop leads. By insisting too strongly, you teach the horse to resist the reins and the legs. You destroy what lightness he may have acquired. Moreover, the horse's resistance proves that you are attempting the change of lead too soon and that he is not yet up to it.

**How and why to continue Training at the Slow Trot.** Gallop Exercises. Review the instructions given under Question XVIII regarding the trot and regarding work at the gallop. Work at the slow trot on the three lines will develop the strength and suppleness of the horse; alternating gallop leads with short intervals, exacted from the trot, the walk, the halt and when backing, will finally perfect his balance and obedience; he will then be *well trained.*

But this work must not be abused. Riding hall work should be of short duration. The horse should be often taken out, galloped over good ground, and jumped over obstacles.

It must not be forgotten that the desirable qualities in an officer's mount are that he shall be perfectly willing, go perfectly straight, and remain perfectly calm, all of which qualities would disappear if he were kept constantly shut up in a riding hall, working at slow and shortened gaits.

# XXI
# How to Teach the Young Horse to Jump

**Jumping when at liberty.** Young horses may be taught to jump when at liberty or on the longe.

Jumping at liberty ordinarily occurs in a straight chute, in which several obstacles reside—at least one ditch and one bar. The trooper quietly leads the horse to the entrance of the chute. The horse enters and proceeds. Near each obstacle, an assistant stands with a longing whip ready to urge the horse that holds back and hesitates. The assistant should not abuse the use of the whip, however, since it bewilders the horse. Plus, after a few lessons, ordinarily it is no longer required. Another man catches the horse at the other end and stops him without frightening him and then offers him oats as a reward.

Jumping at liberty produces horses keen and straight on their jumps. The drawback is that the animals jump too quickly and acquire only a certain amount of skill because instead of observing the obstacles that they jump, they have only one idea and that is to get out of the chute. The system works especially well to train horses for steeplechasing.

If the jumps in the chute are high, then it will be better not to send young horses through until they have had several preliminary lessons on the longe.

**How to teach Jumping on the longe.** Jumping on the longe is a perfect lesson to train a horse for obstacles. Drilled by this method, the horse is cool and clever and forms the habit of observing the obstacle. It is the best system for service mounts and hunters.

This lesson may be given in the hall or in the open and in the following manner:

**High jumps.** Place a bar on the ground. Holding the longe in one hand and the snaffle reins in the other, lead the horse and step over the bar with him several times in succession in both directions. When the horse no longer shows hesitation, move away from him a little, put him on a circle and make him cross the bar on the longe. Later the bar is gradually raised.

To give the lesson properly, it is necessary:
1. To let the horse assume, at a short distance from the bar, whatever gait suits him, and immediately after he jumps to make him resume the original gait of the circle.
2. To advance a step or two toward the obstacle and to open the fingers, so that the longe may slip through the hand while the

horse is approaching his jump and will not be too taut when he leaps; he must never be hampered, but must have complete liberty.
3. To take up the horse on the longe again *gently*, return him to the circle and to the original gait.

It is a good plan to practice the horse in jumping on the longe at a walk before trying him at the trot and gallop. At the walk the horse can best estimate the jump and the amount of effort necessary to clear it; at the walk he also learns how best to assist himself with his head and neck. Jumping at the other gaits then becomes less difficult.

**Broad jumps.** The method of procedure and the precautions to be taken are the same as for high jumps. Begin with very easy ditches and progress to broader and more difficult ones. The first time do not prevent the horse from stopping to examine the ditch. He will feel the ground, bring up his hind legs little by little, and after much hesitation, he will finally enter the ditch. This feeling for firm ground is allowed on the first trial only, and as soon as the first apprehension has disappeared, any halting in front of the obstacle must be energetically corrected. Young horses are much more disposed to hesitate at breadth rather than height.

**Jumping mounted.** After horses have been trained in jumping at liberty and on the longe, they are made to jump mounted. At first, they must be in the snaffle bridle. Always begin with insignificant obstacles. In the riding hall, place the bar on the ground and afterwards raise it gradually according to the confidence shown my man and horse. Out of doors, start with very easy jumps and work up gradually to the class of obstacles that every service mount should clear.

# XXII

**How to Accustom Young Horses to the Saber.** For the first few days, the saber should be worn on the belt and not slung to the saddle. In this manner, the saber may more easily be held away from the horse, in case he becomes too excited, and any dangerous struggles resulting from prolonged contact may be avoided. With very nervous horses, the saber, instead of being attached to the belt, may be held in the hand and the lesson can then be easily continued or stopped at will.

The first lesson should be given in the middle of the work period when the horse's nervousness has already been worn off.

The saber is next slung to the saddle; as soon as the horse has become accustomed to it, the saber's different movements should continue until absolute indifference on the part of the horse is achieved.

**How to Accustom Horses to Fire-Arms and Noises.** Several methods are used. One of the best is to place the mounted troopers on a large circle; dismounted men are placed in the center, some with revolvers, flags and trumpets, others with boxes or sieves of oats. At a given signal the noises cease and the horses are turned to the center of the circle where oats are offered to them.

This same exercise is repeated on circles of smaller radius and when the horses show no further anxiety, they are turned into the center of the circle and fed oats while the noises continue.

Another plan is to place in line the dismounted men with the revolvers, flags and trumpets. They march around the drill field. The young horses, also in line, follow them about, at first at a distance, gradually approaching and finally eating their oats in the ranks.

However, it is not necessary to enter into minute descriptions of details. It will suffice if the following caution is observed:

Avoid a struggle by starting at a distance from the dismounted men and do not insist brutally on the occasion of a horses' first fright.

**Swimming Exercises.** Swimming exercises are difficult to carry out and the results obtained are not always commensurate with the danger to which men are exposed. If, however, the horses must be made to swim, the following schedule should be followed:

1. Make the horse swim, holding him at the end of a longe attached to a halter. In this way you will be more certain to avoid any jerks that would cause him to make false movements. This remark is very important for if a horse in the water is brought up short, he will splash in his struggles and may easily lose his head completely.
2. After the horse exhibits a certain amount of confidence, he should be mounted, bareback and in snaffle bridle, by a man who is an excellent swimmer and taken across a rather narrow stream. In order to have this exercise carried out under favorable conditions, the banks of the stream should have a gentle slope so that the horse can enter the water gradually, get out without difficulty, and not be forced to swim more than a few yards.
3. The same exercise is repeated once or twice only, with the horses saddled and bridled.

# XXIII
# Various Faults of Saddle Horses

**The Hot-Headed Horse.** Ride him alone, calm him by the voice, and by patting. Pull as little as possible on the reins. Bring down the head and neck by protracted periods of trotting. Then, execute in the hall serpentines and figures of eight to accustom the horse to submit to the pressure of the legs and to obey the aids readily.

**The Jigging Horse.** Begin by giving the leg lesson until the horse moves freely to the front. When he is well up on the bit make him half lower the head, keeping the reins taut but following the balancing of the head and neck. Whenever the horse resumes the trot, push him sharply with the legs and then, carrying the body back, exact a half-halt to bring him down to the walk.

**The Horse that Gallops When He Should Trot.** It is almost always because he holds back or because his hind quarters are overloaded that a horse, even a hot headed one, makes trouble at the trot. In either case, make him extend his neck and every time he rises to the gallop push him with the legs, but do not pull on the reins. Then carry the body back, pulling gently on the reins and, by means of the legs, holding the horse's haunches perfectly straight. Loosen the fingers at the first strides of the trot and keep the body erect with the legs firmly set.

**The Puller.** Being at the walk, execute half-halts with lateral effects. When the horse yields, let him straighten himself again and resume the original gait. Repeat this same lesson, first at the slow trot and then at the regulation trot. In this way, the puller's rigidity is broken up. He is forced to bend and to bring his hind legs under.

Work at a slow trot on small circles, serpentines, and diagonals, halts and half-halts, make up an excellent schedule of exercises for the horse with too much weight on his shoulders and that pulls too much on the hand.

**The Star Gazer.** (The horse that pokes his nose out). A horse with this fault has a rigid jaw and holds his head high, approaching the horizontal. A bad neck conformation induces this fault but it generally results from bad riding, the horse being afraid of the hands.

To correct this fault, set the hand, that is to say hold it stationary above the pommel of the saddle, the reins remaining taut; close the legs to push the horse up to the bit and tighten the fingers on the reins until the horse lowers his head slightly; loosen the fingers immediately and slacken the reins. Begin again and continue the lesson until the horse yields at the slightest pressure of the fingers and understands thoroughly that the hand is severe when he pokes out his nose but relaxes completely as soon as he sets his head properly.

**The Horse that Fights the Bit (throws his head).** This fault is found only in the horse that holds back because, in order to make the movement of the head, he must diminish the gait slightly.

To correct the fault, it is not wise to use the hand only, as is frequently done, because any effect of the hands tends to a further decrease of gait. The most rational and at the same time, the most certain method is as follows:

Make the horse move freely and push him energetically with the legs at the very moment that you feel that he is about to throw his head. At the same time, loosen your fingers to allow the neck to extend and the head to lower. If this plan is not sufficient, then hold one rein taut and set the hand that holds it. The method is effective because the head movements can be made only side-wise and become very painful.

**The Horse that Lowers His Head Against His Chest.** It is hard work to correct this fault and much more difficult to raise the head than to lower it. To raise the head, begin by extending the neck in order to open the angle it makes with the head. When the neck is well extended use the snaffle reins to gradually raise the head, *watching carefully that the horse keeps his muzzle to the front*. The upward pull of the snaffle reins must be felt at the corners of the lips. The legs must act vigorously to prevent any slowing of the gait. Exact little at first and ease the hand as soon as the horse raises his head slightly and yields his jaw. Give this lesson several times each ride and at all gaits until the horse holds his head at a proper height whenever the snaffle reins are tightened and the legs are closed.

Dismounted bending lessons also give good results. The trooper stands facing the horse, and taking one snaffle rein in each hand, the trooper steadily raises his hands until the horse lifts the head without backing.

**The Horse that Rears.** This fault begins with halting and squatting. Hence the first thing to do is to prevent this backward movement by a counter attack, that is, by an attack that will produce a movement to the front and that will throw weight on the forehand.

If the horse resists the forward movement, turn him on the spot so as to disorganize the forces necessary in rearing. When the haunches move laterally, no part of the horse can be contracted and his is therefore prevented from throwing the weight on his hind quarters.

**The Kicker.** If a horse has the bad habit of kicking, use the snaffle bit to prevent his lowering the head and at the same time push him vigorously with the legs.

It is a mistake to always hold up a kicker's head. It frequently happens that kicking is caused by some pain in the back or hocks; and if so, then raising the animal's head will merely increase his irritability and incite resistance.

## XXIV

**Requirements of a Good Saddle.** A good saddle should satisfactorily meet the following requirements:
1. The padding should be done in a way to secure perfect balance of the saddle. Too high behind, the saddle will throw the whole weight of the rider into the stirrups. Too high in front, it will throw him back and diminish the grip of the things and prevent proper set of the knees.
2. The pommel arch should be wide enough to allow the saddle to be used on nearly all horses and to be set far enough back.
3. The seat should not be too flat and the rider should not feel the outer edges of the bars of the tree under his thighs.
4. The straps for the girth should be set well forward. If the line of traction of the girth were too far to the rear, the saddle would rock and, rising in front, would work up toward the withers.

**How a Horse Should Be Saddled.** The saddle should be placed far enough back but it is impossible to give any fixed rule. Its proper place depends upon the conformation of the horse. A horse with a good back and a well-marked girth place is easy to saddle; it is the reverse in the case of one with short ribs or big belly or hollow shoulders.

The matter of saddling, although often neglected, is of great importance. Everything in riding hinges on balance and balance will be handicapped from the start if the rider is seated too close to the withers and is unduly overloading the forehand. *(Ed. Note: Gen. Chamberlin and Col. Albert Phillips will reject this claim and modify saddle design to move the center of the saddle an inch forward of the saddle's center in order to move the rider closer to the horse's withers.)*

# XXV

**Holding the Snaffle Reins.** When the horse is ridden in the snaffle bridle, the rider takes one rein in each hand, "the reins coming in on the underside of the little finger, and coming out over the second joint of the forefinger, on which the thumb firmly holds the rein; the other fingers closed on the reins, nails toward the body. *** Hands about six inches apart, on a level with the elbows, backs straight up and down and outward." (*U.S. Cavalry Drill .Regulations.* Par. 294).

**With the double snaffle, the rider takes two reins in each hand.** The reins of the lower snaffle bit (corresponding to the curb bit) pass between the third and the little finger and both reins are held upon the forefinger by the thumb as explained above.

**Holding the Double Bridle Reins.** With horses that pull hard and more especially with horses that struggle or fight, it is a distinct advantage to hold the reins in English fashion, this is, with two reins in each hand as described above for the double snaffle. *

*To take the double bridle reins in one hand (the left) turn the right wrist to the left until the back of the right hand is up; move the right hand to the left and insert the second finger of the left hand between the two reins (right snaffle rein uppermost). All four reins are held upon the second joint of the forefinger by the thumb.

To pass the reins from the left hand to the right hand, turn over the back of the left hand to the right and insert the extended fingers of the right had between the reins in such a manner that there will be a rein *above* each finger (left snaffle rein uppermost), the four reins coming out under the little finger instead of above the forefinger.

If the hand is habitually held back up, as is frequently done, the passing of the four reins from one hand to the other is much simplified. (*The Cavalry Board*).

**Handling the Reins.** It is absolutely necessary to accustom riders to handle the reins skillfully.

All work on the reins must be varied, smooth, and progressive. These results cannot be obtained unless the rider is thoroughly supple in the shoulders, arms, and writs, and has clever fingers. The reins must be changed from hand to hand, must be separated and reunited not only without jerks but also without failing to maintain the proper tension.

It should also be added that handling the reins understandingly and skillfully is an indirect method of making a horse's mouth perfectly straight. Changing hands frequently will prevent the prolonged action that worries the horse and causes faulty bends of then neck. Riders who hold the reins constantly in the same hand and in the same manner always have horses with stiff necks set to one side.

# XXVI

**What is Meant by the Aids?** The *aids* are the different means employed by the rider to convey his desires or intentions to the horse.

**Into What Classes are they Divided?** The aids may be divided into *natural* and *artificial*. The natural aids are the hands and legs; the artificial aids are: the spur, the whip, the voice, the pat, the longe, the longing whip, and the padded posts. (Padded posts are used to train for the *haute ecole*.)

The hands are called the *upper aids* and the legs, the *lower aids*. Some horsemen make use of the terms *principal* and *supplementary* to designate the natural and the artificial aids respectively.

From the standpoint of the execution of a movement, the aids are classed as *decisive* and *controlling*.

The former are indispensable to the execution of the movement and have a dominating action; the latter are merely useful, and participate only in setting the horse to advantage and in making the movement regular.

A final division into *lateral* and *diagonal* aids results from the manner in which the aids are combined. In the first case, the rider uses simultaneously the rein and the leg on the same side; in the second case, the rider uses the rein on the one side and the leg on the opposite side.

**Function of the hands.** It is the business of the hands, through the medium of the reins, to communicate to the horse his rider's will, to regulate the horse's gaits, to halt him, and to back him.

Their principal function is the control of the forehand, the impulse having been given previously by the legs. Considered separately, each rein can produce four important and distinct effects:

1. *Front to rear effect*. The rider pulls on the two reins alike, without pressing them on the neck and without opening the wrists. If the horse is moving, he will decrease the gait or halt; if the horse is halted, he will move backward.

2. *Opening effect.* The rider opens the right rein by carrying the wrist to the front and right. The horse's head will be drawn to the right and he will move in that direction. This is the direct rein.
3. *Bearing or pushing effect.* By pressing the left rein against the neck, the mass (forehand) is pushed to the right and the horse faces in that direction—this is the *indirect rein, sometimes called the supporting rein.* *
4. *Opposing effect.* The rider opens the right rein lightly and then pulls either in the direction of the right haunch or in the direction of the left haunch. He is then said to set the shoulders in opposition to the haunches. The *rein of opposition* comes to the aid of the leg on the same side when the latter's action is insufficient or incomplete.

*In the U.S. Cavalry drill regulations a horse is described as *"rein wise* when he obeys the lightest pressure of the rein on either side of the neck, the bit not being disturbed form its normal position." It is to be noted that the horse has learned to obey this pressure ($3^{rd}$ effect) through its association with the opening of the leading rein as prescribed in paragraph 315 D.R. (2d effect.) When the rider uses the direct or leading rein, there must be sufficient tension on the other rein to prevent the bit from "becoming disturbed from its normal position" and the other rein (*la rêne opposée*) is also pressed against the neck to *support* the action of the direct rein. *In general,* there must be combined action of the reins just as there must be combined action of the legs. (See "Unison of the legs" in the next question), and this fact should be kept in view in the discussion of the distinct effects produced by the reins. The text reads: "Considered separately, each rein, etc." which might be erroneously construed as: "Each rein, acting alone, etc." (*The Cavalry Board*)

## XXVII

**Function of the legs.**—The legs act on the hind quarters. Their business is to communicate the rider's will to the horse in order to move him straight to the front, to make him extend or increase his gaits, and to start him in movements of all kinds. It is also their special business to control the haunches, to restrict them to the direction pursued by the shoulders or to swing them in reference to the shoulders. Finally, they are used to collect the horse by bringing his hind legs closer to the center of gravity.

To recapitulate, the legs have three effects:
1. To produce a forward movement.

2. To swing the haunches in reference to the shoulders.
3. To bring the hind legs under.

The simultaneous action of both legs produces a double pressure to which the horse should respond by moving to the front. The action of a single leg, while it incites motion, forces the weight of the hind quarters toward the opposite side. Thus, for instance, if the rider closes his left leg, he produces two effects: a general forward movement of the mass and a right lateral movement of the haunches.

**Unison of the Legs.** Whenever one leg acts to swing the haunches, the opposite leg must receive the mass in order to limit and rectify the movement. The legs, therefore, should always be close enough to the horse to act without sudden jolts and to lend mutual assistance.

A horse is *in the legs* when he obeys at the slightest indication and when the gentle closing of the calves is sufficient to make him move out boldly to the front. Perfect obedience to the legs is considered the characteristic sign of successful training.

In the use of the horse everything is based upon the movement to the front. The upper aids merely utilize and direct the impulse produced by the lower aids. If this impulse is wanting or is incomplete, then the horse escapes more or less from the rider's control. We have said several times that the lesson of the legs must take precedence over all others and that it is necessary to return to this lesson every few minutes during the whole period of the instruction of the young horse.

A horse is *behind the legs* when he remains indifferent to their action either through sluggishness or unwillingness. A horse behind the legs is, as a natural result, behind the bit. His is completely out of his rider's control. This is the beginning of obstinacy.

**Length of Stirrups.** *(Ed note: Chamberlin's theories render most of this obsolete for military, hunting, Eventing, show jumping and endurance riding purposes. It may still offer useful guidance for the purposes of artistic dressage. The passages do give the reader a clear idea of the theory taught to Chamberlin at West Point and also at the Mounted Service School.)* Our regulations (French) say: "The stirrups are suitably adjusted if the tread of the stirrup is level with the top of the boot heel, when the trooper is sitting properly on his horse, with the knees closed and the legs hanging naturally."

In his treatise on equitation, Count d'Aure admits the same principle but sates it less precisely. According to him, 'the tread of the stirrup, before the foot is inserted, should be at the height of the rider's heel."

In the Austrian cavalry, the stirrups are worn somewhat shorter. Their regulations say: "The trooper adjusts the stirrups so that the tread shall be about one inch above the seam at the heels. If, from this adjustment, the trooper stands in his stirrups, there will be a space of four fingers between his crotch and the saddle."

The German regulations give the same instructions as the Austrian. (See also Par. 346 *U.S. Cavalry Drill Regulations*).

When the stirrups are too long, the rider is said to be *on his crotch* (fork seat). He loses all stability. His legs flap about the sides of the horse and act with neither strength nor accuracy.

When the stirrups are too short, they support more than the weight of the legs. They raise the knees and thighs and force the seat back. The trooper is then said to be *hung up*, and although he has a stronger support in the stirrups, he is less secure because he is not so far down in the saddle. Moreover, the legs necessarily become rigid. They lose all freedom of movement and, in consequence, all nicety (of action as aids).

The stirrups then, should be neither too long nor too short. But of the two faults, the latter is the more serious. A trooper can shorten his stirrups without anxiety, whereas, he feels a certain reluctance about lengthening them. It is to be noticed that the man who loses his suppleness or his confidence always has a tendency to diminish the length of his stirrup straps.

**Position of the Foot in the Stirrup.** At least one third of the foot should be inserted into the stirrup; the heel should be slightly lower that the toe; the part of the sole of the foot included between the joint of the great toe and the little toe (ball of the foot) should rest on the tread.

The support should be secured mainly on the inside portion of the foot; this method results in closing the knee and holding the lower leg in proper position.

# XXVIII

## The Equine Neck

**How the equine neck plays a part in equitation.** When a horse is left to himself and is free to apply his own natural methods, he makes uses of his head and neck as a balancer to keep his forces in equilibrium or to modify their action. If he wishes to go forward, he pushes out his head and extends his neck in order to shift the center of gravity in the direction of the desired movement.

If, on the contrary, he wishes to go back, he pulls in his head and shortens his neck, thus starting the mass in the movement to the rear. In lateral movements, oblique or circular, it is the same; the shifting of the head or neck to the right or left prepares, favors, and controls the animal's action.

At a walk, the head and neck are in constant motion in order to take weight off the legs that are moving to the front and place weight on those that rest on the ground.

At a gallop, the balancer is alternately raised and lowered according as the horse is supported on the hindquarters or on the forehand and is extended or brought in according as the gait is rapid or slow.

This shifting of the head and neck that we observe in the horse at liberty should be noted when the horse is ridden. The rider should be completely master of the neck, and when he gives his horse the signal for a movement, he should be able at the same time to set the neck in the position most favorable to the execution of the movement. The neck is therefore a steering gear as well as a balancer, and suppling exercises that involve this region necessarily take up a large portion of the time devoted to training. But it is to be noted that these supplings must be confined to the upper part of the neck. The neck must always offer an elastic resistance, suitable to its functions. If it were too flexible and too easily moved it could neither react on the hind quarters nor control the movements of the forehand.

**The Kind of Neck to Select.** The importance of the part played by the neck shows the importance that should be attached to its good conformation. A rider should always select a long and powerful neck with the head well set on. And it should be remembered that we said that in training it is more difficult to raise than to lower the head. A high neck branching firmly from a sloping shoulder will diminish the difficulties of training and will permit the rider to produce more easily a brilliant well set up horse.

**The Different Positions of the Neck.** The neck should always preserve its muscled pose and even have a certain amount of rigidity. Its position should be the same as that assumed naturally, when the horse at liberty is in high spirits and standing still.

If, contrary to this principle, the experiment is made of raising the head and neck too high, then the play of the shoulders may be freer, but, at the same time, the loins and all parts of the hind quarters will be weighted down and the haunches and hocks will be hampered in their action. As a result, movements of the hind quarters will be constrained, unequal, and jerky, and the gait will lose both speed and regularity.

If the neck is too low, then the hind quarters will be more at liberty but will not (for that reason) fulfill their functions any better; for since if they cannot be brought up toward the center of gravity except by a special, momentary and forcible application of the lower aids, then they will promptly go back again and will be relieved of the weight which is their proper share in an equal distribution of forces; weight, we repeat, that tends to set the hind quarters; weight that, when the neck is held at a suitable height, naturally and properly falls back from the shoulders upon the haunches. If the hind quarters are too free and do not carry their proper share of weight, then their action is not favorable to smooth gaits.

Therefore, the position of the neck should be neither high nor low. The neck must be able to shorten or lengthen itself accordingly as the face approaches or departs from the vertical. The head, when drawn back, should bend the neck without breaking* it. When extended forward, it should stretch the neck without raising it. When the horse is posed in this manner, the reins will retain full power and both the front and the hind legs will cooperate in any movements, either lengthened or shortened, that the rider may exact. (*Count D'Aure*).

*The bend should be near the poll; the rest of the neck remains practically the same in all positions, or as it is called, "unbroken."

**Different Positions of the Head.** In order that he may feel with uniformity the touch of the rider's hand and in order not to impede his breathing, the horse's face should be set a little forward of the vertical. This position should be taken for ordinary gaits and for simple and regular movements.

The more we wish to shorten the gait, the more the face should approach the vertical plane; on the other hand, the more we wish to increase the speed, the more the face should depart from this plane.

In the last two cases, the position of the head may also be considered as normal since the gaits depend thereon. The head may assume a faulty position. This may be due to defective conformation or the forehand, faulty fitting of the bit, undue sensitiveness of the chin groove or bars; or finally, and this is most frequently the case when horses throw the nose into the air, to a defect in the conformation of some part of the hind quarters.

These faulty positions can be combatted by the rider not only by a judicious use of the aids, but by a careful selection of the bit, an attentive fitting in the mouth, and a studied adjustment of the curb chain. (Count D'Aure).

**The Influence of Conformation.** All horses cannot be ridden in the same manner. General principles of conduct and training remain the same, but supplings vary according to the defects of conformation that must be overcome.

A horse of good conformation is easy to train: all that is necessary is to teach him the language of the aids and when he understands, everything becomes simple to him. When, on the contrary, proper balance is wanting, it is necessary not only to instruct him, but also, by means of protracted and well understood exercises to establish an artificial equilibrium that will correct natural defects. (*Ed. Note: The Italian followers of Caprilli disagree. They argue that exercise, not exercises, enables the horse to achieve his natural balance.*)

A horse with croup too high and whose weight is on his shoulders will not be trained along the same lines as one with high forehand or weak hind quarters. In one case, we must raise the head and force the weight back; in the other, we must lower the head and load the forehand. A good horseman must, therefore, study his horse's conformation and adapt his methods of training to the kind of resistance he encounters. This, in order to develop in the animal, in action, a balance which is rarely to be found in young horses.

# XXIX

**How to Train for a Military Race.** It is impossible to lay down fixed rules for training a service mount to run a military steeple chase. The care of the animal as well as his work will vary with his breeding, but an officer or a non-commissioned officer training his horse must pay constant attention in all cases to:

1. The amount of work;
2. The condition of the legs;
3. The appetite.

**1st, The Amount of Work.** Training a service mount for a military steeple chase does not involve such complete conditioning as is required in training a thoroughbred for a flat race. Moderate work should be sufficient to put him in condition, keeping in view the main object which is to bring him up to his maximum strength and energy on the day of the race. First, it must never be forgotten that the less the horse has of pure blood, the less he should be worked into condition for a speed test.

About two months are required to prepare a horse, following a well-chosen program and working only rarely at full speed. It is better, if possible, to have the horse a little above condition to start with. That is, fat rather than poor because it is easier to take off fat than to gain weight by building muscle.

Each day's work should be of about two hours' duration. Exercise should be given in the morning as far as possible, at any rate in summer, so as to avoid the heat and the flies. Give the horse one, or at most, two quarts of oats about one hour before work.

*1$^{st}$ and 2$^{nd}$ Week.* Exercise the horse at a walk. Work him once or twice every day at a trot for a mile or two, and at a gallop for half a mile. Twice a week give him a mile at a very moderate gallop.

*(Editor's Note: The French recommendations regarding how to cause a fat horse to slim down have been omitted in that a modern rider should consult with a veterinarian for advice based on modern research.)*

*3$^{rd}$ and 4$^{th}$ Weeks.* If the horse's legs keep in good shape and if the appetite continues good, then increase the speed and duration of the gallops, diminishing proportionately the length of time at the trot. Twice a week give a good gallop, but not at full speed.

*5$^{th}$ and 6$^{th}$ Weeks.* Same work, increasing the speed and taking the horse once or twice over a distance nearly equal to that of the race.

*7$^{th}$ and 8$^{th}$ Weeks.* Give several gallops from one-half to three-quarters of a mile, increasing the gait during the eighth week at the end of the stretch. Give also two or three gallops about two miles long, but never force the pace.

Two days before the race, gallop from a half mile to a mile, increasing the pace as much as possible the last quarter of a mile, but of course without over taxing the horse. The day before the race give him only a half mile gallop at a moderate gait. The morning of the race, exercise for an hour at a walk.

Training for obstacles is only secondary, provided the horse already knows how to jump. It is sufficient to take him over a few obstacles at an ordinary gait, from time to time after the second or third week.

During training, it is essential that the horse be calm and that he lower his head and stretch the reins without boring on the hand. It should also be understood that the program of work is subordinate to the horse's appetite and to the condition of his legs; the gallop must be replaced by the trot or walk, entirely or partly, every time the tendons become heated, or the horse refuses his oats.

**2$^{nd}$, Condition of the Legs.** The horse's legs should be examined every day and handled with the greatest care. As soon as one tendon becomes more heated that the other, decrease or stop work and relieve the overworked part with bandages, apply water soaking and other remedies as recommended by the veterinarian. Then change the work and replace the rapid gaits by the walk, increasing the duration of exercise. If the tendons heat again, then it is better to stop training entirely and thus avoid a strain that would lay the horse up for a long time.

**3rd, Feed during Training.** As a general rule, a horse never eats too much during training. But if he eats heartily and if his legs will stand it, then increasing the work is sufficient to prevent him from taking on too much flesh, and training in such case will go on under the best possible condition. This, however, is rarely the case. Increasing work generally decreases appetite and it is difficult to make a horse eat more than 14 quarts of oats a day. As soon as a horse stops eating with relish, the gallop should be decreased or stopped, and resumed only when the horse cleans up his oats. *(Ed. Note: We omit the balance of this section since the recommendations more than 110 years old might not be what modern veterinary science might suggest. The findings of the National Research Council regarding recommendations for feeding horses would provide an excellent point of departure. In addition, the work of Eleanor M. Kellon, VDM regarding the feeding of performance horses also offers excellent advice on the issue of equine nutrition.)*

# XXX

**How to Condition a Hunter.** "I shall take the case of a horse that you have bought with the idea of using him for hunting. He is trained, has been worked, and comes from a dealer or any other similar source. His conformation appears good to you from the standpoint of service and his gaits are natural. He is in good condition, fat. It is spring or summer, June, let us suppose. You wish to condition your horse for the hunting season. What will you do?

"First, run you hand all over your horse, but mainly over the body, and pay special attention to the croup and neck. If you find the flesh soft and yielding under the fingers, the legs rather round and pasty, have your horse saddled, mount him, and ride him into a plowed field or upon a road deep with sand. Put your horse into a slow gallop, keeping him well in hand; make him work his hind quarters and bend his neck a little. The horse immediately begins to blow and in a moment is dripping wet. The sweat is white, and resembles soap suds. Do not go any further; your horse is not in condition, and you must require nothing further of him for the present. Take him quietly back to the stable and for two days put him on bran mash and diet, and on the third day give him a purge. Do not be afraid that I am going to overdo the last.

Perhaps, if your horse is too fat, too heavy, I will allow you more at the end of August, but that is all. For in same hygiene, you should avoid the pit into which many hunting horses in England fall, the destruction of the stomach and intestines by an excess of purges and of drugs intended to give an appetite. Moreover, in France our hunters must be in much finer condition than in England. They are not required to do the same kind of work. A hunter in England must withstand two hours of fast gait and constant effort. The hunter in France is generally required to withstand eight or ten hours of continuous work and effort without eating, but at a much slower gait. Therefore, the question of the condition of a hunting horse in England and in France is very different.

"All summer, you should feed your horse Glauber's salts, one handful in a mash at least once every ten or twelve days. He should have a substantial but gradually increasing feed of ten to sixteen pounds of hay, and ten to twelve quarts of oats every day to begin with, depending upon the temperament of the horse. Give him regular work every day or work him two days and let him rest the third day. His work must last at least two hours; at first, one hour at a walk on soft or heavy ground, preferably over plowed ground, then a moderate but continuous trot over ground that is not too hard, for at least three miles; then at least a half hour at a walk. Continue this work for six weeks, that is till about the 15th of July. Then increase the length of time at the trot and begin to trot in place of walking in the work in the open field, but never push the horse into the rapid gaits.

"Continue this until about the 15th of August. The muscles of your house will already begin to grow harder and firmer; they will be stronger and his endurance and wind will be improved. Begin to increase the speed at which he works and then, if he is still too fat, you may give him another purge. A few days later you may increase his oats a little, up to fourteen or sixteen quarts, depending upon the temperament of the horse. The work is then increased by a gallop over plowed ground, always following a progressive course, beginning with a short and rapid gallop, and ending, on the 15th of September, with a good gallop at hunting speed for five or six miles.

"If the horse is still too fat, if the muscles of the neck, loins, and thighs do not stand out well, if he perspires too freely, if the sweat is a white lather and not a colorless fluid, give him (*Editor's Note: discussion with a veterinarian in the year 2019 suggests that the horse needs to develop better condition slowly along with appropriate modifications to the diet. The following recommendations of Saumur Notes are obsolete and, with the exception of always finishing "at a walk and see that there is a very good grooming when you come in. Put on good flannel bandages after careful hand rubbing of the legs." the balance of this section is not recommended*) two or three gallops under blankets, covering well the parts you wish to lighten. For instance, if the neck is too heavy, too flabby, put on one or two hoods. If, on the contrary, he has too large a belly, put on two or three blankets. Naturally, you should always finish at a walk and see that there is a very good grooming when you come in. Put on good flannel bandages after a careful hand rubbing of the legs.

"By following this course of preparation, your horse should begin to be in condition toward the end of September. He is far from being entirely ready, but he may begin to hunt without much fear of injury. By this time, he has started to shed and is beginning to suffer from the action going on inside of him, which takes away part of his strength and exhausts him. Redouble your care by covering him carefully so that the heat may hasten the shedding *(Ed. Note: discussions with a veterinarian suggest that covering to induce shedding is not recommended)* and above all, give him abundant and substantial feed.

"Accordingly, from the 15$^{th}$ of September to the 15$^{th}$ of October, I recommend a feed of beans every day (two quarts soaked in three different waters) and put iron, nails, horse shoes, etc., in his drinking water. *(Ed. Note: the vet does not recommend supplementing drinking water in this manner.)* All this gives him strength to support the work going on inside of him, for it is very important that the shedding and sweating in October should not put him out of condition. If it does, you will not be able to get him back in condition again the rest of the winter, and in January, he will be completely run down. Consequently, it is from the 20$^{th}$ of September to about the 15$^{th}$ of November that you should feed a hunter the most.

"Now your horse is almost in condition and may hunt. In the interval between hunts, exercise your horse or have him exercised a little every other day, taking care to take him out for a short time the day after each hunt to observe his condition and the freedom of his movements. If for any reason you do not hunt for a time, you should put your hose through the same work that you did in the month of August, giving him short gallops and work at the walk over plowed ground.

"In this manner you keep him fit all winter, giving him good feed and varying it according to his condition and appetite. If he always eats well, continue the oats without overdoing the mashes; the latter should be given only in the evening on coming in from the hunt, and on the next morning feed a cold mash of barley meal. If you horse shows a failing appetite or runs down in condition, give him cooked grain or cooked vegetables.

"Thus you reach the month of April and the end of hunting season. As soon as hunting stops, let your horse rest. Exercise him only at a walk and for his health. Take particular care of the legs and lower his condition by cooling mashes, for a horse cannot be kept with impunity on such substantial and heating feed the year around. You might then turn him out in a paddock without grass or with grass that you have cut short. (*Ed. Note: a grazing muzzle would be more effective. Short grass generates far too much sugar.*) Give him a mash, a full feed of carrots, and only six quarts of oats. Continue this until the 15$^{th}$ of May at least, then stop the carrots and little by little the mashes. Then begin to increase the oats, in order to take up the same work as the preceding year and with the same gradual progress.

"During this period of rest, the horse can be given such treatment as the condition of his legs may require. These are the general instructions for putting a hunter in fit condition for his work." (*Count Le Coulteux*).

**How to Condition for an Endurance Race.** For this training, refer to what has just been said concerning hunters, and to the 29$^{th}$ Question, on training for military races.

The work varies with the length of time available, with the age and condition of the horse, and with the nature of the race. The only general rules to be repeated here are:

- Gradually increase the horse's ration with the work.
- Exercise a great deal at a walk in order to develop muscles.
- Regulate the walk and trot carefully, and have the horse perfectly calm at these two gaits.
- Never use the extended trot.
- Accustom the horse not to pull, so that he will not waste part of his strength fighting the hand.
- The morning of the race, massage the tendons; rub both the tendons and joints with a fatty substance, such as Vaseline; if the race is in the morning, then feed a little grain about one or two quarts.
- During the race, the periods at the trot should be considered shorter than during training, in order to avoid winding the horse.
- Dismount as often as possible, especially going up and down hill.
- Do not be afraid to water in moderate quantities once or several times on the road; there is no danger if you do not take too fast a gait just after watering.

# THE MANUAL OF EQUITATION OF THE FRENCH ARMY FOR 1912
## How to Teach the use of the aids

### Warren C. Matha, Editor

In 1913, Lt. Adna R. Chaffee, Jr., Thirteenth Cavalry, translates *The Manual of Equitation of the French Army for 1912* and the Mounted Service School adopts it as one of its texts. The Manual offers detailed training advice for horse and rider. The teachings and philosophy of Baucher and his followers L'Hotte, de Kerbrech and de Beauchesne exert strong influence upon the manual. The manual's authors intend the work to apply to the training of a trooper who will remain in the French cavalry, as a conscript, for a period of two years. (The future U.S. Cavalry manual *Horsemanship and Horsemastership* assumes that a trooper will be a career cavalryman. The U.S. manual offers, therefore, a much more advanced approach.)

The French manual's authors write:
*"Secondary Equitation* treats of the management of the horse (*conduite du cheval*); it permits a detailed study of the natural aids, with a brief naming of the artificial aids. This chapter has been drawn up following the principles of the School of Versailles, transmitted to the Cavalry School by the Comte d'Aure, whose *"cours d'equitation"* approved by ministerial decision dated April 9, 1853, sets forth the means which a rider has for overcoming or avoiding the difficulties born of the use of the horse."

The School of Versailles originated the diagrams and explanations of the five Rein Effects. Comte d'Aure transmits them to Saumur. Gen. J. de Benoist makes them generally known to the French cavalry as a whole. Later, the authors of *Horsemanship and Horsemastership* and Chamberlin in his books *Riding and Schooling Horses* [Xenophon Press 2020] and *Training Hunters, Jumpers, and Hacks* [Xenophon Press 2019] adopt the concepts and the diagrams verbatim. The diagrams appear later in this volume as part of Chamberlin's 1941 monograph *Breaking, Training, and Reclaiming Cavalry Horses*.

For the right hand, the manual describes in words and diagrams:
- The right opening rein
- The right direct rein of opposition
- The right bearing rein

- The right bearing rein of opposition (in front of the withers)
- The right bearing rein of opposition (in rear of the withers)

Of course, the rein effects follow for the left hand as well.

Of additional interest, the manual offers training pointers for instructors. It offers a protocol to direct their students' use of the aides. For example, the Manual suggests that an instructor might voice specific commands. The instructors at Ft. Riley's Cavalry Replacement Training Center in the 1940's will order their mounted trainees continually as follows:

- "By the right opening rein, by the right flank;"
- "By the right bearing rein, volt to the left;"
- "By the left direct rein of opposition, half turn to the left."
- "Half turn in reverse, leave the track by the bearing rein."
- "Right rein of opposition, on two tracks on the diagonal."
- "Turn to the right, by the right opening rein."
- "By the right opening rein, half turn."
- "By the left bearing rein of opposition, on two tracks on the diagonal."

The authors of the manual write:
"The hand should know how to resist authoritatively when necessary, but should give way as soon as the resistance disappears and should return to the softness which is always the union between lightness and firmness. It is in this sense that a good hand has been defined as 'a force in the fingers equal to the resistance of the horse, but never greater.' (de Lancosme-Breves.)" *French Equitation Manual* p.38

**When to start training a horse.**

According to the manual, the preparation of the troop horse for his career comprises two periods, each corresponding to a very distinct end in view:

1. The *breaking*, to which is devoted the first military year of the colt (4 and 5 years old); its object is his physical development, which is obtained by appropriate work, and formation of his character.
2. The *training*, properly said, to which the second military year is devoted (5 and 6 years old) and whose object is his complete submission to the aids.

**General rules to follow: —**
- Never commence work without being absolutely sure of what is to be done.
- Progress in the horse's education from the known to the unknown, from the simple to the difficult.
- Always use exactly the same effects to obtain the same results.
- Remember that in the execution of every movement position should precede action.
- Never ask anything of a horse which is still under the impression of a preceding requirement.
- Never combat two resistances at once.
- Do not confound the rider's lack of skill with the ignorance or bad will of the horse.
- Demand the new step at the end of the lesson.
- Pat the horse and dismount. *French Equitation Manual* p.54-55

## FILLIS ON THE HANDS AND EQUESTRIAN TACT

To give the reader some idea of the depth into which students at the U.S. Cavalry's Mounted Service School delve into the issues of horsemanship, perhaps a discussion of the concept of "the hands" and their relationship to "equestrian tact" will demonstrate the level and depth of that discussion. In addition, in later years in his own writings, Chamberlin attaches particular importance to the James Fillis discussion of "give and take" with the rider's hands.

Fillis writes in his book, *Principles of Dressage and Equitation* aka *Breaking and Riding with Military Commentaries* [Xenophon Press 2017]:
"…we must continually practice the great principle of *taking* and *giving*; The former to stop resistance, the latter to reward obedience…It is, of course, understood that this work ought to be done with great lightness of hand."

"We can gauge the sensibility of the mouth by an alternative feeling of the curb and snaffle and can thus at once find out if the horse has a hard or soft mouth. In this manner we readily get *good*, that is to say, *light hands*, with which we can manage almost any horse by the continued play of "take and give." It is a great advantage to have good hands, which will be sufficient for all ordinary work."

"But we can take and give for all our life without being able to render an account of what we are doing, in which case neither the hand nor the horse makes any progress. Finally, the action of the hand would be limited to giving when the horse pulls, and pulling when he gives. This faculty may be called the possession of a bell in the hand, and is in fact the movement of a bell in all its beauty."

"The *well-trained hand* acts in the contrary manner, because its *role* is to break in the horse, that is to say, to advance his education. It remains fixed in position by strongly closing the fingers when the horse pulls, but the moment the horse yields his lower jaw, the fingers should be relaxed with the rapidity of an electric flash."

"A *good hand* gives when the horse takes, and takes when he gives."

"A *well-trained* hand gives when the horse gives, and takes when he takes, and that instantaneously."

"Direct flexion should always be preceded, sustained, and completed by the action of the legs pressing the hind quarters on the forehand."

"The legs ought to *take and give* like the hands, and with the hands, that is to say, simultaneously and in the same proportion. This constitutes general movement. If the hands give and the legs continue their action, the horse will be *out of hand*, because the propulsion developed by the legs will no longer be received by the hands. If the hands act without the legs sending them any impulsion, the horse will bring his chin into his breast or will get behind his bit; because his hocks have been left too far behind him."

"The expression "take and give," as I have explained it when speaking of direct flexion, therefore applies as well to the action of the legs as to that of the hands. Legs and hands should always act in harmony, according to the desired result. We get the horse in hand by this combination of the alternate actions of the legs and hands acting on the whole. The entire practice of flexions is comprised in timely *taking* and *giving*."

Later, in his own writings, Chamberlin embraces a slightly different concept regarding the interaction between hand and leg: the "*Baucheriste*" ideal of "hands without legs, legs without hands."

Fillis continues:
"The question is: what proportion of the force ought the hand allow to pass through it, and what proportion ought it retain? We should measure this proportion with absolute precision at each stride, by the correct combination of the "aids," so as to send to the hind quarters only the amount of force necessary to maintain equilibrium with a maximum of propulsion."

*"Equestrian tact consists in doing this.* If the fingers do not work with enough decision, the center of gravity will be carried to the front a little too much, and the horse will be ready to go beyond the hand. If they act too strongly, too much weight will be put on the hind quarters, and the hocks will be brought too far back. In both cases there will be no rassembler. The fingering of the reins should regulate with absolute precision the distribution of the propulsion. We have to solve this problem at each stride, which is not identical to the preceding one or to the following one. Here is the end we have sought."[8]

Chamberlin devours *Breaking and Riding* and highly recommends it to those who desire to refine their equestrian understanding and skills. In later years, he will reject some of what Fillis advocates but keeps those concepts that he deems still valuable. The Fillis book is also known as *Principles of Dressage and Equitation*. Translated by M.H. Hayes.[Xenophon Press 2017]

---

8   Fillis, James, *Breaking and Riding with Military Commentaries.* a.k.a. *Principles of Dressage and Equitation*, Xenophon Press, 2017

# Chapter 3

## The Inter-Allied Games of 1919

**Warren C. Matha, Editor**

**A Turning Point in the American Jumping Style**

As discussed in *General Chamberlin: America's Equestrian Genius*, [Xenophon Press 2020] Chamberlin and other American cavalry officers in France just after the end of World War I first observe the Italian method of jumping obstacles at the Inter-Allied Games of 1919. The Italians make a lasting and deep impression on the Americans.

**Practice Sessions**

With the sole exception of the Italians, the Allied cavalrymen practice for several weeks on the actual jumps they will face in competition. The Italians arrive late and practice for only one day.

***Figure 6.*** *A French officer applies the "close seat" to jump an obstacle. The participants construct the obstacles themselves. Photo from the editor's collection.*

***Figure 7.*** *At the practice sessions for the Inter-Allied Games of 1919, this French officer displays the "close seat" of the French that most of Europe and the Americans apply in jumping obstacles. Photo from the editor's collection.*

***Figure 8.*** *Another French officer applies the "close seat" to jump an obstacle. The obstacles in the practice session duplicate those the riders will confront at the Games. Photo from the editor's collection.*

*Figure 9.* Another French officer applies the "close seat" with his seat bones firmly in the saddle and forming his base of support in this practice session. With the exception of the Italians, all participants practice for weeks over these exact jumps to refine their skills. Photo from the editor's collection.

*Figure 10.* An American officer applies the "close seat" in practice. The Americans, for many years, look to France as the source of equestrian wisdom. Photo from the editor's collection.

***Figure 11.*** *This Italian officer displays the "revolutionary" Caprillist jumping method. The Italians arrive late to the practice sessions.*
*Photo from the editor's collection.*

***Figure 12.*** *Another view of the French Cavalry's "close seat" in practice for the Games. The rider remains glued to the saddle using his seat bones as his base of support. Photo from the editor's collection.*

***Figure 13.*** *Another French Officer who practices over the jumps for approximately two weeks before the Games. Photo from the editor's collection.*

***Figure 14.*** *Another Italian officer surmounts this obstacle with ease a day before the Games begin. His base of support remains over the stirrups and into the rider's heels. Photo from the editor's collection.*

*Figure 15.* Another photo of a French officer in practice for the Games. Notice the difficulty the horse experiences in getting its croup over the obstacle. Photo from the editor's collection.

*Figure 16.* A Belgian officer displays the jumping seat adopted by every European cavalry with the exception of the Italians. Photo from the editor's collection.

*Figure 17.* A Belgian officer surmounts the jump. His heels extend up. His hands seem to support his upper body. He seems to lose contact with the horse's mouth. Photo from the editor's collection.

*Figure 18.* This officer with stirrup irons "home" seems to have slipped almost behind the cantle. Photo from the editor's collection.

*Figure 19.* Notice the tension on the reins as this officer keeps the "close seat" with his back rounded and his feet a bit forward, and his seat bones firmly planted in the saddle. Only the horse's immense effort enables it to clear jump but barely. Photo from the editor's collection.

*Figure 20.* This French officer keeps the close seat, with heels up and legs forward. His buttocks remain on the cantle. He seems to be sitting in a "chair" with his back rounded. Photo from the editor's collection.

***Figure 21.*** *The rider's position over burdens the horse's hindquarters in this practice session. The rider's feet remain forward and his upper body remains behind the vertical as the standard rider position of Saumur until the early 1930's. One wonders whether the horse cleared the obstacle. Photo from the editor's collection.*

***Figure 22.*** *Another French example of the close seat in action at the practice sessions for the Games The rider's weight remains on his seat bones and in the saddle. Photo from the editor's collection.*

***Figure 23.*** *Feet forward. Upper body to the rear in a practice session for the Games This posture displays an extreme position that often results from French method adopted by America and all of Europe except the Italians.*
*Photo from the editor's collection.*

***Figure 24.*** *This Belgian officer also displays the close seat. With stirrup irons "home" but with heels up, he stays on his seat bones with buttocks in the saddle, with weight toward the cantle and over the horse's loins. Photo from the editor's collection.*

*Figure 25.* Another example of the French 'close seat with legs forward and upper body to the rear. Photo from the editor's collection.

*Figure 26.* Another variation on the close seat but with the upper body more forward at the practice session. Photo from the editor's collection.

***Figure 27.*** *Here the French officer goes over the jump with his heels up, his weight in his seat bones and buttocks on the cantle with his leg a bit to the rear, his back rounded, and his upper body almost vertical. Photo from the editor's collection.*

***Figure 28.*** *This Italian officers displays the method of Federico Caprilli at the practice session for the Games. The Italians dominate the stadium jumping competitions with personal triumphs for Major Ubertalli who studied directly under Caprilli. Photo from the editor's collection.*

# The Games: Pairs Jumping Competition
*The Italians astound all with their jumping.*

*Figure 29.* Italy's Major Ubertalli and Major Caffaratti astound the Americans with their pairs jumping at the Inter-Allied Games of 1919. Photo from the editor's collection.

*Figure 30.* Italian Majors Ubertalli and Caffaratti clear another obstacle at high speed in the Pairs Competition of the Inter-Allied Games of 1919. The Americans take note. Photo from the editor's collection.

***Figure 31.*** *Two other Italian officers, Captain Aluisi and Major Antonelli display their revolutionary jumping style at the Games. Photo from the editor's collection.*

***Figure 32.*** *Two more riders display the Italian jumping style in the Pairs Jumping Competition of the Inter-Allied Games of 1919. Notice the straight line from the horse's bit, through the reins, and up the rider's arm to the elbow. Photo from the editor's collection.*

*Figure 33.* Two French officers show their style at the Games. The rider's arm position seems good. His base of support remains his seat bones with his boot "home" in the stirrups and legs in front of the vertical. Photo from the editor's collection.

# The Individual Jumping Competition

*Figure 34.* A Belgian officer competing in the Individual Jumping Competition of the Games. He seems to pivot on his knees with his boot "home" in the stirrups and his buttocks on the cantle. Photo from the editor's collection.

*Figure 35.* Another Belgian officer pivots on his knees as he surmounts a jump in the Individual Jumping Competition of the Games. Photo from the editor's collection.

***Figure 36.*** *This French officer struggles with a close seat to surmount an obstacle. He throws his weight behind the vertical in an effort to "lift" the horse over the obstacle with his legs pushed far forward. Photo from the editor's collection.*

***Figure 37.*** *Another Italian competitor in the Individual Jumping Competition. Italy's Major Ubertalli achieves a personal triumph by winning both first and the third place in the competition. Photo from the editor's collection.*

# Chapter 4

# The Evolving American Jumping Style 1920–1923

Once Chamberlin returns from Europe after the Inter-Allied Games of 1919, he reflects on the riding and jumping style of the Italians at the Games. By 1922, he develops firm thoughts regarding riding and training jumpers. His thinking will progress even further after he attends the French Cavalry's School for Advanced Riding at Saumur and the Italian Cavalry's School for Advanced Riding at Tor di Quinto. The article below, however, demonstrates that even before attending those schools, his thinking progresses beyond many of his contemporaries.

—Warren C. Matha, Editor

### The Rasp, 1922

#### Observations on Riding and Training Jumpers[9]
#### By
#### Maj. H. D. Chamberlin, Cavalry

The basis of this article is the principle that a horse, to become a steady and consistent jumper, must be so trained that he will approach and jump an obstacle as nearly as possible as he would do if running riderless and at liberty. This principle is practiced among all the most successful riders both in America and abroad.

Anyone who has seen remounts trained by jumping them through chutes, when mounted by good riders not holding the reins, has doubtlessly observed how soon all will jump quietly and calmly. It is only when the riders

---

[9] *The Rasp 1922*, The Cavalry School, Army of the United States, Fort Riley, Kansas, 1922.

are not in balance and the reins are poorly used that the horses begin to fear jumping and, as a result, rush, refuse or run out. In other words, the less the horse is interfered with by the rider's lack of balance, or by pulling on the bit, the more calmly, easily, and consistently will he jump. The reason is that he then jumps almost as he would if he were at liberty.

Admitting then that a minimum of interference on the part of the rider—due to his excellent balance (which means "going with his horse"), and to his light, steady hands—produces calm and clever jumping horses, since they are thus given a maximum of liberty, we have two distinct problems involved. The first is to develop the rider's seat, hands and tact so that he is able to ride without interfering with his mount before, during or after the jump, thereby allowing his horse the liberty necessary to jump well.

The second problem is to teach the horse to jump boldly but calmly. This he will do as he gradually learns that he can put forth all his efforts without fear of pain to his mouth (from rider's poor hands), or to his loin (from rider's being out of balance or "behind his horse").

These two problems merge, in the practical solution which we obtain in training men and horses. However, the second problem will never be solved until the first has been. In other words, the horse can never be made to do what his natural ability would permit him to do, if he is handicapped by a poor rider.

The horse jumping at liberty lowers his head and extends his neck in approaching his jump (that is with no direct flexion or bending at the poll). Not interfered with, he also cocks his ears forward and studies his obstacle attentively while approaching it. During the jump he uses his head and neck in an infinite variety of ways, depending upon the sort of take-off he has made, the nature of the obstacle, and the speed at which he has approached and jumped. Suffice it to say he needs absolute freedom in the use of his head and neck while jumping in order to preserve his balance and properly use his muscles. The head and neck serve much the same purpose as the head and arms of a man when he high jumps. In addition, some of the muscles of the foreleg are attached to the neck and he must place his neck as he desires it in order to use those muscles efficiently.

The horse at liberty (meaning not only in a pasture but in a chute, Hitchcock Pen or, to a certain extent on the longe) regulates his speed, as he becomes experienced, with great intelligence according to the size and nature of the obstacle. He is inclined to go too slowly rather than too fast, as a general rule. Yet how many "bolters" we see ridden at all horse shows and in all jumping events! An effort to explain the reasons for this bolting will appear later.

In developing the rider's seat, hands and tact, so that he can ride without interfering with the horse before, during or after the jump, which is the first problem, the method at the Cavalry School is briefly as follows:

About one month of three or four riding hours per day is given before students jump at all. After this first month, the periods of riding without stirrups are progressively increased in length. The slow trot and gallop without stirrups are admitted, the world over, as the best form of riding to develop a firm, supple and graceful seat, without which there can never be good hands. And without seat and hands it is hopeless for a man to try to jump or school a horse well. After the seats and hands of the students have become fairly good, they are put through chutes containing small jumps from one to six in number, without using stirrups or reins. For this purpose, trained jumpers are used. The jumps are gradually raised in height so that at the end of four months students are capable of riding through a cute with five jumps about three or three and a half feet high with ease and suppleness, without stirrups, and either with or without, reins. They are taught to incline the body slightly forward as the horse increases his gait to enter the chute and never to lean back as he starts this increase, thus supporting themselves on the reins, hurting the horse's mouth and discouraging and bothering him when he is studying his jump. This is very important in order to teach riders union with the horse and to avoid destroying and horse's calmness.

In jumping, the grip of the legs is principally below the knees and *not with the knees.* The toes hand down naturally (without stirrups) and are turned out enough—though not excessively—to wrap the lower leg about the horse. Since the knee joint only flexes in one direction, it is obvious that the old teaching of keeping the foot parallel to the horse's sides absolutely prevents strongly closing the calf of the leg on the horse. The knee, perforce, also turns out slightly, but never so much as to prevent keeping the thigh muscles flat against the saddle and behind the femur, not between it and the saddle. It is a case of getting the happy medium and it is absolutely essential to find it in order to develop the drive and grip with the legs, required in good jumping.

At the moment that horse takes off the body bends forward still more, both at the waist by a forward flexion of the back bone and a bending forward at the hip joints, but *without increased gripping with, and a resultant pivoting on, the knees.* However, during all the approach, "take-off" and jump, the rider is sitting "lightly" in the saddle. This is accomplished by a somewhat stronger grip with the thigh, the knee, and particularly the lower leg, and a little more weight in the stirrups when stirrups are used.

If the reins are held, the hands should preserve light contact by the play of the elbows principally, but also by the shoulder joint and wrists, thus following the horse's head and neck in their movements. Leaning forward at the "take-off" puts the rider close to his horse and in a more or less parallel position to the direction of the thrust of the horse's propellers, namely his hind legs.

*This forward position should be held, to a great extent, during the entire jump.* It puts the rider with his horse at the start and he should stay there and *continue* to be with the horse. He should not drift to the rear and be leaning backward at any stage of the jump. The reasons are as follows and a fair trial will convince most good riders of the many advantages in the method.

*First*, at the take-off, as stated above, he carries his body and weight forward so that it is close to the horse and parallel to the thrust of the hind legs. If the rider is *not* forward the mechanical disadvantage to the horse is obviously the same as if a man attempted to put the shot while holding it by a short handle attached underneath it. The backward drag, caused by the lever arm formed by the handle, corresponds to the additional work done by the horse when the rider is leaning back and the center of gravity of his trunk is high above and far out of line of the horse's thrust.

*Figure 38.* Correct Position at Top of Jump. Horses given a maximum of liberty for use of heads and necks. Riders forward, going with horses. Light gentle contact with horse's mouths. Rider's legs in excellent position: heels down, claves close on horses' sides and knees not closed too tightly, hands low.

If the rider is not forward, the horse will jump out from under him, and to maintain his seat, he will usually be pulled over the jump on the reins. This punishes the horse's mouth in addition to all the mechanical disadvantage which it creates.

*Secondly,* during the period that the horse is clearing the obstacle, the rider must keep his trunk inclined forward, as far as possible, *consistently* with maintaining the security of his seat. The trust of the take-off lightens the rider's weight on the saddle by the shock communicated, through it, to his trunk at that instant. Since the forehand is generally clear of the obstacle *before* the rider's total weight again settles into the saddle, it is perfectly evident that the farther to the rear his weight again settles into the saddle, it is perfectly evident that the farther to the rear this weight is put on the horse's back, the more difficult it will be for him to raise his hind quarters over the obstacle. Moreover, as the horse gradually clears the obstacle with his hind quarters, he carries the hind legs forward to a position required for landing and resuming the gallop stride.

*Figure 39.* Wrong Position at Top of Jump. Everything wrong! Rider behind horse. No liberty for horse's head or neck. Horse probably afraid of curb bit and failed to take off with head and neck in normal position. Rider will next crush horse's hind quarters on the jump and hurt his loin and mouth upon landing. Notice horse's ears are back due to pain.

If the rider's weight is allowed to settle far to the rear in the saddle, and consequently crush down the muscles of the loin and back and interfere with their play, this movement of the hind quarters is rendered difficult.

Hence the body should remain forward until the horse is entirely clear of his jump.

Now at the *third* stage of the jump, this is the descent and landing, the weight of the body is carried slightly backward (though the trunk remains inclined forward) in order to keep from falling too far over on the horse's neck at the shock received by the ground of the fore feet. At landing, the body should break forward, but not so far as to lose the balance and force of the rider to support himself by placing the hands on the withers. Continuous light contact with the mouth should be kept when landing. Getting the weight back a trifle, while keeping the body inclined forward, is accomplished by arching the loin and back to the rear while the seat itself remains well forward in the saddle. Leaning far back, as we so frequently see done, gives the horse a very severe blow on the back and loin, and makes him rush away after landing, since he learns to expect and fear this painful shock. The horse uses his forelegs in galloping, and also in landing after a jump, as much as a pole vaulter uses his pole. He simply rolls over the forelegs, so to speak, all, or practically all, the impulsion and power coming from the hind quarters. Hence, the rider's weight during fast galloping and at landing over jumps should be forward, so as to free the back and loin muscles and to constantly help the forehand by rolling forward with it. This is partly the reason for the seat jockey's employ. This keeping the body inclined forward should not be so excessive as to make a fall of the rider imminent in case the horse stumbles on landing, but on the other hand, the trunk must not incline to the rear so as to jolt the back, loin and hind quarters as he lands. In addition to being painful to the horse it prevents his placing his hind legs well forward under his mass on taking his first gallop stride after landing. It is believed that a horse will fall more often after landing when the rider is leaning back than when he is fairly well forward, for the reason that it is the quick, well-forward engagement of the hind quarters which allows the horse to recover after stumbling. Consequently, any weight far to the rear on his back or loin, forestalls this by preventing free play of the back and loin muscles. This overweighting the hind quarters makes the hind feet come to the ground farther to the rear and in a poorer position to lift and propel the mass forward. In any event, a good rider always sees a fall coming and can lean backward, if that appears to be the wisest course, in order to be thrown clear. In addition, a man leaning backward almost always jerks his horse's head when he stumbles, which prevents the animal's using his neck and had at a moment when he needs them most, in recovering his equilibrium.

On other argument for the old fashioned so-called hunting seat, where the rider leans back over the jump and upon landing, has been that it saves the horse's fore legs. This is open to dispute.

**Figure 40.** *Wrong Position at Top of Jump. Rider somewhat behind horse and forced to grip with knees. Reins must be allowed to slip to avoid hurting horse's mouth upon landing.*

The horse is mechanically constructed to "roll" forward over his fore legs and, though no scientific proof can be presented here, it appears and "feels" in jumping that the shock to both rider and horse's fore legs upon landing is less when the rider is forward. The horse's equilibrium is of course more unstable with the rider forward upon landing, since the center of gravity of the entire mass (horse and rider) is father to the front and nearer the front edge of the base of support, (the horse's fore legs). Since the instability of the equilibrium give the measure of speed, the grounding of the hind feet and the first stride after lading will be hastened when the rider's body is inclined forward. However, the quicker the hind feet are grounded the less time will the fore legs be supporting the mass. Moreover, the farther forward under the mass the hind feet are grounded the smaller will be the proportion of weight and shock sustained by the fore legs on the next stride. Any man jumping from a moving car or over an obstacle knows by experience that the shock is less to the legs if he lands "running," this is with his center of gravity advanced, and it is so with the horse. Land inclined slightly forward, going with your mount, *not* leaning back so that your trunk is in a line parallel to and almost in prolongation of, his fore legs, thus intensifying the shock to them and to the back. On the take-off the hind legs do all the work

**Figure 41.** *Correct Position at Top of Jump. At top of the jump after a poor take-off. Rider with his horse, allowing him liberty of head and neck by permitting reins to slip through relaxed fingers Excellent form under the conditions.*

Of thrusting the mass of horse and rider over the obstacles, hence the rider must try to get where that thrust can act most advantageously, as has been discussed. On the other hand, when landing, since the rider seeks to avoid a severe direct thrust on the fore legs, he gets out of the line of their thrust by leaning slightly forward, and permits the momentum of his trunk, as it bends to the front, to help the total mass roll over his mount's fore legs. Instability in the equilibrium thus produced lessens the shock and is not dangerous since the horse is naturally most adept in recovering his equilibrium when the center of gravity is displaced forward. As has been stated, the forward position usually helps him to recover in case of stumbling.

Now, in discussing briefly the training of the horse by the trained rider—let it not be forgotten that the aim is to teach the horse to jump as he would at liberty. Also let it be realized that no finished jumper is produced—and the exceptions are few—in less than three years. It is a long process and generally aged horses of from five to ten years jumping experienced are the winners in shows. They are the survival of the fittest mentally and physically, and certain mental and physical characteristics are necessary to produce a high class show jumper. Power, elasticity, courage and intelligence are necessities for the high class, consistent jumper as a general rule, though some excellent jumpers are found which perhaps lack in one of those traits. Good jumpers come in many conformations however.

Since we have stated before, the poll should not be flexed, the horse to jump well should be in a bridle that he does not fear, and it is the opinion at the Cavalry School that practically all horses, and certainly all green horses, jump better with a snaffle bit, and the larger the mouth piece the better. Watch horses that are jumped with curb bits and see their efforts to escape the punishment of the bit (usually involuntarily administered, be it admitted) as they approach and jump. Generally, they raise their heads and bolt at the jump, and thus place themselves in a position in which they can neither see well nor use the muscles of the forehand, the neck or the loins. (A horse always stiffens the loin in raising the head and stiffening the poll.) If, on the contrary, they yield to the curb and arch the neck, they are again hampered in the use of their forehand muscles and of the necks. Jump your horses in a snaffle bridle if it is humanly possible to do so and they will soon jump in better form and more quietly.

Teach the green horse to jump at liberty and on a longe first. Do not hasten his training as that is the ruination of most jumpers. If they are forced to jump obstacles which they fear, or when they are tired or sore, their generous dispositions soon change to cowardly ones. They then become bolters, refusers or erratic jumpers. Long, long practice, over small jumps, and only a few jumps on any one day, is the surest road to success. Raise the jumps a very little at the time. Give the horse a long rein, and *always, above all things,* keep the hands low. The horse becomes frantic at jumps when he has his head pulled up in the air. He feels himself as powerless to jump as a man feels when held with a "hammerlock." Then too, a horse held in too long when approaching his jump—since he realizes the necessity of quite a bit of speed—becomes nervous over jumping, which tends to produce a bolter or rusher. When the horse is faced towards the jump he should not be held in until he is mentally upset, but allowed and encouraged to approach at a free, bold gait. Teach the green jumper to depend absolutely on himself and do not attempt to regulate his speed to any great extent. If he rushes, he is bound to get a fall, and only a few falls, or bad bruises from tips, will ever teach a horse to respect his jumps. The more rigid the jumps the better as far as training the horse is concerned. Give a jumper light, but steady, support on the bit; if he increases his pace, give the hand a trifle, *keeping the same tension,* making him aware that he can extend the neck and head and take on the necessary speed. He will gradually learn to regulate his gait according to the nature of the obstacle, if he is not pulled. Many excellent jumpers start with a rush (just as a man does), but if they are not pulled, then check near the jump, collect themselves and measure their take-off nicely. If the rider attempts to stop a jumper's rush by pulling, he distracts and worries his mount, and effectually prevents the horse using all his skill as a jumper. Holding in a horse of this type will only make him unreliable and less calm.

When a horse starts with a rush or increases his pace, let the rider be inclined forward and *go with him,* in the manner that has been described, encouraging him with the legs gently so as not to excite him. In landing, absorb the jolt—so as not to hurt and frighten the horse—by keeping the ankles and feet entirely relaxed in the stirrups and the heels well down, thus using the ankle joints as shock absorbers. Absorb progressively the remaining shock by the flexion of the knee, allowing the seat to settle lightly in the saddle, and by the flexion of the loin and back as the body breaks forward.

*Figure 42. Correct Position On Landing. Rider in forward position. Reins lightly stretched, hands low, giving liberty to head and neck. It is to be noted that after a jump the fore feet are grounded and leave the ground again before the hind feet touch.*

Keep your legs in one place all the time and *do not grip the horse too tightly with the calves as he starts at his jump,* or as stated above, he will become excited and think you desire him to rush. Grip very hard with the calves and turn the spurs into him only when you feel him checking or refusing. It takes tact and long practice to be able to use the spurs at the appropriate instant. An increased pressure at the second when he should take off, if the rider sees there is not room for another stride, is useful but takes skill. Clucking at that instant is very useful also, but do not keep clucking for twenty yards preceding the jump as that is distracting.

Never get the idea that you can help your horse over the jump with the reins. It cannot be done. Attempting to do so is—as the old saying goes—like trying to lift yourself off the ground by your boot straps. Let his head alone. All the most excellent rider can do is to shorten the stride a little by steadying the horse to get his take-off correctly. Do not try this unless you are a very, very expert rider. The better method is to urge him forward and by a squeeze of the calves let him know at which stride to jump. Let the horse learn to depend on his own ability and judgment to arrive at his jump so as to get a good take-off.

Use wings until the horse is confirmed in bold jumping as it saves trouble. If you are fighting a horse to keep him straight at a jump, he will never be consistent. He is trying to do something other than jump, and pulling him further prevents his doing his best since he loses his liberty of action.

As recommended before, use the ankles in landing, to take some of the shock, and if the heel is well down, you can keep the body inclined forward and still prevent falling on the horse's neck by the support received from the stirrup. Use your foot as you use it when you jump onto the edge of a raised platform and land on the ball of the foot, prepared to immediately jump backward off the platform. This is precisely the way you use your foot and stirrup in landing after a jump. The legs of course, do not move but are kept close to the horse's side.

After the horse is over his jump, if he increases his pace bring him down quietly, so that he will not expect a painful jerk on the mouth after having jumped. Gallop away with your horse; do not get behind him. He will probably consider being pulled down quickly, or a jerk, as punishment and be at a loss to know why it was administered. Gradually the horse can be taught to slow down and halt after a jump. Backing a few steps after a jump is a good exercise when done quietly and gently, as it takes his attention from the jump and accustoms him to checking.

To sum up:
1. Go with your horse by keeping your weight forward at all stages of jumping. Keeping always supple is absolutely essential to good jumping.
2. Keep the hands low and the reins as long as is consistent with control. Give the horse liberty but not license.
3. Use a light bit, preferably a snaffle, and encourage the use of the head and neck by long reins and light, low hands.

4. Keep the legs in one place and the lower leg well closed at all times. Do not use a varying pressure as that excites him, unless you have to drive a reluctant jumper.
5. Accentuate the galloping movement of the body just before jumping; in other words, do not stiffen as you approach the jump. This stiffening is almost a universal fault.
6. Keep the heels well down, and the calves and knees closed on the horse at all times as this is of vital importance in pushing the timid horse and in keeping the strength of the seat throughout the jump. However, when the horse is clearing the jump relax the knees, ankles and back so as to receive the first shock upon landing through the ankles and progressively through the knee and loin. Do not land on the knees first.
7. Let the horse learn to use his own ability in pulling out of bad approaches. Nine times out of ten your efforts to help him will only annoy and bother him. In case the rider feels a refusal coming he should not lean back as he will then bump the horse's mouth if he does jump (unless the fingers are relaxed) and be "behind him" in any case. Moreover, if the legs are in a correct position and working, the rider can keep his seat even though the horse does refuse. Changing position near the obstacle worries the horse.
8. An important point in jumping and in cross country work is to have the foot correctly placed in the stirrup. Do not have the stirrup against the heel of the boot. On the other hand, have the foot a little farther "home" in the stirrup than in ordinary riding. The tread rests just in rear of the ball of the foot where the sole of the boot slopes upward. Having the foot way "home" against the heel eliminates the use of the ankle as a shock absorber upon landing and makes the rider stiff as a result. The weight should be predominantly on the inner part of the foot so that the calves are forced against the horse's sides. Stirrup straps should, of course, be somewhat shorter for cross country work and jumping than they are for normal hacking or schooling.
9. Remember that only patience, intelligence and tact, which comes with long practice, can make either the man or the horse excellent at jumping.
10. Never trust any horse to jump; always have such control, by the reins and legs, as to defeat any defense he may present.

11. One involuntary jerk on the horse's mouth during any stage of his jump will put back his training a long way. To prevent it, always have the fingers relaxed on the reins during all the jump so they can slip if things go wrong. This is important.
12. Keep your head and eyes up as you jump. See where you are going. This habit will keep your weight equally distributed and may save you a bad fall over rough and unknown country. Moreover, it is better form.
13. Ride for a particular point on an obstacle and let your mental attitude be one of determination. "Throw your heart over the jump and your horse will go too," has much truth in it. Your mental attitude is soon felt by the horse and influences his own.
14. In case of a refusal do not let the horse rush away from the obstacle. Hold him looking at it for a short time. When he jumps the next time, remember which way he turned in refusing or running out and let the opposite direct rein predominate to prevent a repetition. Do not pull with both reins, but keep them in accord.
15. Almost any horse, fit for the cavalry service, can be taught to jump three and one-half feet fairly well and safely, if sufficient time and proper methods are used. Beyond that height and for show purposes, selected individuals must be used, and much patience and time devoted to their training.

This article is, of course, merely an outline. It is believed, however, that the application and mastery of the general rules given will give good results. The results will vary in accordance with the rider's skill and experience.

Special cases, depending on the temperament of the particular horse, are infinite. There, only equestrian tact, coming from long experience and natural ability, can direct the remedies and methods necessary. No rules can be given to cover all cases. Remember, however, that the horse's intelligence is at best very limited.

*Figure 43.* Wrong Position On Landing. Riders trunk too far back. No liberty given to horse's head and neck. Horse will receive a maximum jolt of fore legs and severe blow on loin when hind feet are grounded. Hands too high.

Treat him as you would treat a very small child. You must get his respect and confidence in order to make him jump well and that takes patience, time, and skill.

This article has been concurred in by the Director, Department of Horsemanship, and all other Instructors in that Department at the Cavalry School.

# The Early Evolution of the American Jumping Style in Photos 1907-1923

## Warren C. Matha, Editor

The first photo shows Lt. Adna Chaffee in the descent phase of negotiating a four-foot jump in the French style taught at West Point and the Mounted Service School during the first twenty years of the twentieth-century. In the second photo, Capt. Innis Palmer Swift displays the close seat of the French and the Americans in the middle of a jump as West Point and the Mounted Service School teach in the same era. By 1923, even before Chamberlin returns from the Italian Cavalry's School for Advanced Riding at Tor di Quinto, American practice begins to change.

*Figure 44. Adna Chaffee riding as taught in the first decades of the twentieth century. Chaffee translated the French Manual of 1912 from the French into English for the Mounted Service School. In later years, he will become the "father" of armored forces that George Patton will apply so brilliantly in Europe during World War II.*

*Figure 45. Captain Innis Palmer Swift, Chamberlin's Mounted Service School polo team mate and lifelong friend, displays the "close" seat of the French as interpreted by the Mounted Service School prior to World War I. In later life, Swift will command the 1st Cavalry Division and later a Corps under Lt. General Walter Krueger in the Philippines campaign during World War II.*

The next full sequence of photos comes from The Rasp, 1923 edition. The sequence demonstrates the evolution of the American Jumping Style to this point in time. Keep in mind Chamberlin's 1922 article in The Rasp: Observations on Riding and Training Jumpers, he writes after he see the Italians perform at the Inter Allied Games of 1919 but before he attends the Italian Cavalry's School for Advanced Riding at Tor di Quinto.

In August of 1922, Chamberlin leaves the Cavalry School and attends Saumur. In June 1923, Chamberlin and W.W. West attend Tor di Quinto, the first American officers to do so. Even before Chamberlin's tour at Tor di Quinto, the influence of the Italian performance at the Inter-Allied Games of 1919 on American officers shows itself at Ft. Riley.

The photos three, four, and five show the traditional French "close seat" method that West Point and The Mounted Service School teach to Chamberlin and all other cavalry officers prior to World War I. Photo number three, taken in 1912, demonstrates the French style "close seat" with the rider's upper body behind the vertical. The rider strains his abdominal muscles and puts most of his weight over the horse's loins. Actually, this faulty position seems to reassert itself in many riders while in the descent phase of drop jumps and while going down slides one hundred years later in 2012 at the London Olympic Games.

As shown in photo number four, by 1920, at Ft. Riley, the jumping style begins to show changes. By 1923, one sees more changes. Over the years, Chamberlin will continue to refine this style until by the late 1920's to early 1930's, he finalizes his thinking regarding how to jump obstacles.

—Warren C. Matha, Editor

*Figure 46.* The French style as practiced in 1912 and taught to Chamberlin and other U.S. Cavalry officers. From The Rasp, 1923.

*Figure 47.* This photo, taken in 1914, shows the rider in a somewhat better position but still he puts too much weight on the horse's hindquarters. Photo and actual commentary from the Rasp, 1923.

***Figure 48.*** *Photo taken in 1916. It shows the riders in much the same position as in the 1914 photo. The riders still sit on the cantle and over burden their horse's hindquarters. The Rasp, 1923.*

***Figure 49.*** *This photo was taken in 1920. A tendency to keep the weight farther forward. Rider a little behind his horse in the "close seat." The Rasp, 1923.*

*Figure 50.* This photo, taken in 1923 before Chamberlin attends Tor di Quinto, demonstrates more Italian influence, with the rider more balanced and forward at the top of the jump. No weight on the horse's hindquarters. The rider's forward position gives more freedom to the horse's head and neck.

*Figure 51.* No rider weight on the horse's loins. The Rasp, 1923.

*Figure 52.* In 1923 the rider begins to show the Italian influence. The Rasp, 1923.

*Figure 53.* Horse and rider beginning to descend. The Rasp, 1923

*Figure 54.* "Good position near the top of the jump except that the rider's hands are pressing against the horse's neck. If the rider depends upon hands for support instead of legs, he cannot be master of his balance." The Rasp, 1923.

*Figure 55.* "The rider's body should be inclined more forward…" The Rasp, 1923.

***Figure 56.*** *The rider has lost contact with his horse's mouth and supports his upper body with his hands instead of his legs. The Rasp, 1923.*

***Figure 57.*** *The rider stays with his horse. The Rasp, 1923.*

# Chapter 5

# The French Cavalry School for Advanced Riding at Saumur, France 1922-1923

In August of 1922, United States Cavalry Majors Chamberlin, West, and Rayner arrive at the French Cavalry's advanced school at Saumur. Their term of study extends to June 1923. While the Americans study at Saumur, the French Cavalry School publishes *École d'application de Cavalerie, Saumur, France* to describe the school's curriculum, mode of riding, and facilities. We reproduce the booklet in full. It offers a rare look at the school that the French Cavalry publishes and presents at the very time Chamberlin studies there. In fact, one of the photos that he displays in his own book *Riding and Schooling Horses*, is the photo of the horse-mounted General Thureau, Commandant of the French Cavalry School. You will find that photo on page six of Saumur's *École d'application de Cavalerie*.

Below resides an English translation of the booklet's pages one through three set forth in the same format as the original document.

—Warren C. Matha, Editor

## The Cavalry School of Saumur

Founded in 1771 by the Duke of Choiseul, Minister of Louis XV, the school of Equitation at Saumur was confirmed in 1790 and re-established in 1814 under the title of "School of Instruction," and was commissioned to train instructors for all the Cavalry Corps. As a result of political events, the school was closed in 1822 and transferred to Versailles, but two years later it was reopened in Saumur and this time, with a definitive favor in March 20, 1825 it took the name the Royal Cavalry School.

At that time, Equitation was taught by civilian instructors; since 1855 this teaching has been exclusively entrusted to Military instructors.

In 1826, a school for high ranking officers had been added to the Cavalry School; in 1846, a workshop for horseshoeing and related matters was also added.

The war of 1870 brought about the suspension of the school, which was reorganized on 30 August 1873.

During the period of 1914-1918, the School was placed at the disposal of the American Army, which set up an Artillery School here.

From the cessation of hostilities, the school was restored and the various courses resumed during the year 1919.

The Cavalry School currently includes:

I. The School firstly called the true center of Instruction of the French Cavalry, for work:
   a) Training Courses for High Officers of the Active service and those to be appointed Sub-Lieutenants at the end of the Course (11 months);
   High-Reserve Officers, destined to become Complementary Officers (6 months);
   b) An Application Course (11 months), for Sub-Lieutenants graduated from the Special Military School of Saint-Cyr.
   c) Advanced courses in the transition from one grade to the next:
   Lieutenants of Cavalry (and a number of Lieutenants of Artillery and Genie) to pass to the rank of Captain. (Duration: 6 months).
   High ranking Reserve Officers destined to become Adjunct Officers (11 months);
   Captains and Squadron Chiefs were appointed to the rank of Squadron Leader (Duration: 3 weeks).
   Squadron Commanders and Lieutenant-Colonels for the crossing of the rank of Lieutenant Colonel and Colonel. (Duration: 2 weeks).

II. A Cavalry machine gun school to the Train Officers, Sub-Officers and Troops constituting the cavalry's machine gun personnel.

III. A Veterinary School. Each year a certain number of experienced veterinarians are admitted to tend to the large number of horses of the School and to perfect their art.

IV. A Farrier School for shoeing horses

V. A Workshop, where saddles and harness work are manufactured and operated by the armed forces of the French Army.

The Cavalry constitutes a very complex organization: The Command is entrusted to a General (or Colonel), assisted by a Colonel (or Lieutenant-Colonel) second in command.

With its well-designed buildings including, its spacious riding halls, its training and shooting fields, the Cavalry School is able to provide much equestrian, military, general, and scientific instruction to everyone regarding the duties of the Cavalry Officer.

Without abandoning the traditions of the past, the concern for valor, the passion for the horse and all the sports that relate to it, the Cavalry School, adapting itself to the necessities of modern war, took up the task to make a cavalryman, without taking from him his intrinsic valor, emulate the best infantryman.

Following the strong words of Marshal Petain: "The audacity, the speed, and the employment of the materials of war are the duties of the Cavalry." It is these concepts that the Cavalry School has given to all grades.

The few photographs in this Album are an illustration of this fact.

"It is a duty for the Minister of War to pay homage, in this respect, to the French Cavalry, which, during the great war, has proved worthy of its glorious past...

"By the strength of its military traditions, its qualities of initiative and daring, its magnificent intrepidity, the Cavalry deserves to be considered as an elite weapon. Its role may be modified by adapting to the requirements of the modern military organization, but its usefulness remains, and it cannot be conceived that it has any place in an army worthy of the name."

(Extract from the speech delivered by Mr. Maginot, Minister of War and Pensions, on the occasion of the ceremony of the Cross of the Legion of Honor to honor the standards* of the Cavalry School. May 12, 1922)

*Editor's note: The term "standards" in this context means battle flags.

SAUMUR — École de Cavalerie

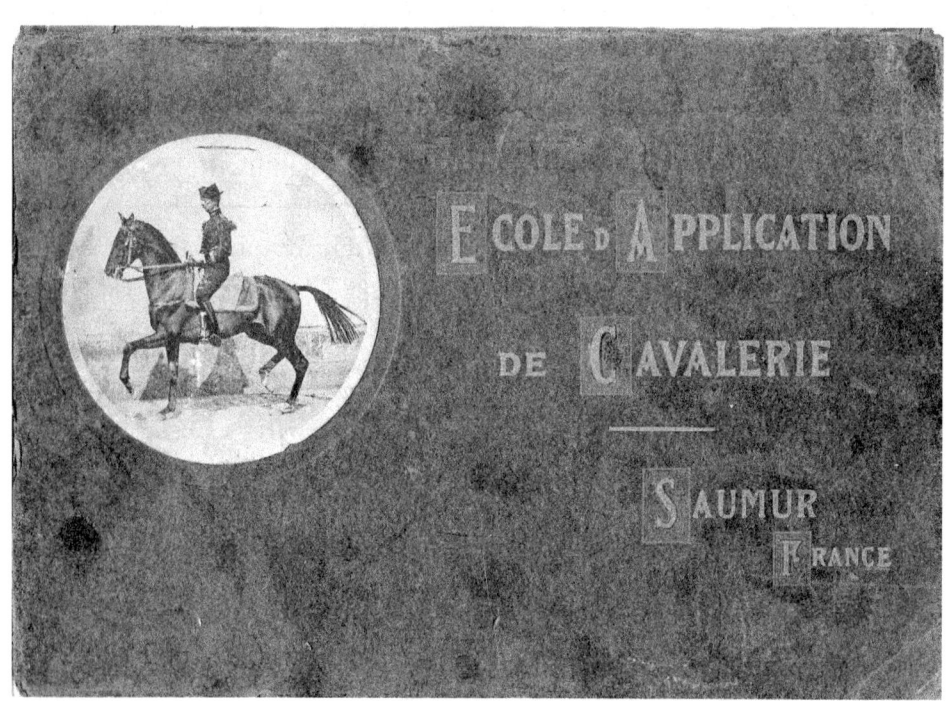

# ÉCOLE D'APPLICATION

# DE CAVALERIE

### SAUMUR
#### (France)

## L'École de Cavalerie de Saumur

Fondée en 1771 par le Duc de CHOISEUL, Ministre de Louis XV, l'*École d'Équitation de Saumur* fut supprimée en 1790 et rétablie en 1814 sous le titre d'*École d'Instruction des troupes à cheval* avec mission de former des Instructeurs pour tous les Corps de Cavalerie. Par suite d'événements politiques, l'École fut licenciée en 1822 et transférée à Versailles, mais deux ans après elle se rouvrait à Saumur et cette fois d'une façon définitive ; le 20 mars 1825 elle recevait le nom d'*École Royale de Cavalerie*.

A cette époque, l'Équitation était enseignée par des Ecuyers civils ; c'est depuis 1855 que cet enseignement est exclusivement confié à des Ecuyers militaires.

En 1826, avait été annexé à l'École de Cavalerie une École de Maréchalerie, en 1846, un atelier d'Arçonnerie. La guerre de 1870 amena le licenciement de l'École, qui fut réorganisée le 30 août 1873.

Pendant la guerre de 1914-1918, l'École fut mise à la disposition de l'Armée Américaine qui y installa une École d'Artillerie. Dès la cessation des hostilités elle fut remise en état et les divers cours reprirent dans le courant de l'année 1919.

L'*École de Cavalerie* comprend actuellement :

I. — L'*École proprement dite* véritable centre d'Instruction de la Cavalerie française, où fonctionnent :

a) Des Cours de formation (Élèves-Officiers de l'active appelés à être nommés Sous-Lieutenants à la fin du Cours (11 mois).

Élèves-Officiers de réserve, destinés à devenir Officiers de complément (6 mois) ;

b) Un Cours d'Application (11 mois), pour Sous-Lieutenants sortis de l'Ecole Spéciale Militaire de Saint-Cyr.

c) Des Cours de perfectionnement au passage d'un grade au grade supérieur :

Lieutenants de Cavalerie (et un certain nombre de Lieutenants d'Artillerie et du Génie), pour le franchissement du grade de Capitaine. (Durée : 11 mois).

Capitaines et Chefs d'Escadrons à titre temporaire pour le franchissement du grade de Chef d'Escadrons (Durée : 3 semaines).

Chefs d'Escadrons et Lieutenant-Colonels pour le franchissement du grade de Lieutenant-Colonel et de Colonel. (Durée : 2 semaines).

II. — *Un centre d'Instruction d'Auto-Mitrailleuses* de Cavalerie chargé d'instruire Officiers, Sous-Officiers et hommes de troupe constituant le personnel des auto-mitrailleuses de cavalerie.

III. — *Une École Vétérinaire*, où passent chaque année un certain nombre d'Élèves Vétérinaires stagiaires qui peuvent, grâce au grand nombre de chevaux de l'École et à une installation bien comprise, se perfectionner dans leur art.

IV. — *Une École de Maréchalerie* pour former des maréchaux de corps de troupe montés.

V. — *Un Atelier d'Arçonnerie* où sont fabriqués selles et harnachements des corps de troupe montés de l'Armée française.

L'École de Cavalerie constitue donc un organisme très complexe : le Commandement en est confié à un Général (ou Colonel), assisté d'un Colonel (ou Lieutenant-Colonel) commandant en second.

Avec ses bâtiments bien compris, ses manèges spacieux, ses terrains d'instruction et de tir, l'École de Cavalerie est à même de donner à ses nombreux Élèves une instruction équestre, militaire, générale et scientifique correspondant à tous les devoirs de l'Officier de Cavalerie.

Sans rien abandonner de ses traditions du passé faites du souci de la valeur morale, de la passion du cheval et de tous les sports qui en découlent, l'École de Cavalerie, s'adaptant aux nécessités des guerres modernes a entrepris la tâche de faire du cavalier, sans rien lui retirer de sa valeur intrinsèque, l'émule du meilleur fantassin.

Suivant une forte parole de M. le Maréchal PÉTAIN : « L'audace, la vitesse et l'emploi du matériel sont les devoirs de la Cavalerie. » Ce sont ces devoirs que l'École de Cavalerie enseigne à ses Élèves de tous grades.

Les quelques photographies de cet Album en sont la preuve.

*\* \* \**

« C'est un devoir pour le Ministre de la Guerre de rendre hommage, en cette École, à la Cavalerie française, qui, au cours de la grande guerre, s'est montrée digne de son glorieux passé.

« Par la force de ses traditions militaires, ses qualités d'initiative et d'audace, sa magnifique intrépidité, la Cavalerie mérite d'être considérée comme une arme d'élite. Son rôle peut se modifier en s'adaptant aux exigences de l'organisation militaire moderne, mais son utilité demeure, et l'on ne peut concevoir qu'elle n'ait sa place dans une armée digne de ce nom ».

(Extrait du discours prononcé par M. MAGINOT, Ministre de la Guerre et des Pensions, à l'occasion de la remise de la Croix de la Légion d'honneur à l'Etendard de l'Ecole de Cavalerie, le 12 Mai 1922, à Saumur).

Décoration de l'Étendard de l'École, le 12 Mai 1922,
par M. MAGINOT, Ministre de la Guerre et des Pensions

Le Général THUREAU, commandant l'Ecole
*(montant "Raquetier" pur sang anglais)*

Hôtel du Commandement

Vue générale de Saumur, prise du Château

Vue générale de l'Ecole et reprise d'équitation par les Elèves

La Salle d'honneur

Vue générale du terrain d'exercices du Chardonnet

Exercices d'assaut à la baïonnette sur le Stade

Infirmerie - Hôpital

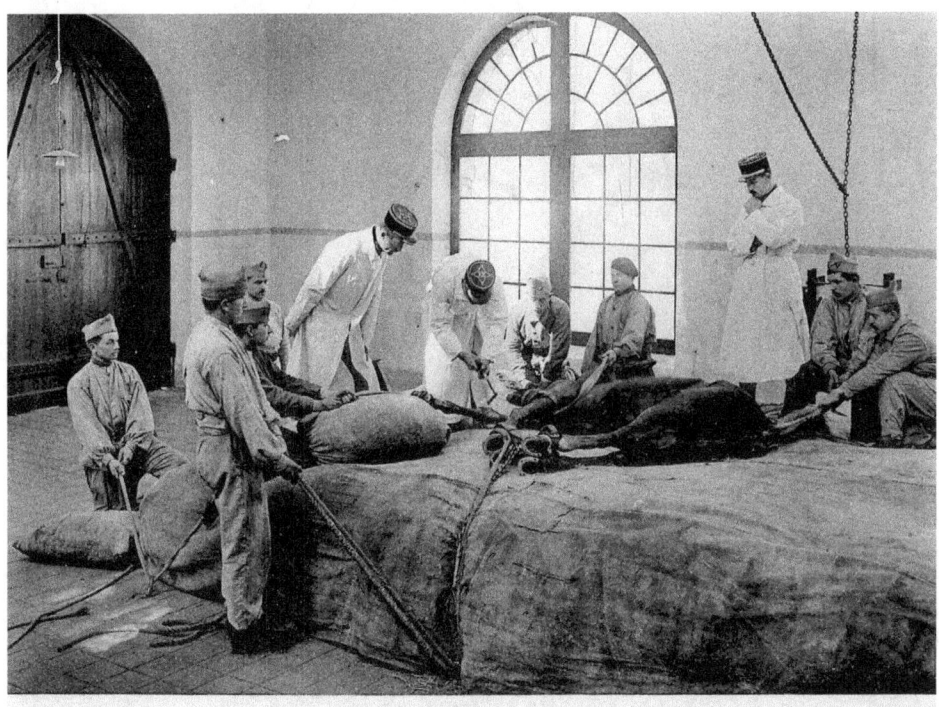

Infirmerie Vétérinaire *(Salle d'opérations)*

Ecole de maréchalerie

Les Écuries du Paddock *(chevaux à l'entraînement)*

Musée du cheval *(squelette de "Flying Fox")*

Musée du cheval

Musée du cheval (*La charge par Richefeu*)

Le Commandant WATEL, Instructeur en chef d'équitation
(*montant "Venus", pur sang anglo-arabe*)

Une reprise d'Ecuyers sur le Chardonnet

Une reprise d'Ecuyers sur le Chardonnet

Un Ecuyer au piaffer

Saut d'obstacle *(Concouzs hippique)*

Saut d'obstacle à l'extérieur
*(Commandant Watel)*

Saut d'obstacle par une reprise de Carrière sur le terrain de Verrie

Une Course militaire à Verrie

Une Course civile à Verrie

Une partie de balle à cheval sur le terrain du Breil

Croupade     Courbette     Cabriole
Sauteurs en liberté

Une reprise de sauteurs en liberté

Une reprise de sauteurs en liberté

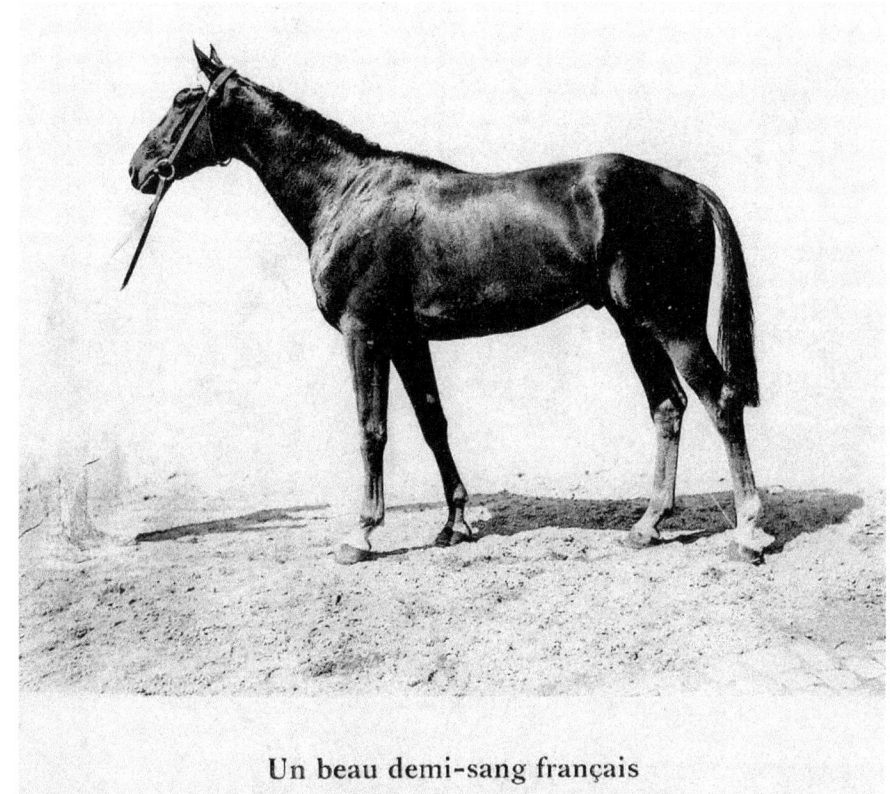

Un beau demi-sang français

Un bel anglo-arabe

Instruction du sabre

Exercices physiques *(Education nerveuse du Cavalier)*

Exercices physiques *(le porter)*

Ecole d'Escadron en terrain varié, à Verrie
(*marche d'approche*)

Passage de rivière

Auto-mitrailleuse de Cavalerie. Voiture de combat ancien modèle

Emploi du matériel (*Exercice de tir de mitrailleuses à Fontevrault*)

Exercice de tir à Terrefort

Auto-mitrailleuse de Cavalerie. Voiture de combat, type White

Rentrée d'un travail de Carrière (*Vezzie*)

# Chapter 6

## Tor di Quinto

## The Italian School for Advanced Riding

After studying at Saumur, Majors Chamberlin and West attend Tor di Quinto to study the Italian methods of riding.
—Warren C. Matha, Editor

*Figure 105.* An instructor at Tor di Quinto, the Italian Cavalry's school for advanced riding. "Students will ride at speeds consistent with the requirements of war." Photo in the Public Domain.

*Figure 106.* The Italian Cavalry demands riders to descend slides at Tor di Quinto with the upper body forward and with weight in the heels. Photo in the Public Domain.

*Figure 107.* Riders remain forward at all times. This obstacle requires horse and rider to ascend up, over, and then down a drop of approximately 4 feet. Photo in the Public Domain.

***Figure 108.*** *This Italian officer at Tor di Qunito shows the Italian style of Caprilli that Chamberlin will learn, master, and then modify. Photo in the Public Domain.*

***Figure 109.*** *Major Ruggero Ubertalli at Tor di Quinto serves as an instructor. He studied directly under Caprilli. Photo in the Public Domain.*

*Figure 110.* Another photo of Major Ruggero Ubertalli who achieved a personal triumph at the Inter-Allied Games of 1919. Photo in the Public Domain.

# The Italian Cavalry School at Tor di Qunito
By
Major H.D. Chamberlin, Cavalry
*The Cavalry Journal 1924*

The Italian Cavalry School is composed of two distinct and separate institutions. The first of these which an officer attends, usually while a lieutenant or as a young captain, is at Pinerola, in northwestern Italy, not far from Turin.

At Pinerola the instruction is of a general nature, comprising tactics, arms, administration, etc., in addition of equitation. It is similar to the present Troop Officer's course at Fort Riley, though perhaps a trifle more elemental.

## School of Application

After completing the nine months' course at Pinerola, certain selected officers are detailed to pass three months under instruction at Tor di Quinto, which is solely a school of application. Riding instruction alone is given with no theoretical work. In principle, all officers of cavalry and some of artillery take the course at Pinerola and many of these go to Tor di Quinto; though not necessarily during the same year in which they have attended Pinerola.

Tor di Quinto is at present under the command of Lieutenant-Colonel Starita, a distinguished officer and a leading horseman in Italy for many years. He was severely wounded during the war, having had one heel shot away during one of the glorious exploits of the Italian cavalry. Nevertheless, he is constantly on a horse and is a superb and fearless rider over any obstacles or country.

In his address to the class at the commencement of the course, Colonel Starita dwelt upon the point that Tor di Quinto was a school of morale, the purpose being to develop those most essential characteristics of a cavalryman—boldness and daring across country at fast paces; hence little elementary instruction is given during the course. The work is all devoted to jumping obstacles and riding the manner and at the gaits which will be necessary during the crises of cavalry employment in time of war.

Tor di Quinto is five miles from the center of Rome. The students live in the city and go to and from work in busses provided by the school. Lunch is served by the school. During the racing season students are given liberty Thursday afternoons to attend the races, where, of course much valuable horse knowledge is gained in a pleasant manner. There are some military races for officers only.

## Riding Time

The actual time on the horse's back at the school averages about five hours per day, which everyone agrees is ample. About thirty students attend each course, and they are divided into two platoons, under two captain instructors.

For ten years or more Italian teams have been winning far more prizes in jumping classes than any other country, at all the large European horse shows, the London show at Olympic included. When one asks why, the envious and unjust answer is, "Better horses"—that old, familiar wail. However, from what I have seen and heard, their horses are no better, and probably not as good, as those of other nations. Certainly, the average horse at Tor di Quinto is far below that at Weedon, the English Cavalry School, and also below that at Saumur, the French Cavalry School. Of course, there are excellent individuals in all countries.

## Reasons Why Italians Win at Shows

The reasons for the Italian superiority are three in number and very simple:

First. From a mechanical point of view, they have developed the most advantageous seat for the horse in getting his own and the rider's mass over an obstacle; hence maximum efficiency from the machine.

Second. Inasmuch as the Italians specialize in cross-country work and also show jumping and spend but little time at anything else, such as schooling and polo, they ride over many more obstacles per day than do the French, English, or American officers. Since the old saying, "Practice makes perfect," holds especially true for riding jumpers (as well as for the jumpers themselves when worked with judgment), the Italian experts have become absolute masters of show jumping.

Third. The training of their horses is eminently correct. The horse is taught to jump when mounted as he does at liberty, and the riding and training are accomplished with this in view.

It is not within the scope of this article to discuss or explain the training of horses or the exact principles of the Italian system of equitation. However, one sees that with a correct seat and correct training, both perfected by an unusual amount of practice over every type of obstacle, the Italians are difficult to beat.

The Italian system of equitation is not, in my opinion, suitable for our cavalry, inasmuch as our use of the pistol and saber and our type of mounted action require a very "handy" horse, which, as a general rule, the Italian system does not produce. However, I believe an adaptation of our military seat along Italian lines, when riding across country and when jumping, is practicable and advisable, for it saves both horse and man and gives better general results.

## Jumping Seat

It is to be noted that the jumping seat taught at Fort Riley has already undergone marked changes since 1919, tending toward the Italian method. This was due to the fact that several of our officers who participated in the equestrian sports during the Inter-Allied Games in Paris in 1919 were quick to see and to profit by the advantages of the Italian seat and the results it obtained. These ideas were carried to Fort Riley, and "going with the horse" has been adopted to some extent, although there is still much difference between the two methods, due principally to the fundamental differences in the seats themselves.

Captain Caprilli, of the Italian cavalry, who unfortunately died before reaching the zenith of his career, founded about twenty years ago the method of equitation now universally employed in the Italian Army. He developed it from what is known in Europe as the "American seat"; in other words, the racing seat which that wonderful jockey, Tod Sloan, first took to Europe. The marvelous success that Sloan gained soon converted all horsemen to the mechanical and practical advantages of this seat, so that today such a thing as sitting in the saddle during a race (as advocated by Fillis) is unheard of.

Lieutenant-Colonel R. Ubertalli has since been one of the greatest exponents and teachers of Caprilli's system. He will probably be in charge of the Italian Olympic team. His galaxy of star performers includes many well-known riders, among whom are Majors Caffaratti, Antonelli, Valerio; Captains Lequio, Fourquet, Valle, Cacciandra, Borsarelli, Santo Rosa, and many others, all of whom are masters of the art of show jumping.

A notable thing in the equipment of the Italian trooper is that his horse is provided with a Pelham bit. The advantages are economy, less weight, and the possibility of the horse's drinking without unbridling. For the rider of the ability of the average cavalry soldier, the Pelham undoubtedly will serve as well, if not better, than the bit and bridoon. In fact, more horses run away from the pain caused by a severe bit than from the lack of control furnished by a mild one.

The horses, as stated above, are not as handy as ours; nevertheless, they go beautifully across country, extending themselves naturally and making the greatest use of neck and head in clearing obstacles. The most remarkable characteristics of the horses at Tor di Quinto are the calmness and willingness with which they jump. These horses are all ridden in snaffle bits, as are all Italian horses in jumping competitions, with but rare exceptions.

## Body Forward

Briefly stated, the Italian rides with a very short stirrup, keeps the heels and knees driven down as far as possible, and at a fast gallop does not sit down in the saddle, only the knees, thighs, and stirrups serving as a seat. Contrary to appearances, this seat is very secure and the legs can be employed very vigorously. The rider does not "tuck under" the seat, as in the French, English, and American schools, but keeps the loin straight or even a bit concave. There is no exception to the rule that the body must be inclined forward at all times, whether backing the horse or racing him. With such short stirrups, the rider not accustomed to the seat becomes tired in the knees and loin at first. After one or two weeks, one finds it a very easy way of riding at fast gaits.

There is an excellent pack of hounds at Rome, and the Hunt Club very generously invites the whole school, staff and students, to attend. The country is quite varied and difficult to negotiate in many places. One finds few obstacles that come down, but as the horses are always trained over fixed obstacles, they jump very cleanly.

Before the war, the Italian Government bought many Irish horses, but due to the necessity of economy in Italy, as elsewhere, and to the high price of Irish horses, especially when bought with the lire at the present low exchange rate, there are only a few very old Irish horses left. The others are principally half-bred Italian horses, with either Italian or imported Thoroughbred sires and native mares. This horse is usually not very large, about 15-0 to 15-3, but very agile, courageous, and remarkably good at obstacles of a reasonable height.

# Chamberlin's Comments Regarding the Italian Method as Contained in an Unpublished Document

Briefly stated, the Italian rides with a very short stirrup, keeps the heels and knees driven down as far as possible, and at a fast gallop does not sit down in the saddle, only the knees, thighs, and stirrups serving as a seat. Contrary to appearances, this seat is very secure and the legs can be employed very vigorously. The rider does not "tuck under" the seat, as in the French, English, and American schools, but keeps the loin straight or even a bit concave.

It is to be noted that the jumping seat taught at Fort Riley has already undergone marked changes since 1919, tending toward the Italian method. This was due to the fact that several of our officers who participated in the equestrian sports during the Inter-Allied Games in Paris in 1919 were quick to see and to profit by the advantages of the Italian seat and the results it obtained.

There is no exception to the rule that the body must be inclined forward at all times, whether backing the horse or racing him.

The French school, while very thorough and excellent in many ways, has tended for years to cling to the classic seat ridden in the "haute ecole." While it has become more forward for cross-country work, as cavalry has become more mobile and equestrian sports have developed, still there has remained a pronounced tendency toward riding with the weight somewhat to the rear, and to keeping the horse closely collected and flexed.

The English hunting men rode with the body inclined to the rear and exaggerated this by leaning back still further when going over a fence. It was done with the idea of taking weight off the horse's forehand when he landed, as well as a matter of safety to the rider. Of course enlightened modern riders know that when a man "rides forward," and does so in good form, he is no more liable to fall off than when he is leaning back.

In addition, the forward position of the weight allows his horse far more liberty in the use of his loin and hind-quarters and thereby gives him a much better chance of negotiating any particular obstacle without pain or difficulty. [10]

---

10   Chamberlin, Harry D. Brig. General USA, personal papers.

# Chapter 7

## The Olympic Games of 1932

### Warren C. Matha, Editor

Chamberlin trains both horses and riders for the Olympic Games of 1932. He also rides in the Three-Day Event and the *Prix des Nations* jumping competition. The U.S. Cavalry team wins the team gold medal in the Three-Day Event. Most significantly, the U.S. team defeats the eventing powerhouses Sweden and Holland—the first time in Olympic history that one or the other of those two teams suffers defeat in eventing. Of special personal note: Chamberlin also wins the individual silver medal in the *Prix des Nations*.

*Figure 111.* Captain Argo of the USA on Honolulu Tomboy. He rides the entire event in excruciating pain with a dislocated shoulder that doctors tape up. Photo courtesy of the U.S. Olympic Committee.

*Figure 112.* Lt. Col. Kido of The Empire of Japan on Kyn Gun.
Photo courtesy of the U.S. Olympic Committee.

*Figure 113.* Lt. Schummelketel of Holland on Duiveltie.
Photo printed with permission of the U.S. Olympic Committee.

*Figure 114.* Captain Yamamoto of the Empire of Japan on Kingo.
Photo courtesy of the U.S. Olympic Committee.

*Figure 115.* Lt. Pahud Mortanges of Holland on Marcroix.
Photo printed with permission of the U.S. Olympic Committee.

***Figure 116.*** *Lt. Pahud Mortanges of Holland on Marcroix. This horse and rider win back to back Individual Gold Medals in Eventing for 1928 and 1932. Photo printed with permission from the U.S. Olympic Committee.*

***Figure 117.*** *Lt. Pahud de Mortanges of Holland on Marcroix. Photo printed with permission from the U.S. Olympic Committee.*

*Figure 118.* Lt. von Rosen of Sweden on Sunnyside Maid.
Photo courtesy of the U.S. Olympic Committee.

*Figure 119.* Lt. van Lennep of Holland on Henk.
Photo printed with permission of the U.S. Olympic Committee.

*Figure 120.* Major Chamberlin on Pleasant Smile.
Photo printed with permission of the U.S. Olympic Committee.

*Figure 121.* Lt. van Lennep of Holland on Henk.
Photo printed with permission of the U.S. Olympic Committee.

*Figure 122.* Major Chamberlin on Pleasant Smile. He lost his hat in a fall at the previous jump. Photo printed with permission of the U.S. Olympic Committee.

*Figure 123.* Lt. Earl "Tommy" Thomson of the USA clears every cross country jump. He walked the entire course twice before the competition. Photo courtesy of the U.S. Olympic Committee.

*Figure 124.* Captain Hallberg of Sweden on Marokan.
Photo printed with permission from the U.S. Olympic Committee.

## Prix des Nations Photos

*Figure 125.* Baron Nishi of the Empire of Japan on Uranus.
Photo printed with permission of the U. S. Olympic Committee.

*Figure 126.* Hallberg of Sweden on Kornett.
Photo courtesy of the U.S. Olympic Committee.

*Figure 127.* The most difficult Prix des Nations course in Olympic history.
Photo courtesy of the U.S. Olympic Committee.

*Figure 128.* Lt. Francke of Sweden on Urfe.
Photo courtesy of the U.S. Olympic Committee.

*Figure 129.* Baron Nishi of the Empire of Japan on Uranus.
Photo printed with permission of the U.S. Olympic Committee.

*Figure 130.* Chamberlin on Show Girl takes the 5'3" wall of the chicken coop.
Photo courtesy of the U.S. Olympic Committee.

*Figure 131.* Bradford of the USA on Joe Aleshire.
Photo printed with the permission of the U.S. Olympic Committee.

*Figure 132.* Captain Hallberg of Sweden and horse Kornett take a tumble at the chicken coop. Hallberg remounts Kornett and they try again!
Photo courtesy of the U.S. Olympic Committee.

*Figure 133.* Chamberlin on Show Girl ascends a 5'3" jump.
Photo courtesy of the U.S. Olympic Committee.

# Chapter 8

# Writings of Harry D. Chamberlin in Periodicals, Letters, and Manuals 1934-1942

During this timeframe, Chamberlin serves as an up-and-coming officer in the United States Cavalry who rises higher and higher in the officer corps. He graduates from the elite Army War College. He starts and begins raising a family. He becomes a squadron commander. Later, he becomes responsible for training the 1st Cavalry Division and makes it the U.S. Army's best trained division. Then, he becomes Chief of Staff for that division. During this time, he writes two books on riding and training horses. He writes articles in periodicals about topics as diverse as the differences in the "seats" of various countries, the jumping seat, dressage, the confirmation of the Three-Day Event horse. He assists in the design of a new saddle for U.S. Cavalry officers.

He then commands the 2nd Cavalry Regiment and writes an influential article on training cavalrymen. He writes another article regarding how mounted units should cross rivers. He then becomes a Brigadier General and commands the Cavalry Replacement Training Center at Ft. Riley. At the same time, he supervises the staff of the Cavalry School in its effort to revise the U.S. Cavalry's manual *Horsemanship and Horsemastership*. In this effort, he writes major parts of the Cavalry manual's sections *The Education of the Rider* and *The Education of the Horse*. Finally, as a Brigade commander, he produces a monograph *Breaking, Training, and Reclaiming Cavalry Horses* which details four exercises to reclaim cavalry horses, polo ponies, eventers, jumpers, hacks, and to transition race horses from racing to eventing.

—Warren C. Matha, Editor

# 1934

## The Modern Seat
## A Discussion of the Differences Between the Seats of Various Countries

*The Cavalry Journal May-June 1934*

by

Major Harry D. Chamberlin, 14th Cavalry
1932 U.S. Army Olympic Equestrian Team

Form is as essential in riding as in any other branch of athletics if a horseman expects to excel. In recent years, coaches in all sports have given much time to analyzing and developing perfect form. The improvement in all athletics which has resulted therefrom needs no comment; many shattered records bear witness to the value of mechanical perfection of movement—which is synonymous with good form. Along with the other sports form in riding, particularly in show jumping, hunting, and steeplechasing, has made vast progress. The amazing thing is that it has been so tardily developed in a sport as old as riding.

In all fairness, the Italians must be given credit for this progress through their evolution of what is generally known as the "forward seat." Our own countryman, that great jockey, Tod Sloan was, however, the first horseman to use it and prove by his many successes the value of keeping the rider's weight forward and over the horse's shoulders, which are by nature his shock absorbers. Major Federico Caprilli, an Italian officer, taking his cue from the racing seat as initiated by Sloan, modified it somewhat and developed a strong and mechanically correct forward seat for jumping and cross-country riding.

Much confusion exists in the United States as to exactly what is meant by such names as the "forward," "Italian," "Saumur," "Fort Riley," and other seats. Even the most accomplished horsemen are in somewhat of a fog as to the differences implied by these denominations. In general, almost any grotesque attitude where a rider is humped forward is called a forward seat. These positions should certainly not be confused with the seats adopted by the Italian or American military show teams.

Many riders in our show rings who ride in the crouching attitudes alluded to above would be utterly unable to control or guide their horses were the obstacles not enclosed by enormous wings and the area by a fence. Usually they support themselves by fixing their hands with short reins on the horse's neck, thus denying him liberty in using his head and neck as a balancer during some phase of the jump. On the other hand, where riders allow the reins to remain very slack, they completely surrender control. In the first case, with the fixed hand and short rein, the horse receives a blow on the mouth from the bit at each jump and in the second case he can run out or refuse at will if the obstacle does not suit his fancy.

In general, it may be said that the art of equitation and all scientific seats have been developed at the cavalry schools which have existed in Europe for centuries. There is no doubt that the officers graduated from the Cavalry School at Fort Riley during the last two decades have done much in developing good form and sound equitation in the United States.

The Riley school has for many years been patterned after the French school at Saumur, France. Adoption of French methods resulted from the fact that American officers for many years past have been detailed by our government to take the complete Saumur course, which lasts about ten months. Two of the first officers to be sent there are now distinguished generals of the United States Army—Major-General Guy V. Henry, Chief of Cavalry, and Brigadier-General Walter C. Short of the First Cavalry Division, El Paso, Texas. These excellent horsemen became instructors in equitation at Fort Riley, and to them is due in a great measure the initiation of methods which have accomplished such marked improvement in horsemanship among our mounted Army officers in the last twenty years.

The French school, while very thorough and excellent in many ways, has tended for years to cling to the classic seat ridden in the "haute ecole." While it has become more forward for cross-country work, as cavalry has become more mobile and equestrian sports have developed, still there has remained a pronounced tendency toward riding with the weight somewhat to the rear, and to keeping the horse closely collected and flexed.

The Italians, on the other hand, have since Caprilli's time gone to the extreme in training the mounted horse to move as he does when at liberty, and to seek his own balance while carrying a preponderance of the rider's and his own weight on his forehand. In this connection it is noteworthy, notwithstanding popular opinion to the contrary, that a horse can use his hind-quarters and throw his weight onto his hocks with greater ease when allowed to carry his head in a normal and fairly low position than when the rider keeps it raised with the bits. There is much misconception as to what "being on the hocks" and "jumping off the hocks" really mean. A discussion of this, however, would require more time that can be given in this article. Suffice it to say that raising a hunter's or jumper's head, unless he has been properly trained to engage his hocks in response to action by the rider's legs is very faulty procedure.

In our country the majority of hunting people, for many years, copied the riding methods and seat handed down from England. The English hunting men rode with the body inclined to the rear and exaggerated this by leaning back still further when going over a fence. It was done with the idea of taking weight off the horse's forehand when he landed, as well as a matter of safety to the rider. Of course enlightened modern riders know that when a man "rides forward," and does so in good form, he is no more liable to fall off than when he is leaning back.

In addition, the forward position of the weight allows his horse far more liberty in the use of his loin and hind-quarters and thereby gives him a much better chance of negotiating any particular obstacle without pain or difficulty. Even if a rider feels that he is not quite as secure with this seat it is certainly more sportsmanlike to ride it if he considers the benefits accruing to his horse. In almost every European nation the military riders, who are always the models for their civilian associates, have adopted the Italian seat or some modification thereof. Many of those who have not adopted it in its entirety have failed to do so, quite probably, through failure to completely understand it and the principles of mechanics involved, with their resultant advantages.

Old horseman hate to change methods, probably sensing their inability to learn new ones! Moreover, almost every man who has hunted or even hacked for a couple of years feels some Heaven-sent equestrian omniscience settle on him! He should remember that a recruit rides more in his first six months than the ordinary rider to hounds does in two years.

In the last ten years, both the French and our own Cavalry Schools have tended toward more forward inclination of the body in outdoor and cross-country riding. There is still a tendency in both these schools, however, to ride with the buttocks too far forward under the rider, with a consequent convexity to the rear of the loin. This position forces the rider to "hump" the entire back in attempting to ride a forward seat. The position is most faulty and unfortunately has existed in American military riding for many years. It is to be hoped that all military and civilian riders will soon realize the vast advantages inherent in keeping the backbone in a normal erect position and in obtaining forward inclination by bending forward *from the hip joints only*. This is one of the distinctive characteristics of the Italian seat which

Piero Santini has very well described in his book entitled "*Riding Reflections,*" published in The Derrydale Press.

Military riders among the Swedes, Poles, and Germans have all adopted some form of forward seat, and most of them have apparently incorporated in their system some of the Italian ideas. Still, the Italians, more than the others mentioned, leave the horse at liberty in regard to movements of his head and neck through having exceedingly light hands and following the horse's mouth as his head and neck execute their natural movements.

The Swedes in recent years at the Olympic Games and at Madison Square Garden in New York have not used nearly as much forward inclination of the body as the Italians and have maintained much heavier support on the horse's mouths. As a result, many of them seem to be habitually "behind" their horses and attempt to "place" them too much. The Germans, on the other hand, have a pronounced forward inclination, but demand much more collection from the horse than do the Italians. The polls of the German horses are more flexed, but at the same time their necks are in a natural position and are not distorted by unnecessarily high head carriage. While some of the English are excellent horsemen, they do not, as whole, have as good form as the riders of the other nations mentioned and consequently fail to attain the best results. The same is true of the Irish, although each year at the National Horse Show they have shown improvement, and at the Chicago World's Fair Horse Show in October, they did exceedingly well.

There are, of course, many excellent riders among civilians in our country as well as abroad, but they ride with every conceivable style of seat and almost all would do much better if they studied and practiced form. Be it granted that an experienced and natural horseman can ride any sort of seat and get along with his mount, still he certainly cannot do well over obstacles and cross country as if he rode in good form. This, to the knowing, thinking man, is indisputable and there is no doubt that correct seats account for the numerous successes of those certain well-known riders from the various countries who habitually excel.

Few men really have "hand," since few have enough security and balance to their seats and sufficient coordination to avoid involuntary and unnecessary actions of the reins during stress and excitement. These actions upset and hinder the horse, oftentimes when he is making his greatest effort. The result of these poor seats and hands is such that 85 percent of the hunters and jumpers in the field and show ring would be considered exceedingly poorly trained horses by high-class riders. As stated before, the average horseman soon becomes satisfied with himself and fails to make any attempt to improve. It is greatly to be regretted that most of them do not realize that none ever becomes perfect and that every real horseman can learn something new and improve his tact, skill, and seat every day he rides.

Briefly, the seat taught members of the United States Horse Show Team of 1932 is as follows:

a) The heels forced well down. This is an absolute requisite to accomplish superior riding of any type, for if the heels are not down the calf muscles cannot be powerfully contracted and the rider's seat and legs are weak.

b) Feet turned out naturally, about 45 degrees from the horse's side. No effort is made to splay the outside of the foot upward and depress the ankle bone inward. This stiffens the ankle and tends to throw the calf of the leg away from the horse.

c) The calf normally clings lightly to the horse's side, but is used with vigor when necessary to push him ahead.

d) The knees are as low as the stirrups permit and remain fixed in position by slight pressure. They are pressed strongly against the saddle when the horse slows down, "pecks" or attempts to refuse. The knee joint is *relaxed*, except when the rider is purposely standing in his stirrups while galloping across country or between obstacles.

e) Thighs are flat against the saddle. The muscles on the inner side of the thigh should be back of the thigh bone. This is easy to accomplish if the rest of the seat described is adopted.

f) The fleshy part of the buttocks should not be pushed under the rider by convexing the loin to the rear but should be kept well to the rear.

g) The backbone is held in a normal erect position with the loin slightly hallowed out.

h) The pelvis bones rest lightly on the saddle.

i) The upper part of the body is inclined forward from *the hip joints*.

j) The length of the stirrup strap depends upon the type of riding. Beyond a certain point shortening the stirrups lessens the rider's security. In flat racing the stirrups are extremely short in order that the riders may throw all possible weight forward and keep off the horse's back. This increases the horse's instability to the front and instability is the measure of speed. Of course, the jockey's seat is very insecure if the horse makes any sudden lateral movement. In show jumping the stirrups, while slightly longer than in flat racing, are also very short because they permit the rider to keep his weight off his horse's back during the entire jump. In steeplechasing, where security is more important than a clean performance, the stirrup is longer than in show jumping. In hacking, a little more length is given, and in high school work and in the early training of a colt an extremely long stirrup is required so the rider's legs can be used efficiently in applying the necessary aids.

k) The chest and head should be kept raised, which tends to hold the backbone in proper position and makes the rider master of his balance.

l) Normally the rider, due to his relaxed knee and forward inclination of the body has his weight resting on the pelvis bones, the thigh, the knee, and the heel. One should disregard the stirrup and have the sensation of carrying the weight in the heel of his boot. This keeps the heels well depressed.

With the very short stirrup used in flat racing the body inclination to the front is extreme because the center of gravity of the unstable portion of the body, namely the trunk, must, in order to overcome momentum, be in advance of the center of the rider's base of support. The longitudinal measurement of the base of support is the horizontal projection of the distance between the point where the knee is in contact with the saddle and the pelvis bone. The more the stirrup is shortened the greater his length becomes, and consequently the greater must be the inclination of the body.

The seat described is easy to acquire, although one unaccustomed to it will at first become tired in the loin. After having acquired it thorough practice, however, both the rider and his horse will outlast the man who leans backward and the horse which carries the weight on his loin.

# 1935

### Excerpt from Chamberlin Letter to Col Albert Phillips Regarding the Phillips Saddle Design 1935

In 1934, Chamberlin suggests that the U.S. Cavalry adopt a new saddle for officers. Col. Albert Phillips, the designer of the Phillips Pack Saddle, takes the challenge and designs a new saddle. The U.S. Cavalry calls it the M–1936 Officer's Field Saddle. Chamberlin recommends that the saddle's deepest part be one inch forward of the saddle's center (and thus departing from French practice.) Chamberlin insists that no matter what the size of the rider, the saddle should measure 18 inches. Anything smaller fails to distribute properly the rider's weight. Anything larger extends into the loin of the horse and, in time, harms the horse. —Warren C. Matha, Editor.

Chamberlin writes:
"One of the greatest errors which prevents the rider's assuming a correct forward seat, and which leads to the grotesque positions often seen, results from two things: first, saddle seats are frequently too short for the riders; and second, the rider endeavors to push his crotch and buttocks too far forward in the saddle. The crotch would be in the throat or deepest part of the saddle, and the fleshy part of the buttocks should be kept well to the rear, but due to the rider's constant forward inclination of the body from the hips there should be practically no weight on the cantle. Assuming a proper seat on the other hand necessitates a properly made saddle with the throat or deepest part of the seat a little in front of the center. The forward seat is easy to acquire, although one unaccustomed to it will at first become tired in the loins, after having acquired it through practice, however, both the rider and his horse will outlast the man who leans backward, and the horse which carries the rider's weight on his loin." [11]

Chamberlin concludes that the deepest part of the saddle's seat should be one inch forward of the center so as to put the rider as close to the horse's withers as feasible.

—Warren C. Matha, Editor

---

11  Chamberlin, H.D. Brig. General. Personal papers.

# 1937

## Article Regarding the Conformation of Three-Day Horses

The following article Harry Chamberlin penned in 1937 as part of a series of articles by cavalrymen on the topic of conformation for the Three-Day Horse. Of particular interest is Chamberlin's suggestion that the short-backed horses favored by the Cavalry for field campaigns do not meet the needs of the event rider; that a longer backed horse will do better in the Three-Day Event but will not perform as well as the cavalry's favored horse in long-distance campaigning. Also, Chamberlin favors smaller horses as opposed to larger.

—Warren C. Matha, Editor

### *The Conformation of Three-Day Horses*
### *The Cavalry Journal 1937*
### By Lt. Col. Harry D. Chamberlin

To discuss the requisites of a three-day horse in a few words is not exceedingly difficult, but to find a horse which possesses all to a high degree is almost impossible. I have at hand a copy of Major Cole's comments which are brief, sound, and need no expatiation.

It is impossible to get away from the all-important value of correct conformation. In 1932, after trying out approximately one hundred horses of one type and another and finally selecting those we considered best for shipment to California prior to the Games, it was soon discovered that, almost without exception, those with some obvious fault in conformation, such as pasterns too upright, poor feet, not sufficient tendon and bone below the knee, etc., quickly proved the soundness of our theories in conformation by being eliminated for lameness. The three horses finally used on the three-day team—*Jenny Camp, Pleasant Smile,* and *Honolulu Tomboy* were all, in general fairly well conformed. Jenny Camp, however, has proved herself the miracle horse, in that, as stated by Major Cole, she is on the small side, short-gaited, far from prepossessing from the knee down (particularly in her front pasterns which are quite upright), and undoubtedly the poorest of the three horses in general conformation. Yet she did the best work then and lived to repeat in 1936. Captain Earl F. Thomson must share generously in her glory, for such things do not happen to any horse unless superbly and intelligently ridden.

In general, it may be stated that upright pasterns, since they serve so little their function of absorbing shock, are a grievous fault in a horse required to go great distances. However, Jenny is somewhat compensated in that she is well-balanced, standing high at the withers: this distributes more weight on the hindquarters, thus saving the forelegs. In addition, she possessed that greatest of all virtues, true *quality*. The word is frequently misused and misunderstood. When used generally about a horse, as "that horse has 'quality,'" it means something that can be determined only by test. It is a matter of the circulatory, respiratory, nervous, and digestive systems, substance of the tendons, muscles, bones, etc., and their proper functioning under tremendous strain, requiring particularly endurance and maximum effort. In quality, the gallant little mare proved a marvel, having that final and all-important virtue embraced in the term "quality"; i.e., great courage. She also has the innate and impossible-to-develop attributes of agility and quickness.

*Pleasant Smile* is a superb horse but too long in the back for carrying weight for a long period of time. Were he two inches shorter in the loin region he would have been a perfect performer in a three-day event. Major Cole is on sound ground, I believe, in stating that some length of back and loin is necessary for jumping. It also allows the horse to stand over more ground and stride farther. However, Pleasant Smile was *excessively* long. In other words, the back must not be too long or too short for a three-day horse. Yet it must be understood that for a cavalry troop horse a short back is most desirable. Then too, *Jenny Camp's* back and loin merit a glance. Certainly they are on the short side which seemed to bother her in no way except as the possible cause of her short strides at all gaits.

*Honolulu Tomboy* has fairly good conformation, except for one feature, easily overlooked, which was obviously defective. Her nostrils were very small. This was surely responsible for her difficulty in completing certain phases of the cross-country test in the required time. The toxins generated in the muscles by long continued exertion which brings fatigue if not eliminated by the lungs, could not be rapidly enough removed, due to the limited quantity of air inhaled through her too-small nostrils.

The only test of a horse regardless of his beauty and presumable quality is actually riding him thought the phases involved in the particular competition. This alone will determine his fitness. If he has true quality, he may be 15-2 or 16-2. It comes in all sizes and, I believe, most often in smaller horses. In general, however, the medium-sized thoroughbred horse from 15-2 to

16-1 is best for three-day purposes. In this connection, it is noteworthy that our method of measuring a horse's height is not highly rational. For instance, many horses, practically the same size and weight will show a discrepancy of from one to three inches in the height at the withers. In other words, a 15-2 horse may be bigger than a 16-2 one. It is a question of length and height of body relative to the length of legs. High withers (not high horses) are a most valuable attribute in any horse for any work. Also, for a jumper and distance performer, the height of the horse at the withers should be greater than that at the croup. This invariably makes a lighter-going, better-balanced, better-jumping horse over rough country, despite the fact that the old "ideal horse" of Jacoulet and Chomel and other authorities stood the same height at withers and croup. To be sure, many very fast race horses, particularly sprinters, are lower at the withers than at the croup which is favorable to great speed inasmuch as it creates instability toward the front.

### What of the Newest Prospects?

Having at hand the picture of *Reno Helmet*, it is difficult indeed to state just what kind of a performer he will be. To comment on him, as I have been requested, takes temerity. Only observation and riding can tell the way of going and quality which no picture can show. From the picture (which may or may not give a true likeness of this horse), *Reno Helmet* appears to have several characteristics in conformation which, to my mind, indicate the possibility of a great three-day horse. Disregarding the ugliness of his croup (which is nevertheless rugged, shaped to jump, and powerful), and perhaps too much length of leg, especially between knee and fetlock, he, on the other hand, apparently has high, well-shaped withers; a flat, long shoulder; and a fairly upright arm, which is very essential. His body is well-shaped and of proper length with long, well sprung ribs. His top-line indicates strength and suppleness; direction of the back is excellent; neck and head appear well set on, being neither too light, too heavy, too long, nor too short to serve as an excellent balancer. His head and expression indicate boldness and alertness. His croup appears a trifle short, but it must be remembered that the true length of croup is the length of the *ilium* plus the length of the *ischium*. When the angle formed by the two is acute the croup may appear short when actually long. Such a croup favors jumping.

## Little Jenny Camp Could Lay No Claim to Being The Perfect Picture Horse

As previously stated, to make the above observations from a photograph, having never seen the horse, takes great audacity, and all the observations may bell be in error. "Beauty is as beauty does." Little *Jenny Camp* could lay no claim to being the perfect picture horse. Nevertheless, she, with the assistance of her handsome rider, so performed during two most difficult competitions as to please any horseman's most esthetic ideals. Colonel Henry R. Richmond, when senior instructor in equitation at the Cavalry School, once told the students, "A good horse is a good horse." The more this sententious remark is considered, the more broad-minded a horseman will become and the less committed to a type.

The study of conformation is most engrossing. Unfortunately, however, it is but superficially undertaken and understood by many horse lovers; in fact, by many who fancy themselves as judges. Even the genuine, knowing horse judge is never infallible. Nevertheless, his thorough knowledge does help him to make fewer mistakes and to make very few indeed if he rides and tests the horse whose conformation meets theoretical requirements.

All know that a flat, long, sloping shoulder is desirable—but such a shoulder is of little value if not correctly proportioned to the length of the arm—or if the angle of the arm and shoulder is too small—or if the withers are not high and correctly placed relative to the upper end of the cartilage of prolongation, etc. There is neither time nor space to discuss these many co-related facts concerning conformation which only careful study, experience and an observing eye can give a horseman.

If after a sound thoroughbred of the type illustrated is found, and if after schooling he possesses the several great attributes which, although partly hereditary, are also our training objectives, i.e., calmness, relaxation, suppleness, boldness, balance, agility, and long low strides at all gaits, and if he also can do well the school work and jumping required, he still must receive the final test of going through a trial more difficult that the three-day Olympic test. This alone will prove whether he *appears to have, or truly has quality*. If there is any doubt after such a test, replacement is in order.

# High School for Horses
## By Lieut.-Col. Harry D. Chamberlin
### *The Cavalry Journal*

The pinnacle of perfected skill in equitation is the high-school. In the United States but little understood and consequently unappreciated, it is even ridiculed by certain persons who consider themselves horseman; this attitude, of course, is an offensive defense of their own ignorance. Whether or not one is interested in high-school work, it is perfectly apparent that it is an equestrian art requiring much practice and natural ability.

There is nothing that gives greater joy to a horseman's soul that to see his horse's training improve under his guidance, and it is high-school work which develops the skill in a rider which permits him to bring his horse to the height of beauty and brilliance. It also rapidly increases a horseman's ability in all other forms of riding.

Usually, poor work on the horse's part is the result of mediocre riding and training on that of the rider. Unfortunately, a great many people have seen circus "trick" horses go through a series of movements taught with a whip by a dismounted trainer, and erroneously believe that these poor creatures, laboriously dragging their hind legs, are high-school horses. The true high-school horse is taught all his "airs" by a mounted rider, and he executes them with a technique as exact as that of a perfectly trained member of the ballet.

The expression *"haute ecole"* is partly self-explanatory, meaning "the school of high gaits." Teaching a horse the movements, or "airs," as they are usually called, requires great skill and extreme patience, and progress is painstakingly and methodically accomplished. The horse must do his work with perfect precision and perform each movement with the utmost grace and lightness. When properly trained, he offers no resistance to the rider's demands, but gives himself over generously and unconsciously, and becomes so supple and graceful that he appears to enjoy his work and to perform the most difficult requirements of his own free will. Rarely can a person be found, who whether devoted to horses or not, will fail to become enthusiastically appreciative upon seeing a well-executed high-school performance.

A young horse being trained in this work is first taught to go with exactly cadenced steps at all gaits; walk, trot and canter. As matter of fact, this "cadencing" should be part of every colt's training, although few trainers realize the importance of this fact, or know how to accomplish it. It improves immeasurably any horse' gaits and appearance.

Very early the high-school horse is taught at all gaits to engage his hind legs and feet well forward under his body, and to carry his head and neck raised to a graceful position, with the latter arched at the poll, (the region of the neck just back of the ears). This manner of carrying himself at the demand of his rider is called "collection," and permits the horse to throw more of his weight on the hind-quarters than he can with a low head carriage and with the hind legs "dragging," or not well-engaged.

While "collected," the front line of his face approaches the vertical, due to the arching of the poll, and the forehand appears light and graceful as a result of his balanced relaxation and impulsion. Higher knee and hock action result. The head carriage somewhat resembles that of a well–trained saddle horse, except that the high-school horse takes much less tension on the reins; in other words, his is far lighter on the hand. This is because he is better balanced, and his impulsion is more restrained; consequently, he never pulls.

If a well-trained high-school horse is given a longer rein, he immediately stretches out and lowers his head and neck without excitement of increase of speed. Simultaneously, however, his strides become longer and lower, while the flexion of knees and hocks diminishes. If one observes the above points, he will soon be able to tell whether a schooled horse is truly relaxed and balanced through having a "good," "light" mouth. A good mouth is the prime requisite in a high-school horse. Also, it is to be noted that a horse which gives himself over to his rider without resistance generally has his ears up and appears alert and contented while working.

A second characteristic of the finely schooled horse is the enormous impulsion and action developed by his hind quarters. They appear "vibrant" and transmit that vibrancy to all parts of the body throughout the whole exhibition. The marked and continuous impulsion which produces the vibrancy, results from the horse's engaging his hind feet well forward under his belly. The engagement is taught by the rider "using his legs" or spurs with tact and finesse throughout all training. These should be an appearance of power, springiness, exact cadence, and great elasticity at all gaits and in all movements; particularly must these qualities be noticeable in the action of his hind legs. Some horses, of course, have more natural impulsion and brilliance than others. They make the "showiest" high-school horses. An active Thoroughbred with personality and beauty is the ideal instrument.

There are in general two types of horse: those which have innate impetuosity and fire, and as a result, usually have great natural impulsion. These are often called "hand" horses, since their training requires little action from the rider's legs, but much skill and delicacy of his hands. The other type consists of those horses with phlegmatic dispositions. These require strong and persistent action from the rider's legs to instill the necessary amount of impulsion and "go" during their training. With either type, however, each high-school horse, (as well as every other horse), never-endingly should be taught that the rider's legs and spurs must be instantly obeyed by energetic engagement of the hind-quarters and forward movement. This can and should be accomplished without brutality or cruelty.

Collection, which is the foundation of haute ecole, demands equestrian skill and tact. It is produced by the hands' accurate and timely working on the relaxed and soft mouth, in order to regulate the strong vigorous impulsion generated by the hind legs. In response to the rider's legs, (the movements of which become imperceptible as training nears completion), the horse gradually learns, while remaining balanced, to increase the power of his hind legs to act on his mass by engaging them at each step far forward under his belly. The impulsion so generated is regulated as stated previously by the rider's hands. Part of it is allowed to carry the horse forward, while part of it, being restrained by the bits, is turned into loftier action The knees and hocks are little or highly flexed, and the strides are long and low, or high and short depending on how much impulsion the rider allows to escape in forward movement and how much his hands' resistance turns into elevation. The horse is always "in front of the ride's legs" and "on the hand," but *lightly* on the hand. In the most difficult movements, as for instance galloping in place, the hands are exquisitely light and delicate in their resistances. If they are heavy or rough the horse will be thrown off balance.

In executing the reprise called for in the Olympic Games, movements begin and end at specific spots in the 60 x 20-meter rectangular arena. For instance, a horse may be called upon to go at an extended trot along one side of the arena; then, when six meters from the end of that side, he is required to come to a collected trot as the rider's body arrives opposite the set point six meters from the short end. The change of speed must occur exactly at that point. He now maintains a smooth, cadenced, collected trot. After passing the far corner of the short side and turning down the other long side he may be, for example required at a point six meters from the corner to take the passage, continuing at that gait until he reaches the center of the long side, where he is called upon to slow down and execute the piaffer, (or trot in place). Here he "piaffes" for the number of steps; no more and no less.

This example illustrates how accurately each movement must be executed; for any faults, such as overriding the point where the change of gait is to occur; not keeping the horse rigorously straight; the horse's head being too low or too high; failing to maintain the cadence of the gait; changing from the trot to the gallop unintentionally, or not smoothly; or any such poor execution of the details cause the judges to make a cut in the performer's mark for that movement.

It is to be hoped that our large horse shows will soon have classes for high-school horses, as is the case in all the big shows in France, Germany, Sweden and certain other foreign countries. They will prove very popular with the public and aid in the dissemination of equestran knowledge.

## 1940

In the following article, Chamberlin addresses what he believes to be weaknesses in the U.S. Cavalry's training procedures for new recruits. This article proves influential in changing the Army's training practices. Ultimately, this article, as well as Chamberlin's private lobbying, leads to the creation of the Cavalry Replacement Training Center at Ft. Riley. The CRTC becomes the central training facility for all cavalry recruits during World War II. The CRTC proves most influential: Gordon Wright, Morton Smith, William Steinkraus, and a host of other notables learn the modern cavalry way of riding here. Throughout the late 1940's through the 1960's, Wright, Morton, and others teach students the riding methods of the CRTC. Olympic Gold Medalist William Steinkraus maintains that the CRTC, taught him "how to ride all over again."

—Warren C. Matha, Editor

**Cavalry Training**
**by**
**Colonel Harry D. Chamberlin, 2nd Cavalry**

*The Cavalry Journal*
*September–October 1940*

**Forward**

In view of the numerous articles recently appearing in our newspapers and periodicals, written by self-styled and theoretical "military experts," it seems apropos to express some thoughts on cavalry training which, despite inherent deficiencies, at least are based on facts and experience. While neither new nor original, these thoughts need attention at this particular time. It is believed that the final recommendations are constructive and, with the introduction of selective service will be entirely feasible.

Incidentally, when reading current destructively critical articles, it is well for Regular Army personnel to bear in mind a sententious statement once made by a great cavalry soldier and former Chief of Staff, Major General J. Franklin Bell, to wit: "Any fool can criticize."

If our able and conscientious cavalry officers, as well as those of the other branches, permit themselves to be perturbed by the present flood of acrimonious and erroneous comment, they unnecessarily will suffer. For although the Army, like any other human institution, has its imperfections, nevertheless, it serves as a noble and fine leavening element in this great country and when the truth is fully known—as it ultimately will be—few, if any items of unpreparedness or lack of foresight can honestly be placed to its account.

Moreover, *officers of the horse cavalry should maintain abiding faith in our arm!* Until something yet unheard-of appears on the field of battle, the horse cavalry—properly trained—has definite and vital functions and missions which no other arm can execute with similar speed or thoroughness. The Germans have realized these facts and even on the small and cramped battlefields of Europe, have continued to use this indispensable arm. Many contemporary critics apparently have not learned as yet that the Germans have employed *hundreds of thousands* of horses in Poland, Belgium and France.

*At the Third Army maneuvers in Louisiana, the lack of thorough combat security and reconnaissance, which oftentimes could only have been accomplished by horse cavalry, was the reason why motorized, and even marching infantry columns were "blind" and consequently easily susceptible to surprise attacks. Had the two opposed corps been approximately equal in infantry strength so that the* 1st Cavalry Division (attached to the weaker corps) might have been assigned independent and more typically cavalry missions, it undoubtedly could have created many surprises and great havoc for the "enemy" which usually had available only one squadron of horse cavalry.

If the reconnaissance elements recently organized for the Infantry divisions are to remain entirely without horse cavalry, it is hard to believe that they can prove of much value for close-in or combat reconnaissance. Scout cars by themselves are hopelessly road-bound, are an easy prey for a clever enemy, and if not reinforced are normally capable of rendering only rather indefinite road information.

While the importance of mechanized and armored forces is evident to all, many officers were struck by the vast amount of terrain found in the Louisiana maneuver area of approximately twenty-four hundred square miles—an area far larger than that comprising the final phases of the Retreat to Dunkerque—over which it was utterly impractical to employ tanks. It was also obvious that almost invariably the horse cavalry could have maneuvered with ease and usually under concealment across those very areas not passable for mechanized troops. Consequently, the two forces generally should be used to complement each other when terrain or other causes prevent their operating in conjunction. In the future, much thought and practice should be devoted to the combined use of mechanized forces and horse cavalry, reinforced in many cases by motorized infantry. A corps of this type, with proper air and artillery support, would present great flexibility, mobility and power.

In our spacious and diversified country, *there is great need and much room for several divisions of horse cavalry. This statement applies even more strongly to vast portions of the western hemisphere occupied by our sister republics, were they someday to call for our assistance, where roads are few and terrain is most difficult.*

### Training in General

Since thousands of years before Christ every great military leader has taught that a high standard of individual discipline and training is the basic essential of a successful army. Napoleon's oft-quoted remark, "Man in war is everything; men are nothing," emphasizes this precept. Today, the German army once again has shown that its exceedingly rigid discipline, which is the basis of its through training, has developed a military team, the power and drive of which easily overwhelmed the half-disciplined, weaker-willed and physically less-strong elements interspersed among the Allied forces.

Discipline, to the minds of many, is apparently associated with brutality. Our people must be taught that this is not true. *Military discipline is simply the habitually prompt, thorough and willing performance of every soldierly duty always in the same precise and proper manner.* Such social discipline as is concomitant with the military is only that practiced by any person whose good manners are founded on respect for authority and courtesy towards superiors in rank. Military discipline must be generated by intelligent and meticulous training. Soldiers soon realize that it gives their unit's superior combat efficiency and that this superiority brings both to the individuals and to the unit, confidence and strength. Genuine discipline is cheerfully put forth and is evolved through good leadership. Its existence becomes a matter of greatest pride to members of an organization wherein it exists.

It must be realized, however, that the perfect discipline and training which make a soldier brave and self-assured on the battle field cannot be developed in a month or six weeks. As Major General Fox Connor recently indicated in a newspaper article, notable for its keen accuracy and fund of military facts, it may be possible to train the individual soldier quite thoroughly in one year but in that brief time an entirely new *regiment* cannot be organized and thoroughly prepared for war. Due to the volume and intensity of firepower in modern warfare, individuals frequently are called upon to perform battlefield duties where they are separated by considerable distance from their comrades. Such lonely, terrifying crises put a man's courage to the supreme test. His morale can withstand these tests only when it is built on confidence in his own physical strength, on knowledge that his own and his comrades' training are perfect; and finally, on that intangible something existing in his unit called *esprit de corps*. This can only become part of each man's consciousness through long associating and training.

The difficulty of perfecting the team work, conditioning and individual training of a football team in five or six months, is well known. Rarely when the season ends will a coach have convinced himself that his team has at any time reached its potential peak. How then, assuming all conditions favorable, may it be hoped to perfect in one year a far more complex team of a thousand men and horses—a team which probably will never be called upon to make the same play twice? The consummation of individual training and of the team play of a regiment as a whole requires much time, and time alone produces a background sufficiently colorful to engender that organizational esprit which, on the field of battle, lifts each man to his greatest heights of physical and moral courage. No officer can honorably afford to deceive his men, and least of all himself, as to the amount of time necessary to put his military team in such a state of training that he may expect to have it function successfully in war.

In absolute frankness, how many cavalry officers can state that they have seen a cavalry regiment trained to the high standards which should exist in the regular Army; standards desirable before committing a regiment to battle? The regrettable fact that not many, if any, have seen such regiments is neither the fault of the officers nor of our splendid enlisted personnel. The cause lies in conditions existing in our service which undoubtedly have been irremediable. However, with the passing of the Selective Service Act it appears probably that most of these conditions can be either eliminated or ameliorated.

## Present Conditions Prevent Thorough Training

As our present Chief of Cavalry has indicated, every officer who has been fortunate enough to serve with troops over any considerable length of time in recent years will recognize and appreciate the discouraging obstacles to training which are listed as follows:

1st: *Receipt of recruits by posts or units in driblets, usually from one to ten in number and at constantly varying intervals of time.* This single condition continuously prevents the commander, of even so small a unit as a troop, from having it completely trained. For a regimental commander, the situation becomes increasingly difficult.

Assuming a course of recruit instruction of eight weeks' duration as a minimum requirement, and the usual *weekly* influx of a few recruits, it is necessary to provide instructors and horses for from six to eight recruit groups, since all are at different levels of instruction. Whether instruction be conducted by post, regiment or smaller unit, this method of distributing recruits in driblets is excessively costly in overhead. Recruit instruction, certainly a tremendously important duty, calls for the most able officers and noncommissioned officers. On the other hand, these can be ill spared by the habitually under-officered troop organizations. A compromise generally results which neither gives an appropriate number of superior instructors for recruits, nor leaves a sufficient number with the troops.

Moreover, when a group of recruits graduates to duty with its troop, the members have missed all training up to that date which has been covered by the troop's annual schedule of instruction.

2nd: *The continuous detail of a great number of combat personnel on detached service or special duty.* It is well realized that the duties performed by such absentees are, for the most part, absolutely necessary, and under present conditions no replacements for them are available. The effects are nevertheless pernicious, in that many members of combat units constantly are absent, and hence remain at best only partly trained soldiers.

In addition to enlisted personnel, frequently officers must be taken from combat units for necessary post staff positions. Schools, staff jobs, special duty and civilian component details, together with a minimum amount of close contact with, and command of troops inevitably tend toward producing highly theoretical officers. Practicality, common sense and observing eyes are three most necessary requisites of military leaders. Only by actually practicing one's profession with troops will those requirements be developed.

3rd: *Too frequent changes in officer personnel.* This policy works a severe hardship on enlisted personnel, especially on the noncommissioned officers who barely have time to become acquainted with their commanders and to readjust themselves to the alterations in routine administration and training introduced by new officers, before others arrive. These frequent changes are most detrimental to organizational *esprit*, the value of which is often emphasized more in theory than in practice.

4th: *Too few officers of troop grade on duty with troops.* With the prescribed number of officers never present for duty, training suffers greatly and the complete team never practices. This deficiency probably will be remedied by the influx of young reserves for one year's troop duty, and as a result of the Selective Service Act. Most of these young men, while potentially fine material, are initially more of a liability than an asset. Regular officers must be utilized to give them courses in basic training, which incidentally, should begin with the actual performance of all duties of the soldier and non-commissioned officers. It is absurd, if not futile, for an officer to attempt teaching what he has never practiced.

In selecting men for commissions, greater importance should be attached to the physical and mental attributes which make superior leaders and fighters in actual warfare, and less to those which permit successful results in written tests. Often the latter only prove that those receiving highest marks are blessed with better memories for studied theory, rather than with the courage, endurance, quick wits and natural attributes essential in battle.

5th: *Insufficient rank and pay for platoon sergeants.* When men are outstanding instructors and leaders, they are the most valuable platoon sergeants. Such men are extremely difficult to find. Many of their necessary qualities and traits are innate. They are the real backbone of a unit; and the men who will win its battles. Under our system, the really superior platoon sergeant sooner or later is promoted to the second or third grade and thereupon receives a clerical position. Administration must be carried on, but fighters and leaders of great competitive ability undoubtedly are more essential to an organization which primarily is designed to make war. Recent inclusion of the staff sergeant grade in line troops is a step toward such reward.

6th: *Training inspections of small units are not made by any War Department agency nor by Corps Area commanders.* The War Department has no agency for this purpose, while Corps Area commanders simply have not the time to inspect the training of each unit, much less that of its individuals. Where regiments are actually in a division, the commander of that division and his brigade commanders can make these inspections; but with separate regiments this is not the case.

Post commanders change station frequently and often are officers of branches other than Cavalry. Since there are no official, well-defined standards of training, it is practically impossible at present to have uniform standards throughout the service.

Master schedules giving number of hours pre subject and the number of training cycles per year, prepared by the Chiefs of Branches and approved by the War Department, would help to standardize and improve training. In the Cavalry, this idea also applies emphatically to the training of remounts. Too much is now left to idiosyncrasy of the individual in the means and methods.

## Suggested Remedies

Possible means of improving the above-mentioned conditions are recommended as follows:

1st: *Recruit depots, or training centers, should be established where training in all basic subjects is completed and qualification courses are fired with principal arms.* Except for mounted work, Cavalry recruits could be trained at infantry depots, since the various items of basic training in the two branches are either identical or very similar. Minor differences in technique and mouthed work could then be taught after recruits have joined their regiments.

All men deficient mentally, morally or physically should rigorously be weeded-out. Physical training should be stressed. In the accomplishment of Germany's recent successes in land warfare, full credit has not as yet been given to the universal physical training provided for all German youth, which was systematically begun in 1919. The youth of our country are soft. A few participate in athletics; the great majority look on. This fact has given many who think of the United States as an athletic nation a dangerous and false impression.

The time required for recruit training at the depots which should be superior, is largely a matter of the *quality* of instruction. Hurrying through instruction in his basic duties does not tend to make a good soldier. Regiments should spend a maximum amount of time in the field training which all so urgently need.

Cavalry training and organization should be complete in every detail *in time of peace*. Quickly organized units or partly trained replacements or recruits will prove costly, as their helplessness will only adulterate the organized, well trained units they join. Above all, each regiment should be furnished with ***its** requited quota of recruits in not over two increments annually. To receive the entire quota on one known date would be ideal.* Regimental and troop training cycles could then begin shortly after the recruits arrive. Training at the depots, including processing and target practice, probably would require for eight to ten weeks.

This rational, efficient recruit training system is normal in other armed forces of our own country and should be practicable in the Army under prevalent conditions.

2nd: *At all camps and posts, sufficient service personnel, either civilian or military, should be provided to relieve combat troops from detached service, special duty and all non-military work.* Not only is it ruinous to training, but it lowers morale to make clerks, firemen, gardeners, janitors, messengers, recruiters, laborers, etc., of men who join the army to become soldiers. Sufficient officers for necessary post staff duty also should be provided so that troops will not suffer from lack of officer personnel.

3rd: *Officers should be left on duty with troops to which assigned for at least four years; and normally when ordered back to troops from detached service, they should be returned for service with the same regiments.* This would greatly increase morale and assist the training of a regiment as a team. It also would steady and improve the roles of noncommissioned officers and soldiers.

4th: *Sufficient troop officers to fill unit quotas according to Tables of organization should be constantly on duty with troops.* The organization of military machines is the product of evolution, and each cog has been carefully fashioned through years of experience. It is impossible for the machine to function properly when the parts are missing.

5th: *At least three platoon sergeants should have pay and rank equal to those of staff sergeants.*

6th: *Centralized master schedules containing the subjects and number of hours to be developed thereto should be prepared by the Chief of Cavalry and issued after approval of the Chief of Staff.* Schedules should leave a large amount of time to the commanders of lower echelons and be prepared (1) for units from the regiment to the troop, inclusive (2) for recruits at depots or posts (3) for remounts. Almost all European nations give their remounts two years of standardized training before they go to combat units. Ours are fortunate if they receive two months. No remount, except in an emergency, should leave the post for hard maneuvers or extended marches in less than eighteen months. Working young, unfit horses not only ruins them physically, but temperamentally as well.

Veterinarians of great experience, such as Colonels John A. McKinnon, Daniel B. Leininger, Jacob E. Behney, among others, agree with this statement. *In an emergency, of course, all available horses would have to be used and the Remount Service presumably will only purchase horses seven years of age or older during war.*

Training and tactical inspections of regiments or smaller units should be made by a War Department agency, preferably, the Chief of Cavalry. He, by visits of one week or more to each regiment, could definitely determine the state of training in each, and assist greatly in bringing all up to the required standards. The Chief of Cavalry could then furnish the War Department, Division or Post commanders, and the regimental commanders concerned with a report of the conclusions resulting from his inspection. Such procedure would help raise and standardize the level of training of both men and horses in the Cavalry.

## Recruit Training

Experiments in regiments at various posts has proven that recruits, through an intensive course of eight weeks, can be trained sufficiently to join and function with their troops, either in garrison or in the field. However, this is a minimum allowance of time and unless instructors, both officers and noncommissioned, are superior, the recruits will be awkward, very superficially trained, and decidedly "in the way" when working in ranks. The difference in *quality* of instruction in various units is amazing. Standards in certain organizations are often far below those in others. It should be understood by all that soldiers, almost without exception, greatly admire, and desire to attain West Point standards. In the regular army, no other standard should be tolerated. The logical, intelligent and feasible objectives of any schedule obviously should make instruction in field duties concurrent with that in other basic duties and to demand high proficiency in all. Other than in extreme emergency the period should not be reduced beyond a point where every recruit is soundly and well trained and able to function in his troop without embarrassment, either to the troop, or to himself.

Consequently, certain fixed Standards of Proficiency, rather than an arbitrarily fixed number of weeks, should govern the time necessary for completion of recruit training for each individual. Those less adaptable must be dropped back to groups on lower levels of instruction so that they ultimately acquire the same prescribed proficiency. If certain ones cannot reach the prescribed standards after a fair trial, they should be eliminated. Since horsemanship is fundamentally and vitally important, it must be thoroughly learned; otherwise, the arm is not worth the cost. No assumption should be made that a cavalry recruit can be trained as soon as an infantryman. It simply is not possible in a few days to teach men to ride well enough to become efficient cavalrymen.

In conducting recruit training, just as in all military work, the enthusiasm and interest of all concerned, from the post commander and colonels down, are essential. Diversification of instruction, continuous detailed planning, careful daily orientation of all instructors on the next day's work, persistent insistence on attaining highest standards and never-ending efforts to improve the whole system, are the objectives of those charged with training recruits. The quality of instruction is vital, for the material is young, impressionable and very valuable.

*Editor's Note: It is regretted that the comprehensive and complete Course Outlines for Recruit Instruction, Master Schedule and Daily Schedules covering the progressive and thorough eight weeks' recruit training as minimum essentials for the 2nd Cavalry, are too voluminous to publish in this issue of The Cavalry Journal. Unit commanders and other desiring copies, however, can obtain them by writing directly to Colonel Chamberlin, at Fort Riley, Kansas.*

The "Editor's Note" above is from the original article as published in *The Cavalry Journal.*

—Warren C. Matha, Editor

# 1941

Chamberlin's experience in crossing rivers dates back 1912–1914. During these years, he serves as a Second Lieutenant with the 7th U.S. Cavalry in the Philippine Islands. On the island of Luzon in Pampanga Province rivers prove to be daunting obstacles to the Cavalry's forward movements. There, Chamberlin learns the importance of crossing rivers and the best methods of doing same.

—Warren C. Matha, Editor

**Crossing Rivers**
*January-February*
*The Cavalry Journal 1941*
*By Colonel Harry D. Chamberlin, 2nd Cavalry*

River crossings by horse cavalry have been discussed many times, but relatively few have been accomplished. In fact, a high percentage of those few have been executed under such artificial conditions—that is, stripped saddles, no pack animals and frequently no weapons—that little was learned. In order to be effective, river crossings must be practiced under conditions as similar as possible to those which probably will be encountered in actual campaign.

Last fall, the 2nd Cavalry furnished a war strength platoon with attached light machine guns for the purpose of demonstrating a river crossing to the Basic Horse and Mechanized Class, then at The Cavalry School. This demonstration was ably directed and staged by Captain Henry R. Westphalinger, a member of the Academic Division staff, Department of Tactics, while First Lieutenant Wm. F. Beaty, "E" Troop, 2nd Cavalry, commanded the platoon.

The first essential in training of this type, just as in any other training, is much practice. As far as the men are concerned, if they are good swimmers and soldiers, their roles are readily learned. For average horses, however, quite a bit of preliminary work is required. They must be accustomed to enter water boldly and to swim calmly. All horses, if properly handled, will quickly learn to do this.

**Preliminaries**

The first step can be accomplished quite easily by the use of a large pit, similar to the dipping vats used in Texas for killing ticks. Essentially, it should be narrow enough to maintain the horse's sense of direction and long and deep enough to require a short swim of approximately one dozen strokes. In addition, the approach and exit should be firm, gently shelving and not slippery. The use of such a vat tends to make the horses water-conscious, bold and strong swimmers, and eliminates the possibility of accidental drownings. If a good stream, river, or lake exists nearby, all horses can be taught to swim quite as well in them. The vat is simply a good idea if available at a post for the first lessons, or to build where there is no natural swimming place at hand. These first lessons should be carefully supervised and conducted by the best horseman. A timid, poor horseman spoils a horse at any kind of training.

After the preliminary training described above, those horses which have progressed suitably should be required, where it is feasible, to swim larger bodies of water, and longer distances. At first it is best to "herd" groups across rivers or lakes, the herders riding or swimming alongside the leading animals known to be strong swimmers. Snaffle bridles or halters only are used for this first practice. Feeding the horses on the opposite bank as soon as they land encourages and interests them in their work. This reward also aids in teaching them to swim a straight course. It is well to bear in mind that horses are attracted to groups of people or other horses. Consequently, if spectators are present or some horses are already of the far side of the stream, they should be placed at such a point that the horses, when attracted to them, will swim in the proper direction.

Upon graduation from this intermediate stage, the horses next should be taught to cross stretches of water while saddled and equipped. Again, the most capable horsemen should give the first lessons, and *stripped* saddles, snaffle bridles and halters are used initially. It is advisable to fasten the snaffle reins to the square ring of the halter rather than to the snaffle bit. At all times when riding into the water, the men should use their legs strongly in order to drive the horses boldly ahead. Timidity on the part of the rider merely teaches balkiness. As soon as the horse walks to a point over his depth and must start swimming, the rider slips off on the up-current side and swims alongside his mount, holding onto a stirrup strap, saddle pommel, or the halter-shank which is left knotted loosely around the horse's neck. If the horse attempts to turn downstream away from the rider, the latter gently pulls the horse's head by the rein towards himself. If the horse turns toward the rider, he may be diverted in the proper direction by splashing water against the side of his face or pushing his head in the opposite direction. The rider may also reach across the withers and pull the horse's head in the desired direction by the far rein. After a horse has been taught to swim straight, the rider may allow himself to be towed by hanging to the tail. With horses that swim well, men may remain mounted in swimming over short distances. However, horses are like humans—the fat, round ones are very buoyant, while the thin muscular ones of high specific gravity have great difficulty in swimming under a load. *It is much better to teach all soldiers to swim alongside the horse, or by holding onto his tail, because this is the only feasible method which will avoid overturning and drowning some horses if the swim is long and difficult.*

When horses swim well, lightly equipped as described above, the full packs should be added, along with arms, and tactical exercises may be conducted with the river-crossing as an incident thereto.

### Combat Situation

In a unit the size of a platoon such as was used at Fort Riley, a security detachment of from six to eight me is first sent across, their crossing being covered by suitable firepower. This detachment should logically be a part, or all, of the advance guard. Of course, local, all-around security on our own side of the river is understood to have been effected upon halting. Since, the initial bridgehead to be formed, speed and fire power are highly desirable, this advance group must have both. For speed, they should either leave pommel and cantle loads on the saddle or drop them off to be brought across the river by others and only men with powerful swimming horses should form the detachment; horses that can swim do so with their riders mounted. No time should be taken for safety precautions advocated later on for troops that follow the bridgehead group or groups. For fire power, all must carry rifles, pistols, and ammunition. If the horse is known to be especially expert and bold at swimming and the distance is short, the rifle may be carried overhead to keep it dry, while the soldier remains mounted. Pistol and cartridge belt are carried in the usual place, buckled about the waist. In this connection experiments indicate that both rifle and pistol ammunition may be submerged in water as long as twenty-four hours and still fire. As a matter of fact, it appears likely that a submersion of months will not damage the cartridges. The important point, however, is to be certain that all the water is blown out of the barrel before the weapons are again fired. Also they must be thoroughly cleaned at the earliest opportunity.

Upon the successful crossing of the initial crossing force and their establishment of a bridgehead on the opposite side, the movement of the remainder of the patrol may be begun. First, means for floating the packs—cantle roll, light machine gun, administrative, etc.—must be provided. There are several ways of carrying these across. If lumber is available, then rafts may be made. This, however, is a condition so seldom encountered that it may be disregarded for instructional purposes. Fortunately, enough material is carried within troop organizations in the cavalry regiment to construct "canoes" or "floats" which will easily take care of all equipment and some personnel.

### Construction of Floats

The two-man float is simply made of two rifles, two shelter halves and one coat-strap. The rifles, bound together in the form of an X, form the framework. The two shelter halves serve to keep the water out. The lighter material, such as blankets, saddles, saddle bags, grin bags, etc., are first placed in the center of the shelter halves, these latter being placed one on top of the other, triangular flaps at opposite ends. The edges are then folded carefully up and bound to the rifles, thus forming the float. Its main purpose is to carry equipment across the river in case horses have become casualties, or to carry rations, ammunition, etc. The men in charge of equipment swim across, pushing the float in front of them. If care is used in making the float, the contents should be relatively dry and undamaged upon reaching the shore.

*(Editor's Note: we have cut those further paragraphs dealing with the construction of floats since most reading* The Chamberlin Reader *will never need to build one.)*

### Precautions

Of course, in peacetime practice and training the big thing in a river crossing is SAFETY. In a war, the main consideration is given to dangers from the enemy. These are avoided by proper tactical dispositions. During peacetime, we must consider dangers from natural sources. Since an ounce of prevention is worth a pound of cure, the obvious steps to take—during practice crossings—are: First, to organize a lifeguard force in several boats, composed of good swimmers, at least two to a boat. Each boat should be equipped with boat-hooks, life preservers, rope, oars, and outboard motor if possible. Second each trooper should wear a kapok jacket (obtainable from the engineers) and a campaign hat. A man may easily be struck on the head by a struggling horse, and the hat will break the force of the blow. The jacket will keep him afloat if knocked unconscious.

In either a practice crossing or a crossing during maneuvers, when the weather is cold, some means should be provided for the men to dry and warm themselves. A tent with a heater—which may be improvised from a No. 10 can and gasoline or alcohol—should be set up on the far side of the river. If possible, dry clothing should be provided.

After maximum safety for the men, attention should be directed toward safety for the horses. First, all curb reins should be removed. They should never be knotted about the horses' necks. They may be used as tow ropes, for lashing, as improvised breast straps, or for any other suitable purpose. Second, snaffle reins should be unbuckled so the horse cannot get a foreleg caught in them. It may be well, in addition, to fasten the snaffle reins to the halter D-rings rather than to the bit, as previously mentioned. Some men will involuntarily "tighten up" to such an extent that they may pull the swimming horse over backwards. Third, cinches must be good and snug, since saddles tend to slip back much more in water than at any other time. On herring-gutted horses a breast strap, either G.I. or improvised should be used. Fourth, stirrups must be crossed over the saddle and all loose strap ends well secured, so that the horse will not become entangled while swimming. Fifth, men must be instructed NOT to use the reins as a handle, NOT to try to turn the horse abruptly, and NOT to pull led horses' heads around to the rear if they swim ahead. They must be turned loose and if some men are riding swimming horses then they must slip off (on the upstream side) at the first sign of trouble or when the horse's head is about to go under water. They may hang on to mane, saddle, stirrup, or tail, but never to reins. If necessary, let go entirely and swim ashore. It is far better for all men to be taught to slip off and swim alongside their horses holding to a stirrup or strap.

If horse cavalry is to justify the many claims made for it, we must give much more thought to the subject of swimming rivers. With that thought must go plenty of practice to enable the crossing to be carried out smoothly, quickly, and efficiently. This work should be compulsory in all cavalry commands.

# Last Writings on The Rider's Seat

As the U.S. Cavalry's preeminent horseman, and while commanding the Cavalry Replacement Training Center at Ft. Riley, Chamberlin supervises the revision of the Cavalry's manual *Horsemanship and Horsemastership*. He contributes writings to both sections of the manual: *The Education of the Rider* and *The Education of the Horse*. He appears in photographs for the manual to demonstrate the military seat as well as the proper jumping style. This document represents Chamberlin's last thoughts regarding the rider's seat. Throughout the cavalry, the seat becomes known as "The Chamberlin-Military Seat." For the excerpt printed below, Chamberlin made revisions to the earlier manual's discussion of the Military Seat.

The description of the Military Seat, also known as the Chamberlin Seat, we reproduce below substantially as it appears in Chapter IV of the U.S. Cavalry manual *Horsemanship and Horsemastership* published by The Cavalry School at Ft. Riley in 1942. We have clarified the organizational outline somewhat for ease of reading.

—Warren C. Matha, Editor

Excerpt from *Horsemanship and Horsemastership 1942 Edition*.[12]

**The Military Seat**

A. General Principles.

(1) The correct seat. — The correct military seat permits the rider to remain master of his equilibrium, whatever may be the actions of his horse. It must be secure in itself and provide ease and comfort for both horse and rider. Such a seat is dependent upon balance, augmented by suppleness, muscular control of the body and the use of the legs.

(2) Adaptability. — The military seat, while obligatory in the Army, is also admirably adapted to all kinds of riding such as hunting, polo and jumping. For certain of these activities a different adjustment of stirrups may be necessary.

---

12  *Horsemanship and Horsemastership*, The Cavalry School, Ft. Riley, Kansas 1942.

(3) Importance of saddle. — Without a properly constructed saddle, the deepest part of which is approximately in the center, it is extremely difficult to acquire or retain the correct military seat. The McClellan saddle is properly designed. Many flat saddles are too low at the cantle, or at the pommel. These faults place the deepest part of the seat of the saddle too far to the rear or too far to the front, making it difficult, and in some cases impossible, to assume the correct seat. Usually all issue flat saddles can be altered by changing the amount of padding at the cantle or pommel so that the deepest part will be correctly centered. *(Editor's note: Chamberlin recommends that the deepest part of a saddle should be one inch forward of the center of the seat. This puts the rider closer to the horse's withers which Chamberlin maintains offers the optimal rider position. Since cavalry troopers rode in the M–1928 McClellan saddle, Chamberlin's concept is modified to meet the configuration of the McClellan which puts the deepest point approximately in the seat's center. For his pleasure riding and jumping, Chamberlin rode in a Pariani saddle. For his military riding toward the end of his career, he rode in the M–1936 Phillips Officer's Field saddle which is fashioned pursuant to Chamberlin's recommendation.)*

(4) Principal elements. — The principal elements entering into this discussion are the rider's upper body, his base of support, his legs, and his equilibrium or balance.

(a) The upper body is considered to be that part of the body from the hip joints up.

(b) The base of support is formed by those parts of the rider's body in contact with the saddle and the horse, from the points of the buttocks down along the inside of the thighs, to and including the inner knees and legs. The fleshy parts of the buttocks are forced to the rear and in no case form part of the seat.

(c) The leg is that part of the limb between the knee and the ankle.

(d) Equilibrium or balance. — It is quite evident that the rider, since he is constantly receiving impulses from the moving horse, frequently is in danger of losing his equilibrium and can retain it only by the clinging of the knees and thighs, reinforced by a sufficiently strong leg grip. Balance obviates the necessity for continuous leg grip, saves the legs from undue strain and fatigue, and is the principal requisite of a secure seat.

Balance requires that the center of gravity of the upper body remain as nearly as possible over the center of its base of support. With the horse in motion the center of gravity must be further advanced than when at the halt in order to compensate for the force of inertia which tends to over-balance the upper body to the rear and to leave the rider "behind his horse." When the center of gravity passes outside the limits of its base of support, the rider's balance is in danger of being lost and he must maintain it by gripping with his legs. A rider with a poor seat makes the grave mistake of pulling on the reins. *Balance must be entirely independent of the hands and reins.*

B. Position Mounted.

(1) The rider sits with his crotch squarely in the center of the saddle, his weight distributed forward from the points of his buttocks into his crotch and down onto the inner thighs, knees and stirrups.

    (a) At the halt, the upper body, *due to a slight forward inclination from the hip joints,* is just in front of the perpendicular. Thus, its center of gravity is placed in front of the points of the buttocks. This facilitates the correct placing of the thighs and the proper distribution of weight.

    (b) When in motion, to be in balance, the upper body is inclined farther forward from the hips. The lower thighs, knees and legs remain in close contact with the horse. The knees, ankles and heels sink at each stride, absorbing part of the shock and fixing the rider securely in the saddle. Inclining the upper body to the rear, or convexing the loin to the rear, places the center of gravity of the upper body in rear of the center of its base of support and causes the rider to sit on the fleshy parts of his buttocks. This faulty position tends to raise the thighs and knees, weakens the seat, concentrates the weight toward the cantle, and is unmilitary in appearance. It is fatiguing to the horse and often injurious to his back. The rider is "behind his horse".

(2) The thighs extend downward and forward, their inner sides resting without constraint on the saddle. With the buttocks to the rear and the upper body inclined to the front as has been described, the thighs are naturally forced down, and the center of the saddle comes well up into the rider's crotch. The large fleshy muscles of the inner thighs are thus forced to the

rear, and the flat of the thigh is permitted without muscular constraint to envelop the horse. Thus seated, a proper proportion of the rider's weight is distributed down his thighs, and the tendency to grip with them is avoided.

If the thighs are turned outward excessively, then contact of the knee and lower thigh with the saddle is lost and the rider has neither the correct distribution of weight nor the proper base of support. Instability and lack of security result.

(3) The knees are forced down as low as the adjustment of the stirrups will permit, without causing the stirrups straps to hang in rear of the vertical. Knees are neither limp nor stiff, nor is there normally any effort to "pinch" with them. Flexed and relaxed, they rest with their inner sides in continuous contact with the saddle.

Properly placed thighs, as described in (2) above, naturally and correctly place the knees. Knees excessively turned out produce the same faulty results mentioned for similar incorrect positions of the thighs. Knees excessively turned in force the heels out and cause the calves of the legs to lose proper contact. Knees too high cannot form a proper part of the base of support. They place the rider behind his horse. Such a fault is an indication of the fact that either the stirrups are too short, the rider is sitting back on his buttocks, or that the forward inclination of the upper body is insufficient. If the knees are stiffened, or straightened, then the calves of the legs lose proper contact with the horse and the rider's seat is forced out of the saddle. If the knees are limp, the legs go too far to the rear and the stirrup straps are no longer vertical. The heels come up and the crotch and buttocks slip too far forward in the saddle. Thus, a faulty position of the knee is an indication of the fact that the entire seat is incorrect.

(4) The legs, ankles, feet and stirrups are disposed as follows:

(a) The legs extend downward and backward with the calves in light, elastic contact with the horse. The calves naturally fall into this position if the knees are flexed and relaxed. This contact of the calves is a means of communication between rider and horse and also assists security. When the legs are not in contact, communication is lost and their swinging confuses a well-trained horse; irritates a nervous one; and renders the seat insecure. Correct adjustment of stirrups assists materially in preserving leg contact.

(b) Stirrup leathers are approximately vertical. The length of stirrup is normal and approximately correct if the tread hangs opposite the lower level of the ankle bone when the rider is seated as described above, with his feet out of the stirrups and his legs hanging naturally, well down and around his horse. This is not a fixed rule as the conformation of both horse and rider call for slight modifications.

(c) Stirrup leathers for special forms of riding may be longer or shorter than described.

> (i) For schooling, a longer stirrup should be used. For show jumping, steeple chasing, and racing, the stirrups should be shortened. Too long a stirrup diminishes the riders base of support, renders balance from front to rear particularly difficult, and interferes with the proper use of the legs. Too short a stirrup raises the knees excessively, makes the seat insecure as to lateral reactions and causes undue fatigue when employed over long periods of time.
>
> (ii) With very short stirrups, unless the forward inclination of the upper body is increased materially so as to keep the center of gravity of the mass over the horizontal distance between the knees and heels (see Diagram of the Rider's Base of Support), the rider is placed behind his horse with his weight towards the cantle of the saddle. All requirements of military riding may be met by the normal adjustment of the stirrups as described above. Short stirrups should not be used except for the special purposes mentioned.
>
> (iii) The McClellan saddle is not suited for use with very short stirrups. Its high cantle prevents the buttocks from going to the rear as they must when stirrups are markedly shortened.

(d) The heels are well down, the ankles flexed and relaxed. The feet, turned out naturally, rest with the ball of the foot in front of the center of the stirrup tread. The rider normally supports the weight of his feet, legs and a portion of the weight of his thighs and upper body in the

# Diagram of the Rider's Base of Support

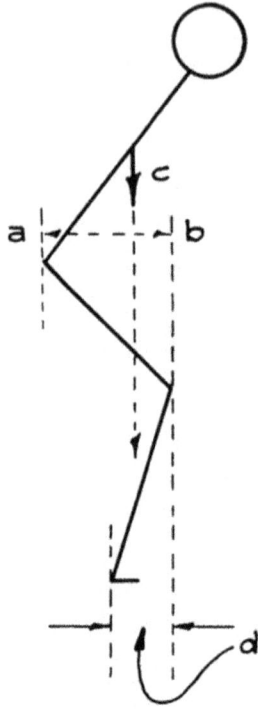

a-b - Represents horizontal length of base of support when seated.
d - Horizontal lenght of base of support when seat is out of saddle
c - Center of Gravity

stirrups. This weight in the stirrups results from the forward inclination of the upper body, and not from "standing in the stirrups".

The ankles naturally break slightly to the inside, thus allowing the calves of the legs to rest against the sides of the horse. They should be relaxed, in order that the downward thrust on the stirrups will pass into the heels, causing them to sink below the level of the toes and allowing the ankle joints to flex freely with the movements of the horse. Ankles which are stiff cause the rider to carry the heels too high and result in unsteady legs and frequent loss of stirrups. They also restrict the rider in the proper use of his legs in the control and management of his horse.

Toes turned in stiffen the ankles, force the heels out, and cause loss of contact of proper parts of the calves of the legs. This fault reduces the security of the rider and makes the correct use of the legs impossible. Excessively turned out toes stiffen the ankles, put the knees out of contact, place the rider on the backs of his thighs and disrupt the seat.

The toes should not press down on the soles of the boots, but on the contrary, should be relaxed, thus aiding materially in obtaining a relaxed ankle.

It must be realized that when riding with stirrups, the calf muscles cannot be powerfully contracted except when the heels are driven well down. "Strong legs" and a strong seat are indicated by well depressed heels. They brace the rider against losing balance to the front and facilitate correct driving power against a stubborn mount.

(e) Without stirrups the legs and feet hang in a natural manner, except that the knees are flexed sufficiently to bring the legs into light, elastic contact with the horse in order to secure the seat and assist balance. The ankles are relaxed, thus permitting the toes to hang lower than the heels.

(5) The posture of the upper body is as follows:

(a) The rider assumes the posture of the dismounted soldier at attention *except for a habitual forward inclination from the hips.* This position distributes the rider's weight evenly over his base of support and so saves both horse and rider unnecessary discomfort and fatigue.

(b) If the upper body is inclined too far forward, the rider easily becomes unbalanced since at any violent reaction his legs slide too far to the rear. On the other hand, the center of gravity of the upper body should never be so far to the rear as to be directly over the points of the buttocks.

(c) The chest is lifted.

(i) The shoulders are square without stiffness and carried in a plane at right angles to the long axis of the horse. Lifting the chest with the shoulders as described facilitates the maintenance of a correct posture of the upper body.

(ii) Rounded shoulders cramp the chest, invite a general slumping of the back and loin and cause the elbows to fly out from the body. Shoulders forcibly carried back result in general contraction. Failure to lift the chest is often the cause of a poor seat, particularly in riding across country and over obstacles.

(d) The head and chin are up, eyes looking to the front.

(i) Due to its position and weight, the head has a great influence on the balance of the upper body. For this reason, it is important that it be correctly placed. If it is dropped down, the resulting tendency is to round the shoulders and back, thus destroying the ease and balance sought in the military seat. The chin is held up without being thrust out or stiffening the neck.

(ii) The eyes are lifted, so that the rider may see where he is going. The bad habit of looking down at the horse's head and neck is dangerous for the rider and all others in the vicinity.

(6) The arms, elbows, wrists and fingers normally are relaxed, the elbows falling naturally in front of the hips.

(a) As long as the horse is going at the rate, gait and in the direction desired, only sufficient muscular energy is used to keep the forearms lifted to the proper position and to maintain the reins securely. A natural relaxation of the arms insures freedom and quietness in the use of the hands.

(b) Any involuntary contraction quickly communicates itself through the hands to the horse's mouth, resulting in loss of that calm confidence which the horse should always have in his rider.

(7) The reins are held in either or both hands, fingers softly closed. Backs of the hands are up and out at angles of about 30 degrees inside of the vertical.

(a) The reins in both hands. — The hands, with fingers relaxed, are separated about 8 or 10 inches and normally held slightly above the withers. The wrists are straight and supple; the forearms, wrists, hands and reins form almost straight lines from the points of the elbows to the horse's mouth. Sometimes, for corrective purposes, hands may be carried higher than just described. *However, they should never be carried any lower.* Hands carried too low give the impression of pushing down on the reins and cause the horse to seek to escape the downward effect of the bit on the bars of his mouth by raising his head and thrusting his nose into the air.

The elbows are carried slightly in advance of the points of the hips. Their position will vary from time to time in guiding or controlling the horse; but, with reins properly adjusted, they should never pass in rear of the hip joints.

When riding with a snaffle bit, maintaining a direct line from elbow to mouth is facilitated if the reins are taken into the hands between the third and fourth fingers, rather than underneath the little fingers.

(b) Reins in one hand.— If only one hand is used, the free arm hangs naturally.

(c) Good Hands. — Good hands are impossible to acquire without a good seat. Softness is an essential characteristic of good hands and must be developed. Relaxed arms, which permit the soft and elastic opening and closing of the elbow joints, combined with the lazy play of the wrists and fingers, give soft hands.

As long as the horse is going at the speed and in the direction and manner desired, such hands smoothly follow the movements of his head and neck while maintaining soft, continuous contact of unvarying intensity with his mouth. Rough hands are unsteady and quickly communicate unintentional impressions to the horse's mouth, making him nervous and difficult to control.

(8). Balance. — When a rider so disposes his weight as to require the minimum of muscular effort to remain in his seat, and when the weight distribution interferes least with the horse's movements and equilibrium, the rider is said to be "with his horse" or "in balance." This condition of being "with the horse" is the keynote of riding.

When passing from the halt to motion, and when the horse is moving, the seat undergoes certain modifications. The rider must assume positions which assure his retention of balance and which keep him "with his horse". The knees, legs, ankles, and to a great extent the thighs, remain fixed in position. The upper body—the unstable part of the rider's mass—remains in balance over its base of support by appropriate variations in its degree of inclination towards the front, and thus overcomes the disturbing effects of the horse's movements.

Any change in the inclination of the body modifies the distribution of weight on the various parts of the base of support. As forward inclination increases, the rider's center of gravity is carried forward and downward. There is an increase in the weight borne by the knees and stirrups until finally when galloping fast across country or racing, and in certain phases of posting and jumping, the knees and stirrups support the entire load. Through the medium of the stirrup hangers this weight is distributed properly along the back of the horse.

(9) Inclination of the Upper Body.

(a) General.

(i) In forward movement, the degree of forward inclination of the upper body should vary with the speed of the horse and with the gait. This inclination always should be such that the rider remains in balance over his base of support. When the inclination of the upper body is not sufficient to maintain this balance, the rider is not "with" but is "behind" his horse. If it becomes excessive the rider is not "with" but is "ahead" of his horse.

(ii) The upper body is inclined forward from the hip joints. *The back should not break to the rear at the loin.* The eyes, chin, and chest are lifted in order that the back, while inclined to the front, may retain its normal posture and the field of vision be not reduced. To allow the back to break rearward at the loin and to permit the shoulders and head to drop forward, places the weight on the fleshy part of the buttocks and tends toward loss of balance to the rear. This in turn concentrates the weight of the rider at the rear portion of the saddle, and, in marching will result in undue fatigue and often injury to the horse's back in the region of the loins.

(iii) Suppleness, muscular control, and the opening and closing of the angles at the hips, knees and ankles supplement the inclination of the upper body and enable the skilled rider to remain in balance with his horse. In the case of unforeseen movements, such as shying or bolting, which tend to unbalance or unseat the rider, security is provided and balance retained, or regained, by an increased grip of the legs.

(b) The upper body at the various gaits.

(i) Transitions. — When passing from the halt to one of the various gaits, or when changing gaits or rates, the degree of inclination required of the upper body is dependent upon the suddenness of the change. In increasing gaits, the inclination must be sufficient to prevent inertia from carrying the center of gravity of the upper body in rear of the base of support. The change in inclination is made just prior to the change in gait.

(ii) At the walk the upper body is inclined forward very slightly more than at the halt. As a result, despite the constant tendency to drift to the rear, caused by the horse's forward movement, the rider remains in balance. Thus seated, he neither slouches, concentrates his weight on the cantle, nor gets "behind his horse". The upper body has the same erect, alert appearance as that of the smart dismounted soldier at attention.

(iii) At the slow trot or trot (not posting), with stirrups, the upper body remains practically erect without stiffness and has just sufficient forward inclination to keep its center of gravity over its base of support. Its forward inclination is approximately that assumed when at the walk. At the slow trot, without stirrups, the beginner must lean back slightly in order to remain in balance. This is due to the change in position of the lower leg when riding without stirrups.

(iv) At the posting trot the rider's center of gravity under goes more varied displacements than during any other gait. The length of his base of support varies from the maximum when he is in the saddle to the minimum when he is at the top of his rise. At this latter phase his base of support consists of his inner knees, legs and stirrups.

Sufficient forward inclination must be taken at all times to be in balance over the minimum base of support.

The rider's body moves *forward* and slightly *upward*, then *backward* and *downward* in cadence with the beats of the gait. In rising to the trot, the angle at the hips should be opened as little as necessary, and the buttocks should remain to the rear. The upper body should maintain its inclination without appreciable change. *Excessively opening the angle at the hips during this movement causes the upper body to approach a vertical position and the buttocks to move too far to the front. These grave faults must be avoided.*

The upper body remains fixed in posture and there is no sinking to the rear at the loin. Lifting the head and chest and keeping the hips and buttocks well to the rear produces an easy and natural posture. The chin is raised so that the plane of the face remains vertical. The rider sinks into the saddle very lightly on the upper thighs and crotch, and the points of the buttocks barely touch the saddle at each beat. The knee and hip joints serve as springs to make the reactions soft for both horse and rider.

A rider is said to be posting on the right diagonal when after rising, he comes back into the saddle at the instant the right forefoot comes to the ground.

(v) At the ordinary gallop, when fully seated in the saddle, the upper body is inclined slightly farther forward than at the walk or slow trot, but not as much as at the posting trot. The rider's thighs and crotch maintain continuous light contact with the saddle. At each beat of the gallop, that part of the rider's weight coming onto his thighs forces the *relaxed knees* downward, and they in turn transmit weight through the relaxed ankles into the heels.

This automatically forces them down and causes the legs to maintain their proper position. The back and loin are straight without stiffness. The buttocks are forced well to the rear. The reactions of the gallop are absorbed by the play of the hip joints and not by the relaxation of the loin. Leaning backward at the gallop, or allowing the loin to break rearward, concentrates weight on the cantle and places the rider "behind his horse". He will then ride "heavily" instead of "lightly".

(vi) As the speed of the gallop is increased, the upper body is inclined farther forward from the hips. The points of the buttocks are lifted clear of the saddle until the crotch is just out of contact. This places all the weight on the lower thighs, knees and especially in the stirrups. "Pounding" the saddle is eliminated, the rider is more comfortable, and the horse moves with more ease and freedom.

Rounding the back and loin entails loss of muscular control of the upper body and results in loss of balance. If balance is lost to the rear, the rider gets "behind his horse" and sits heavily, close to the horse's loins. Being "behind the horse" makes galloping laborious and painful to him and places the soldier in an unfavorable position for employing his weapons. When riding over-balanced to the front, the seat is insecure and the rider has difficulty in using his legs or hands to control his horse.

(vii) In decreasing rates and gaits, in halting and in backing the rider must not lean back. If necessary, the forward inclination of the body decreases just sufficiently to enable the rider to remain in balance. As the horse decreases his speed or halts abruptly, the rider stiffens his back muscles and keeps his buttocks to the rear. He pinches momentarily with his knees and obtains a brace against his stirrups as a result of his low heels. These combined actions prevent him from losing balance to the front and permit him to remain off the cantle.

(10) Summary.

(a) Seat: Forward part of pelvic bones rest on saddle; crotch well back so as to be deep in throat of saddle; fleshy part of buttocks forced rearward toward the cantle at all times, and never allowed to slip forward under the rider. Rider does not sit on buttocks but on the inside of thighs and forward points of pelvic bones.

(b) Thighs: Flat; heavy muscles to rear of femurs; continuous contact down to, and including, inner sides of knees.

(c) Knees: Inside of knee bones are snugly against saddle skirts; pushed down as low as possible with stirrup leathers remaining vertical; not allowed to turn outward so as to leave space between them and saddle; normally do not grip tightly but sufficiently to keep whole thigh softly against saddle skirts. Knee joints are almost completely relaxed, except when necessary to keep seat from being displaced forward or sideways as in stopping suddenly before an obstacle, etc.; must not be entirely limp or lower legs will slip too far to rear, heels come up, seat slides forward, and the rider will hump his back.

(d) Lower legs: Inner and upper portions of calves always remain in soft contact with sides of horse; no great effort required to keep them there. Calves squeeze to drive horse forward, and to maintain seat in case of emergency. In latter case, knees also increase grip. When stirrup leathers are vertical, knee joints relaxed, and heels thrust down to absolute limit permitted by relaxed ankle joints, position of lower legs is correct. Heels should be kept down when squeezing or gripping with calves. Spurs are used just in rear of girth — not far back against the flank.

(e) Ankles: Habitually relaxed, allowing weight transmitted down thighs, through partially relaxed knees, to sink into heels of boots. If trunk is correctly inclined forward at the hips, portion of rider's weight necessarily runs down through thighs and automatically flexes ankles and drives heels down.

(f) Feet: Turned out so that upper, inner sides of calves rest against horse. Toes make angle of twenty to forty-five degrees with longitudinal axis of horse. Stirrups slightly in rear of the ball of the foot, permitting all weight to sink into heels. For schooling, balls of feet may rest on stirrup treads.

(g) Heels: Thrust far down. Give brace to feet against the stirrups if horse checks suddenly, so the seat cannot slip forward. Receive all weight coming into stirrups if feet and ankles are correctly relaxed.

(h) Trunk and Loin: *Carried in same posture as when standing erect in the "Position of a soldier," except that whole trunk is inclined to front from hip joints.*

When fully seated in the saddle at halt, walk, slow trot or canter, the center of gravity of the trunk falls just in front of pelvic bones. At posting trot or gallop, the center of gravity is approximately over knees, and the trunk's forward inclination is greater. The loin is habitually "hollowed out" in its normal, natural position; it never remains convex to rear. The buttocks should be well in rear toward cantle of saddle, but due to body's forward inclination no weight is on them. The buttocks provide rear counterbalance for the forward-inclined trunk. The knees, over which trunk and buttocks are balanced, are the center of motion when posting, galloping or jumping.

(i) Chest, Head and Chin: Lifted. The whole body is carried lightly. *There should be a feeling of stretching the spine upward and making the body tall.*

(j) Length of Stirrups: After some slow trotting without stirrups (when seated as prescribed above for slow paces) and with the legs hanging down in a natural position by horse's sides, the treads of properly adjusted stirrups should hang even with center of large bones on inner sides of ankle joints. A little variation in length is inevitable due to differences in conformation of both people and horses. For fast cross-country work or jumping, the stirrups are shortened from one to four holes. The shorter the stirrups are adjusted, the greater must be the inclination of the upper body.

(11) Important Points:

(a) Any faulty attitude of one part of the rider will cause faults in other parts, thus throwing the whole seat out of adjustment.

(b) When the horse checks suddenly, goes down a steep incline, or lands after a jump, the knee joints should stiffen a trifle, and in conjunction with the lower heels, permit the feet to brace the whole body against the stirrups. The knees also should grip the saddle more tightly and the back muscles should stiffen in order to keep the spine straight. These actions prevent the body's toppling forward, and hold the seat secure.

The above actions are easily accomplished after practice, and also serve to prevent the buttocks' slipping forward and the lower legs going to the rear which disrupt the whole seat and involve surrender of balance and control of the horse. *If the heels are thrust down and the back is kept swayed, the forward inclination of the body, even when checking the horse very quickly, can, and should, be maintained.*

The rider's knees, when in the position described, are approximately in the transverse vertical plane containing the horse's center of gravity. Hence with the rider correctly seated, their centers of gravity fall approximately in the same vertical line. During movement there is of course oscillation of the centers of gravity of both, but they remain approximately in the same vertical line if the rider is constantly "with his horse".

(c) Stiffness should be avoided. As much relaxation should exist throughout the whole anatomy as is consistent with maintaining muscular control of the body, balance, and the seat steadily in place.

(12) Position at Walk and Trot: In order to lessen fatigue to the horse, *it is absolutely vital to maintain slight forward inclination of the body at the walk and trot.* This keeps the rider's weight distributed down his thighs; whereas leaning backward or sitting bolt upright concentrates it far back on the cantle, which is very tiring to the horse.

(13) Liberty of Head and Neck: In addition to using the correct seat every effort should be made to allow horses maximum liberty of head and neck. At the walk in particular the reins should be very long permitting the horse to stretch his head and neck into a low, extended position favorable to long strides and comfort. The hands remain still at the trot; at the gallop they move back and forth with the horse's movements, "following the mouth". Elbows must be partly flexed so as to be soft and elastic.

(14) How to Test the Correctness of the Rider's Position.

(a) If the rider is in balance as a result of his upper body's being properly inclined forward, then he is able at the walk, trot or gallop, *without first leaning farther forward* and without pulling on the reins, to stand in his stirrups with all his weight in his depressed heels.

(b) In executing this exercise the seat is raised just clear of the saddle by stiffening the knees but keeping them partly flexed. The upper body remains inclined forward at hips. At the trot one hand should touch the horse's neck lightly to assist in remaining in balance. At the walk or gallop the rider, if his seat is correct, should be able to stand in his stirrups without the aid of his hand. A rider who can execute the above exercise at all gaits and without first changing inclination, is in balance and never "behind his horse". The majority of those not in this position partly maintain their balance by hanging onto the reins, thus unnecessarily punishing their horses' mouths as well as their backs.

(15) Manner of Holding the Reins.

(a) Single Rein. — With a single rein, such as generally is used with a snaffle bit alone, the reins enter the two hands between the little and third fingers, passing up through the palms, and out over the index fingers. The thumbs are placed on top of the reins, pressing them against the middle joints of the index fingers, which prevents the reins from slipping. When both reins are held in one hand, the rein from the empty hand enters between the ring and middle fingers, or between the middle and index fingers, as desired. The two bights, (loose ends of the reins), then pass over the index fingers, and are held in place by the thumb, as in the case when the reins are held in the two hands.

(b) Double Reins. — If the reins are held in both hands, when using a double bridle, (one having both the curb and snaffle bits, often called "bit and bridoon"), the snaffle rein enters each hand underneath the little finger, and the curb rein enters between the little and ring fingers. The two reins run up together through the palm and out over the index finger, and are held in place by the thumb.

If all reins are held in one hand, one curb rein enters between the little finger and the ring finger, the other between the ring and middle fingers; one snaffle underneath the little finger, the other between the middle and index fingers. The bights pass out of the palm over the index finger, and are held down by the thumb. Thus the snaffle reins are always outside the curb reins, relative to the horse's neck and to the fingers. There are numerous ways of holding the reins, many of which may be satisfactory. However, those just given are thought to be as good as, if not better than, any of the others.

(16) Posting.

(a) Posting, or rising to the trot, has been quite generally adopted as a means of reducing the shock of this gait for both horse and rider. It is accomplished as follows: As the horse takes up the trot, the rider inclines the upper part of the body forward, supports himself by pressing the knees against the saddle, and then permits himself to be impelled upward by the thrust of the horse's hind leg (the left, for example). He remains up during the stride of the right hind leg, and sits down just in time to be impelled upward again by the next thrust of the left hind leg. He continues in this way, avoiding the alternate thrust of the hind leg.

(b) When learning to rise to the trot the beginner will make more rapid progress if, at each effort to rise, he strokes the horse's neck. Stroking the horse's neck assists the rider to catch the rhythm of the motion; it also causes him to incline the body forward at about the correct angle. In rising to the trot, the buttocks should be raised moderately from the saddle; contact with the saddle should be resumed gently and without shock; the knees should be pressed snugly against the saddle; the lower leg should be kept perfectly still, the ankle joint supple, and the heel slightly lower than the toe. The rider's head should be up, and his eyes glancing well out to the front; he should not lower the head and look down toward the horse's front feet.

(c) When the rider sits down in the saddle each time the right forefoot strikes the ground, he is said to be posting on the right diagonal; when he sits down each time the left forefoot is planted, he is posting on the left diagonal. The rider should frequently alternate diagonals in order to insure equal development and power in the hind legs of the horse. On straight lines it is immaterial which diagonal he posts upon; provided he uses both diagonals equally; but in a riding hall or enclosure it is essential that a fixed rule be insisted upon.

(d) A horse when worked in a hall travels a great deal of the time on a curve in such a manner that his outside lateral travels a greater distance than his inside lateral, his outside hind leg further than his inside leg. On the left hand, for example, the rider should post on the outside or right diagonal, receiving the thrust of the left hind leg, which has the shorter distance to travel, and thus equalizing the work of the hind legs. The converse is true if the horse is on the right hand."

The document which follows, *"Breaking, Training, and Reclaiming Cavalry Horses"* constitutes Chamberlin's last writing on the education of the horse.
—Warren C. Matha, Editor

## November 1941
## Breaking, Training and Reclaiming Cavalry Horses

Second Cavalry Division
Camp Funston
Fort Riley, Kansas

# Breaking, Training
# And
# Reclaiming Cavalry Horses
# Headquarters 2d Cavalry Division

**Camp Funston, Kansas**

12 November 1941

The following exercises for breaking, training and reclaiming cavalry horses, prepared by Brigadier General Harry D. Chamberlin, are prescribed for general use by all organizations of the 2d Cavalry Division.

By Command of Major General Millikin:

> W.B. Bradford,
> *Lt. Col., CSC,*
> *Chief of Staff.*

*OFFICIAL:*
    J.M. Glasgow,
    *Lt. Col., AGD,*
    *Adjutant General.*

# Breaking, Training & Reclaiming Cavalry Horses

## Four Simple Exercises to Break, Train and Reclaim Cavalry Horses

*Note: Before studying this article, Changes 1, F.M. Animal Transport (25-5) should be carefully studied and each detail thoroughly understood, also the rein effects verbally described and graphically depicted attached hereto.*

The four simple exercises to be described below will not only serve to break and train all colts and remounts, but also will render older horses obedient and supple for military and all other equestrian purposes, such as polo, hunting and jumping. In fact, before negotiating a single obstacle with a hunter or jumper, or before practicing with stick and ball on a polo pony, these four exercises should be thoroughly taught, and practiced over and over again. Many remounts, jumpers, and polo ponies are permanently injured physically or spoiled temperamentally because they are placed in ranks, started at jumping, or put in a polo game before having been taught to execute properly and calmly the movements required in the four exercises.

Provided the work is under the supervision and direction of capable horsemen, these four exercises for breaking, training, and keeping horses relaxed and obedient can be executed by mediocre riders. Many spoiled and headstrong horses can also be reclaimed by the same simple system.

The reader will discover that the exercises not only break, train, and subdue the horse, but also teach him and the rider the five rein effects as well as the effect of the legs used either singly or in conjunction.

## Exercise No. 1

The first exercise consists in riding the individual horse on a circle of about fifteen to twenty-five yards in diameter. He is guided solely with *the inner "opening," or "leading" rein.*

The principal purpose of the exercise is to "take the edge off the horse," thus without a fight, rendering him calm, obedient, and attentive. However, many other benefits which result as by-products will be pointed out.

Always begin at the walk, until circulation in the feet is assured. As soon as this is accomplished, take up the trot. *The opening rein must be employed, not the direct rein; that is, there is no tension on the rein unless absolutely necessary to control the horse.* For example, when circling to the right, the right rein is carried out and to the *right front* and is used with "alternating" effects (not a steady tension). The leading effect is applied and continued until the horse both follows the desired path and bends his neck to the right *with relaxed muscles*. At the exact instant when the relaxation of the neck occurs the rein effect ceases momentarily. As the rider "feels" the horse about to branch off on a tangent to his circle, he re-applies the leading effect and continues it until the horse again concedes as just described. This is what is meant by "alternating" effects of the rein. Total relaxation cannot be expected until the horse's first friskiness and exuberance have worn off. He soon learns that when he obeys the rein and relaxes, he is *instantly* rewarded by escaping the annoyance of the bit. This is the basis of all horse training, i.e., instantaneous reward to obedience through ceasing all use of the aids when the horse obeys. The reward must be instantaneous—never so much as one second after the *horse obeys*. If the reward is a fraction of a second tardy, he will not associate this concession with the relief from the annoyance of the aids.

Thus the light leading effects used with *just sufficient frequency and intensity* to keep the horse on the chosen circle. The left rein is entirely passive and "floating"—rather than stretched taut. (It is amazing to note how few riders can keep one hand entirely passive while the other one is active!) The left rein is only used in two cases. First case: if the horse's trot becomes so rapid that there is danger of his breaking into a gallop, a *minimum amount* of direct tension on both reins must be applied momentarily in order to prevent his so doing. Increase your forward inclination when applying the tension in order to ride lightly rather than leaning heavily backward, which results in "pounding" the horse's loin and provokes his resistance. Reins should work exactly parallel with each other in this case and the bit be gently sawed ("vibrated") through the horse's mouth. The moment he settles to the trot, resume the leading rein. Permit him to trot freely and faster rather than fight his mouth to maintain a regulation or slow trot. Second case: if a horse is inclined to be rubber-neck (i.e., bend his neck too far to the right in answering the right leading rein), the left rein should be lowered so that the left hand is near the upper part of the horse's left shoulder and just enough tension intermittently applied to the left rein to prevent the horse's bending his neck exaggeratedly to his right. The left rein thus exerts a limited effect to the bend of the neck. (This is also the one and only case when the hand is lowered to a point where the rein and forearm do not form a straight line. The hands are very frequently raised to secure the correct effect on the bit but only lowered in this specific instance.) See paragraph 9 I, (1), Changes 1, F.M. 25-5.

As the horse becomes calm, the neck should bend uniformly from the shoulder to poll and gradually become entirely relaxed and soft. As indicated above, do not endeavor to compel the horse to trot slowly. Always ride well forward, with weight somewhat over the inside shoulder. This frees the horse's loin from irritating pounding and helps to induce a maximum extension and a lowering of his head and neck. *Calmness is never obtained with a spirited or nervous horse until he is taught to work with an extended and naturally carried head and neck.* Soft relaxation of the jaw (chewing on the bit) and a lateral bend of the neck usually develop soon with this exercise if the rider's hands are clever and soft.

The hand is kept rather high so that the leading rein tends to act approximately *parallel to the long axis of the horse's head.* A low hand acts perpendicularly to this long axis and will usually over-flex the neck and poll, rending the horse fretful from constraint. Inevitably, the right leading rein occasionally will have to be used with a little tension to the *right and rear,* (direct effect), particularly with an impetuous horse. Remember, however, to limit all tension to an absolute minimum.

Thus, with minimum rein annoyance the horse is allowed to trot on the circle until his playful exuberance has subsided. The exercise is then repeated on a similar circle to the left hand. *If the horse has any tendency to carry his head high, the rider's inside leg should predominate, pushing the croup slightly to the outside of the circle.* This requires the horse to lighten his hind quarters (mobilize the haunches) because they are forced to cover more ground than the forehand. Consequently, he will soon automatically increase the weight on his forehand by lowering his head and neck. As the horse becomes calm and obedient, the rider begins to establish light tension on both reins in order to secure very delicate contact with the horse's mouth. Thus, he is gradually taught to "accept the bit"—with his head and neck in a natural, graceful, and extended posture. *Remember that if he raises his head too high, your hands also move higher in order to make his mouth uncomfortable by slowly and moderately sawing the bit with slightly increased tension.* He should not be allowed to escape the bit for so much as a second until finally he seeks relief by lowering the head. Instantly, he is rewarded by softening the hands and allowing him to lower his head to a natural position. You must sustain the gait by appropriate use of the legs while holding the horse's head high, as the additional pressure on the bit tends to slow or stop him.

Depending upon the energy and condition of the horse, exercise on the circle will take from 5 to 20 minutes on each hand, or a total of from 10 to 40 minutes. Where the horse is very "high" or very sensitive, stubborn, etc., he should, prior to any mounted work, *always be worked on a longe until calm and relaxed.* The longe, properly used, is of enormous value and all officers and noncommissioned officers should be skillful in its employment. Many an old but energetic and difficult horse can be quieted and made pleasant to ride by plenty of work on a longe each day before he is mounted. Longeing also will subdue and reclaim many so-called "bad" horses. If necessary, longe him three or more hours daily in two or more periods until through boredom and fatigue he comes around to going quietly under the saddle.

After having worked a horse on circles such time as is necessary to cause him to trot quietly with his head and neck extended and low, he should be allowed to walk on a *loose rein* for several minutes and caressed by pats on the neck. Many riders are quick to punish and far too slow to reward. He is then pushed into the canter and again worked on both hands around the circle until completely soft and amenable at this gait.

In taking the gallop depart on circles, the rider should switch to the outside direct rein and outside leg aids. Use the "direct" rein effect very lightly in order to weight the outside shoulder just as the legs are used to force the horse to break into the gallop. The outside leg is used more vigorously than the inside and a little farther to the rear. The leg aids, just as the hands, should always be employed alternating—yielding instantly to obedience—resisting (acting) instantly against resistance or disobedience.

Naturally, long periods of work can only be given to a remount after he has been conditioned by longeing and leading until his wind, legs, and muscles are fit. Early lessons should always be short and frequent. Three short lessons daily are of much more benefit that one long lesson. Often it is necessary to longe an older and fairly well trained horse, which through being without exercise for some time is bursting with fire and exuberance, for several days before he will be sufficiently quiet and relaxed to ride even on a circle without fighting your hand. Moreover, after all this longeing, it will be found that the trot *only* can be used when mounted for several more days because the horse is still too lively to gallop without fighting the bit and resisting in other ways. Patience and intelligence on the part of the rider and hours of slow work both on the longe and by leading prior to riding will gentle, relax, and make manageable most any horse. With an intelligent group of men, a remount squad can be organized in a troop, squadron, or regiment which will produce amazing results by the system here advocated with either remounts or rogues in an astoundingly short period of time.

It will be noted that this first exercise accomplishes the following:

1. Calms the horse through:
    a. steady work on circles without unnecessary restraint
    b. permitting an extended and natural head carriage
    c. not annoying the mouth so as to provoke resistances

2. Teaches the horse:
    a. relaxation of his neck in obtaining a lateral flexion
    b. relaxation of the jaw by vibrating the reins
    c. obedience to the leading rein
    d. obedience to action of rider's inside leg through mobilizing the haunches
    e. relaxation of the spine as he bends lightly around the rider's inside leg
    f. natural extended carriage of the head and neck as well as acceptance of the bit (a well-trained horse only needs the lightest sort of support from the hands)
    g. the gallop departs and the aid therefore

### 2nd Exercise

*(Note) This exercise is not attempted until the horse is calm at the trot on the circle.*

The greatest difficulty in riding horses either for military purposes or for sports, such as hunting, jumping, or polo, is to regulate the gait (commonly called rating), to change the gaits, and to halt. *Absurdly enough while these three items are the most difficult to execute, few riders ever attempt to train their horses thoroughly to go at only the desired rate, decrease the gait readily or to halt under all conditions promptly without resistance.* Needless to say, all should be practiced over and over again. Instead of riding a young horse for an hour or more and halting only upon returning to the stable he should be halted and required to change gaits and rates *literally hundreds of time during that time.* If the routine to be described below is followed, there will be few horses which will not only halt quickly and decrease gaits readily when being ridden alone but most will do likewise in ranks, at polo, hunting, jumping, etc. Not only does the following exercise teach the horse regulation of gait and rate but it develops his ability and balance. *Again let it be stated for emphasis that everything described hereafter should be repeated over and over again.*

After the horse has become relaxed and calm on the circle and accepts contact with the hand, the 2nd exercise is begun as follows: The horse is put at the walk on a long rein and halted every few steps. The instant he halts the fingers completely relax and the reins are allowed to hang entirely loose while the horse is permitted to rest in place for several seconds, and is patted on the neck. Next, he should be again moved forward in response to the rider's legs. As soon as he learns to halt promptly and stand quietly, the periods during which he rests should be made progressively briefer so that he halts only a second or fraction thereof before being urged forward again by the riders' legs.

Next, changing from the trot to the walk and vice versa is practice. After walking quietly for a few moments, he is squeezed into the trot and as soon as he settles into steady, balanced movement, he is brought back to the walk, continuing at this gait until complete calmness occurs. Do not forget to pat him on the neck when he obeys and is calm. The periods at the walk or trot should be briefer and briefer. After a few such lessons much practice also should be given at *extending* the trot little by little, then bringing the horse gently back to a slow trot; then to a halt. When this exercise is executed well, the horse should be brought directly from the *normal* trot to the halt, then put promptly at the normal trot again, with no intermediate steps at the walk. To reiterate, these exercises must be repeated over and over and over again. *Also the rider's hand must give the horse's mouth entire freedom the moment he halts.* If the hands and legs are skillful the horse will soon obey the lightest effect. *As soon as resistance or displacement of the head develops in halting or slowing the rate, similar work at a slower pace should be resumed.* In other words, if the horse resents halting directly from the trot, more work in changing from the trot to the walk and from the walk to the halt is necessary. *The preparation for the halt from the trot has not been complete.* The exercises can be greatly elaborated and made more difficult as obedience and calmness become habitual. For example, more: (a) from halt to normal trot, to extended trot, to normal trot, to halt; (b) from halt to extended trot, to halt. When the horse is fully prepared, he should come to the halt from the extended trot in about six or seven trotting steps, with none at the walk, but such tests are not attempted until after good condition is acquired with calmness and obedience normal. *The prompt moving out after a halt and prompt increasing of speed after it has been reduced, are vitally essential to teach the horse to collect and balance himself.* Without displacing his head unnaturally, he very soon learns to check or halt with his hind legs well advanced under his belly ready to spring quickly forward. He moves and handles himself as does a horse at liberty and so works at maximum efficiency.

These gymnastics can be executed on circles, straight lines, or on the serpentines and zig-zags, to be described under Exercise 3. If a horse is exceedingly "hot," it is usually best to keep him on circles until he becomes perfectly calm at the elementary halting exercises. After all the work involving the halts and changes of rate and gait described above is performed easily and promptly, similar work at the canter and gallop, etc., should be given as: (a) from canter to gallop, back to canter; (b) from trot to canter to gallop, and reverse; (c) from canter to trot, to walk, to halt, and reverse; (d) from canter to walk and reverse; (e) from canter to halt and reverse and (f) finally, when the horse becomes strong, conditioned, obedient and calm, *he should halt in a few yards from the extended gallop with no steps at the trot,* promptly back a few steps, and spring forward again softly and gracefully into the gallop.

From this exercise the horse learns:

(1) Obedience to the "direct rein," then halting or slowing down in answer to direct tension or resistance by both hands.

NOTE: Care should be taken that the hand Resists and Does Not Pull. In other words, if the rein, held by a resisting hand, were cut, the hand would not fly to the rear; whereas in the case of the pulling hand, it would.

(2) Obedience to the legs—i.e., moving forward frankly, energetically and promptly in answer to the pressure from the rider's calves or spurs.

NOTE: The horse should gradually be taught to fear an attack from the rider's legs more than anything else in the world.

(3) To engage his hocks naturally at all appropriate time in order to spring forward easily and quickly.

(4) To move lightly in good balance without displacing the head grotesquely.

(5) To slow the gait or halt almost instantly in answer to *light rein indications.*

## 3rd Exercise

The third exercise consists in schooling the horse, first on serpentines described on large curves, and later as his training progresses on zig-zags which are arrived at by progressively reducing the radii of the serpentine curves until sharp changes of direction of approximately 180 degrees are executed on the hind quarters as a pivot.

In these movements, the "bearing" or "neck" rein only is employed. In using the right "bearing" or "neck" rein when turning to the left for example, the right hand is carried just across the crest of the neck, and acts toward the left front.

To be most effective, it should bear against the right side of *the upper half of the neck,* as this part of the neck is more sensitive than near the shoulders. It is an artificial effect and not powerful. It is habitually used with cavalry horses and polo ponies and whenever riding with the reins in one hand to change direction without changing speed. By first using the left opening rein and immediately thereafter alternating it with the *right bearing rein,* obedience to the *right bearing rein* alone is quickly taught. The effect is to turn the horse's nose upward and to the right, and force the bulk of the weight of the neck onto the *left shoulder.* While this effect is not strong the horse's balance is shifted toward the left front causing him to turn on a large curve to the left. The rein is used intermittently and in cadence each time the left foreleg is moved, when working with a green colt. If the riders right (outside) leg is used in conjunction with the right bearing rein the horse soon learns to engage his haunches and pivot on the hind quarters in changing direction.

Since the horse during the first part of his lesson has been calmed by work with the opening rein on circles and by halts, the exercise on serpentines and zig-zags may be begun at the trot. In this work, the rider *habitually uses the outside leg to engage the haunches. In other words, the haunches are kept on the inside of the curve of the serpentine.* Since the haunches travel over less ground than the forehand, the horse as a result must lighten the weight on his forehand at the expense of his hind quarters which tends to improve his balance and renders him light to the effects of the hand. As soon as he appreciates the significance of the bearing rein, the inside hand (leading rein) is entirely passive. For example, as he turns to the left, the right bearing rein and the right leg are used; as he turns to the right, the left bearing rein and left leg. Of course, if the horse attempts to escape the hand and whirl around too rapidly or to cut inside of the path which the rider desires to traverse, effective corrective measures must be applied by the inside leg and rein. As a variation and to obtain complete control, the rider should occasionally *mobilize* the haunches on a serpentine. *Never permit a horse to become routined.* Later on when serpentines and zig-zags are used at the gallop, the horse should be brought to the trot just prior to changing direction, otherwise he will be required either to change lead or gallop false on the half turns. Until complete obedience and much experience are gained, no attempt should be made to require the change of lead at the gallop. In fact, when necessity demands, the trooper's horse and the polo pony as a matter of self-preservation will learn the changes of lead at rapid gaits without special schooling.

As the horse becomes obedient, calm, and relaxed in changing directions by use of the outside leg and neck rein, turns should be made sharper and sharper until the polo pony turn is made by pivoting on the hind legs. Since the horse has been given many lessons in halting, each sharp change in direction should be executed by first indicating a partial halt with both direct reins (using the hand in a *high position*) and immediately thereafter by applying the neck rein and outside leg to secure the half turn on the hind quarters.

Many, many halts should be executed while exercising on the serpentines or zig-zags. Inevitably, horses will sometimes resist the turn, in which case the neck rein must be changed to what is known as the "indirect rein of opposition in front of the withers." With the right rein, for example, the right bearing rein instead of acting to the left front acts to the left rear across the horse's neck *but in front of the withers.* Such *tension* as is necessary is applied in order to secure a sharp turn to the left, remembering always that the right leg assists in holding the haunches in place. It may be necessary to employ the left direct rein in combination with the right rein after the horse presents marked resistance. Remember, however, after all, resistances are certain signs of insufficient training at slower gaits and preceding exercises.

This exercise teaches the horse:
 1. Obedience to the bearing rein.
 2. Obedience to the rider's outside leg.
 3. Lightness of the forehand.
 4. Engagement of the inside leg on all turns.
 5. Agility and natural balance.

## 4th Exercise

## Shoulder-In

This exercise is not difficult and it is the *most valuable of all gymnastics given a horse.* Having taught mobilization of the haunches on circles and occasionally on serpentines, there will be no difficulty in securing the shoulder-in from any horse by even a mediocre rider who is properly supervised and directed.

Taking right shoulder-in as an example: *the horse is bent symmetrically throughout his spinal column from poll to point of the croup, around the rider's right leg, and moves toward his left front with his body set obliquely to the lines of motion.* This requires him at each step to cross his fore and hind feet, respectively. The movement is obtained by: 1. Shortening the right rein; 2. Beginning a turn to the right with the right opening rein; 3. Just as the horse's forehand is led off the straight line which he has been following, the leading rein is changed into a *"rein of opposition in rear of the withers,"* which acts in the direction of the left haunch; 4. At the same instant, the rider's right leg is carried back a few inches and used to force the horse's croup to the left; 5. The left rein, with combined leading and direct effects, assists in conducting the horse in his oblique attitude along the same straight line he had been following; 6. The left leg aids the right as necessary to sustain impulsion.

The horse thus is bent around the rider's right leg so that his right shoulder is inside the curve made by his own spinal column. Obviously, his right fore and right hind legs must cross over in front of the left fore and left hind, respectively. If the rider is unsuccessful in obtaining shoulder-in along a straight line, further preparatory work in mobilizing the haunches, and in schooling with the "rein of indirect opposition in rear of the withers," while moving through the corners of an enclosure is indicated. The horse is simply pushed into the corners by the action of the rider's inside leg and the rein of opposition in rear of the withers so that his whole spine from ears to point of the croup are bent outward, coinciding with the line over which he travels.

The benefits of shoulder-in are manifold. If the horse is gradually *required to carry his head in a low position, a soft, relaxed lateral bending to the right of the well extended neck occurs. Alternate resisting and relaxing of the fingers,* which is necessary to keep the horse oblique to the direction of motion, *will secure complete relaxation of the jaw,* as well as a *slight flexion of the poll* as the horse entirely gives himself over to his rider. The crossing of the fore legs involves a raising, and an unusual swinging, of the whole right foreleg across and in front of the left fore, necessitating suppleness and relaxation of the right shoulder and knee. Also the horse is required to obey the rider's right leg and to bend his whole spine laterally as he moves in a sidewise direction. To cross his right hind over the left hind calls for engagement of the former far forward under his body. This supples the joints of the hind leg. *The horse, in working at right shoulder-in, is simply over-balanced to the left because of the attitude forced on him by the aids, and consequently is compelled to chase his own center of gravity in order to maintain balance.* When fully trained, a shying horse can be pushed into an object which frightens him by applying shoulder-in to the shoulder away from the object.

Shoulder-in, although here described while moving on a straight line, should be practiced on curves, serpentines and circles. On circles it is simply an exaggerated mobilization of the haunches. *The horse's curved attitude, and not the particular direction in which he moves, constitutes shoulder-in.* His spine is bent like a bow with the rider's arm and rein functioning as the bowstring and his inside leg as the hand holding the bow. As it is most difficult to execute on a straight line this movement is taught last. Practice on circles first, next on oblique lines, and finally, straight to the front with the horse oblique to the line of movement.

The principal points to be observed in right shoulder-in are:
1. Shortening the right rein and using the rein of *"indirect opposition in rear of the withers"* predominately so as to bend the whole spine (to do this the right hand should be held low and near the top of the right shoulder-blade, not across the withers);
2. Limiting the bend of the neck with the left rein so that it is uniform with the curve of the backbone;
3. Maintaining impulsion;
4. Endeavoring to keep the neck low, well extended and relaxed and the jaw soft with frequent flexions, using the right spur just before the right hind starts to cross the left;
5. Stopping the exercise before the horse, through boredom, shows resistance.

As always, the rider's fingers and legs "act" or become "passive' as required: to break any resistance; to maintain the correct position; to follow the prescribed path; to reward obedience.

In right shoulder-in at the walk, the fingers relax as the right fore crosses the left fore, since this difficult movement of the right shoulder requires its freedom. They tighten more or less as needed at the instant the left fore stops to the left front, which prevents the horse from moving on a curve to the right. Just at the time the fingers tighten, the rider's right leg, or spur, pushes the right hind across the left hind. Since the right hind moves immediately after the left fore, the action of the rider's leg is timely. At the trot, similar timing of the aids is essential, remembering that the diagonals move simultaneously.

Shoulder-in is obviously almost universal in its relaxing and suppling results. *Taught first at the walk as all exercises* should be when feasible, *it is most efficacious when executed at a free, long-striding* trot. The long strides and impulsion make agility, relaxation, suppleness and good balance imperative. At the gallop, the exercise obviously is confined to left shoulder-in when the horse is leading right; right shoulder-in when leading left. The work has no value unless his position is correct and all resistance is absent. The horse should be utterly relaxed and contentedly obedient.

Where the rider's inexperience makes it advisable, advantage may be taken of a wall or fence to give first lessons in shoulder-in. In so doing, the horse's head is turned toward the wall so that he cannot escape obedience. Great care, however, must be taken to prevent the crossing of the right fore and the right hind *in rear, instead of in front*, of his left fore and left hind, respectively. The wall should be utilized only at the walk for interference (hitting on leg with the foot of the other) easily may occur. Moreover, the horse is controlled largely by the wall and not the aids.

Shoulder-in is, in fact, a very simple exercise to execute for either horse or rider. Each horse develops, on one side or the other, certain stiffness and resultant resistances, or vice versa.

If for example, he stiffens his neck and jaw to the left front, he generally increases the resistance by thrusting his left hip to the same side. The quick remedy is shoulder-in. In this case, left shoulder-in is indicated, but in practice it will be found that some work at right shoulder-in will also be beneficial. This exercise is immeasurably helpful in breaking up all such resistances and a few steps at shoulder-in will reveal to the rider who mounts a strange horse, where the resistances lie—whether in the croup, jaw, shoulder, or elsewhere.

It is an excellent idea at the beginning of each day's work to require a few steps of shoulder-in at the walk on an oblique to one side of the way and back to the other shortly after leaving the stables. Complete relaxation of the jaw, neck and spinal column are quickly obtained. This puts the horse in a pleasant mood and he becomes calm, obedient and agreeable in the work to follow. Thus, the exercise of shoulder-in accomplishes complete relaxation in the neck, poll, jaw, shoulders, spine and hocks and, in addition, secures complete domination in most emergencies.

## Conclusion

As the schooling of the horse progresses and after he presents no resistances upon first being saddled, work on the circles need occupy but a few minutes. However, a little of it is always helpful since it promptly and without resistance produces lateral relaxation of the horse's neck and spine. Thereafter, the four exercises should be mixed and intermingled in every possible combination. Just which exercises are most needed by a particular horse is a matter requiring constant study of the rider. As horses possess entirely different physical and mental characteristics, one should disabuse himself of the idea that they are as similar as motor cars.

Be careful not to overwork young horses. Study them minutely each morning to see that no tiny swelling has occurred round the fetlocks, knees, or hocks. If such is the case, it is a certain sign that the horse is being overworked. If immediately rested, these swellings will usually disappear. Always trot the young horse on a halter the first thing in the morning immediately after taking him from his stall, on a level, hard road. If the slightest bit of stiffness or lameness appears, again remedies are immediate rest and attention. Above all, use your brains and eyes in breaking, conditioning and training horses. They unfortunately cannot talk and explain their disabilities and pains. Consequently, the true horseman must have abnormally observing eyes. The old adage which says "The condition of the horse is in the eyes of the master" had much truth.

In closing, attention is again called to the fact that these four exercises teach the horse and rider the use and significance of every rein and leg effect.

SKETCH 1.

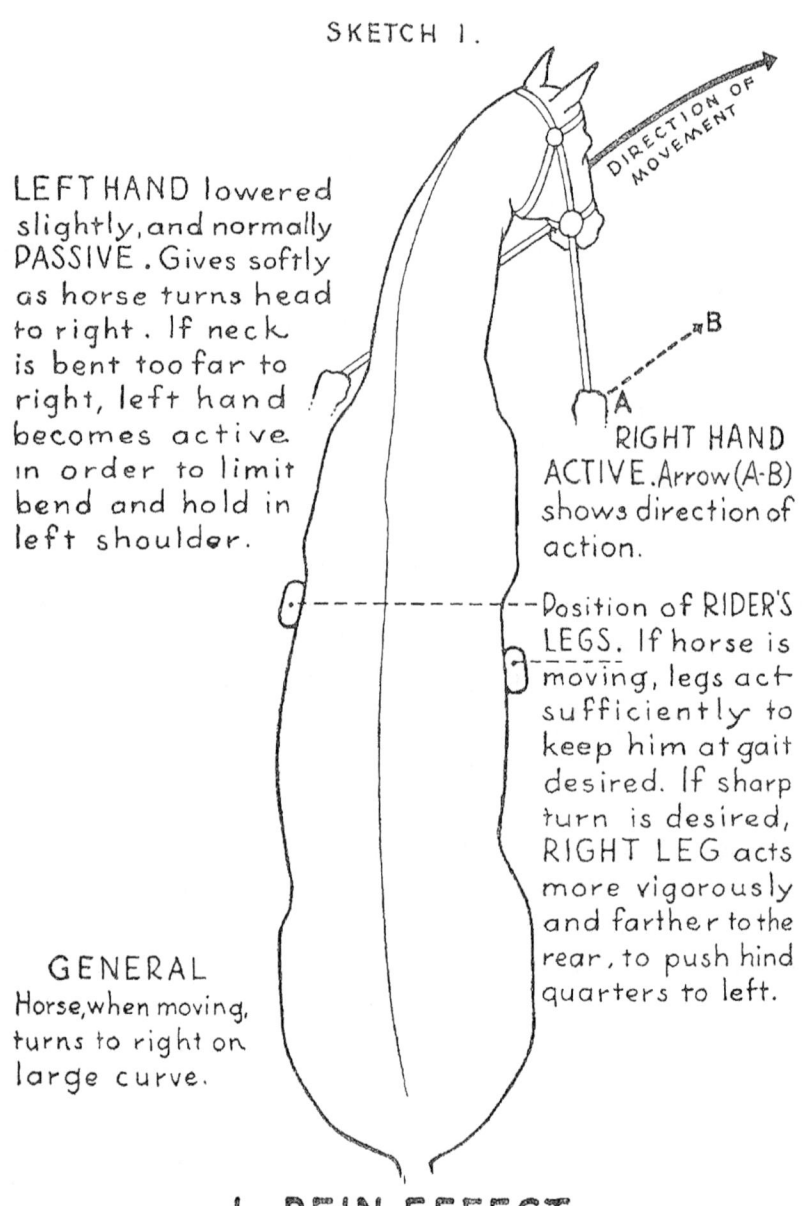

DIRECTION OF MOVEMENT

LEFT HAND lowered slightly, and normally PASSIVE. Gives softly as horse turns head to right. If neck is bent too far to right, left hand becomes active in order to limit bend and hold in left shoulder.

RIGHT HAND ACTIVE. Arrow (A-B) shows direction of action.

Position of RIDER'S LEGS. If horse is moving, legs act sufficiently to keep him at gait desired. If sharp turn is desired, RIGHT LEG acts more vigorously and farther to the rear, to push hind quarters to left.

GENERAL
Horse, when moving, turns to right on large curve.

## 1st REIN EFFECT
Right Opening, or Leading Rein

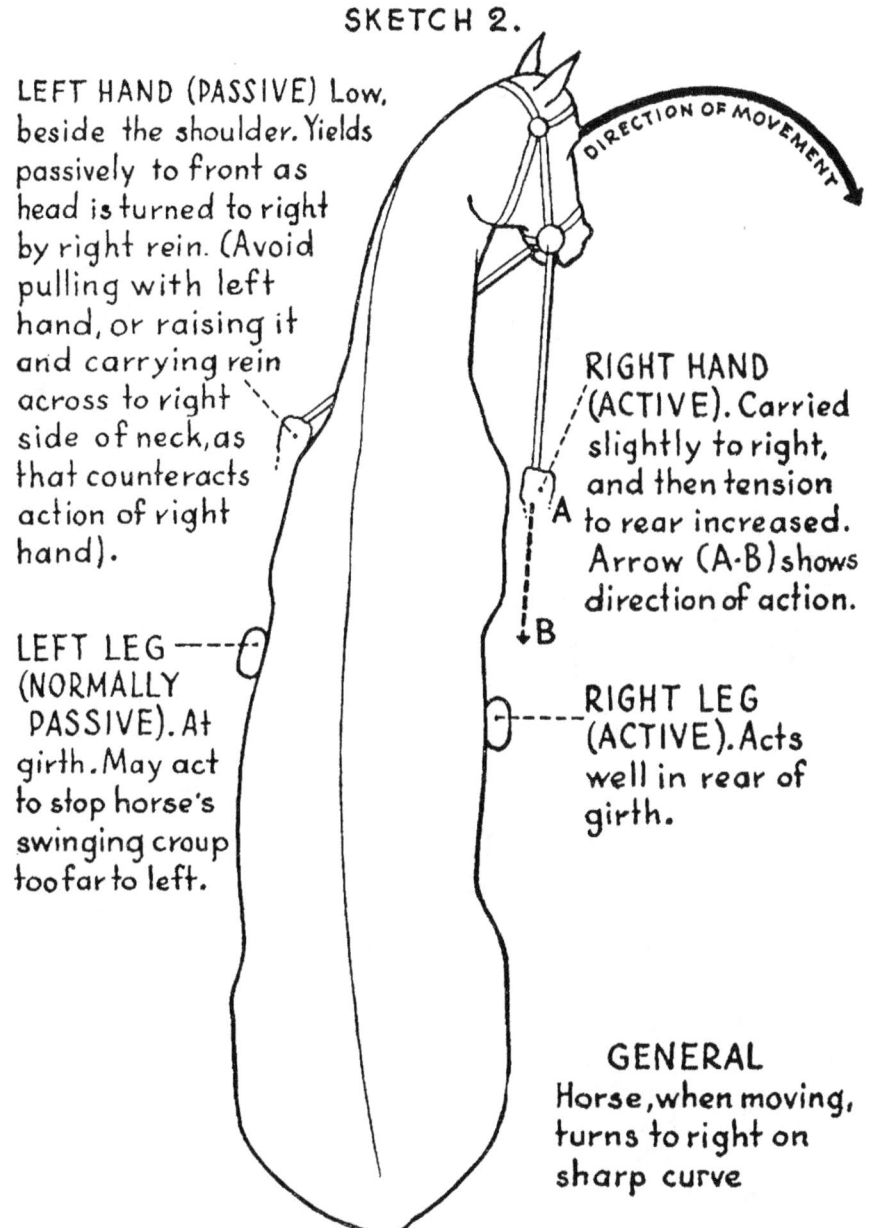

SKETCH 2.

LEFT HAND (PASSIVE) Low, beside the shoulder. Yields passively to front as head is turned to right by right rein. (Avoid pulling with left hand, or raising it and carrying rein across to right side of neck, as that counteracts action of right hand).

LEFT LEG (NORMALLY PASSIVE). At girth. May act to stop horse's swinging croup too far to left.

DIRECTION OF MOVEMENT

RIGHT HAND (ACTIVE). Carried slightly to right, and then tension to rear increased. Arrow (A-B) shows direction of action.

RIGHT LEG (ACTIVE). Acts well in rear of girth.

GENERAL
Horse, when moving, turns to right on sharp curve

## 2nd REIN EFFECT
Right Direct Rein of Opposition

SKETCH 3

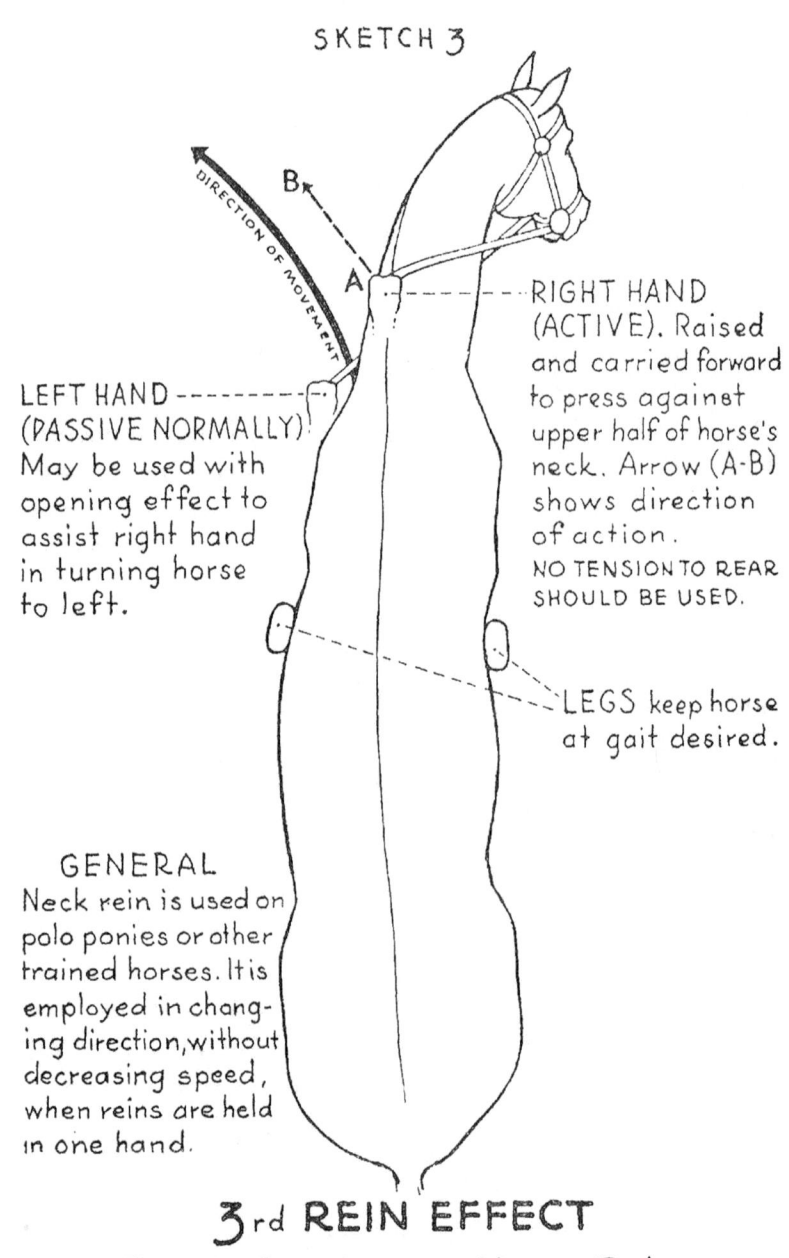

DIRECTION OF MOVEMENT

**RIGHT HAND (ACTIVE).** Raised and carried forward to press against upper half of horse's neck. Arrow (A-B) shows direction of action.
NO TENSION TO REAR SHOULD BE USED.

**LEFT HAND (PASSIVE NORMALLY).** May be used with opening effect to assist right hand in turning horse to left.

**LEGS** keep horse at gait desired.

**GENERAL**
Neck rein is used on polo ponies or other trained horses. It is employed in changing direction, without decreasing speed, when reins are held in one hand.

## 3rd REIN EFFECT
### Right Bearing or Neck Rein

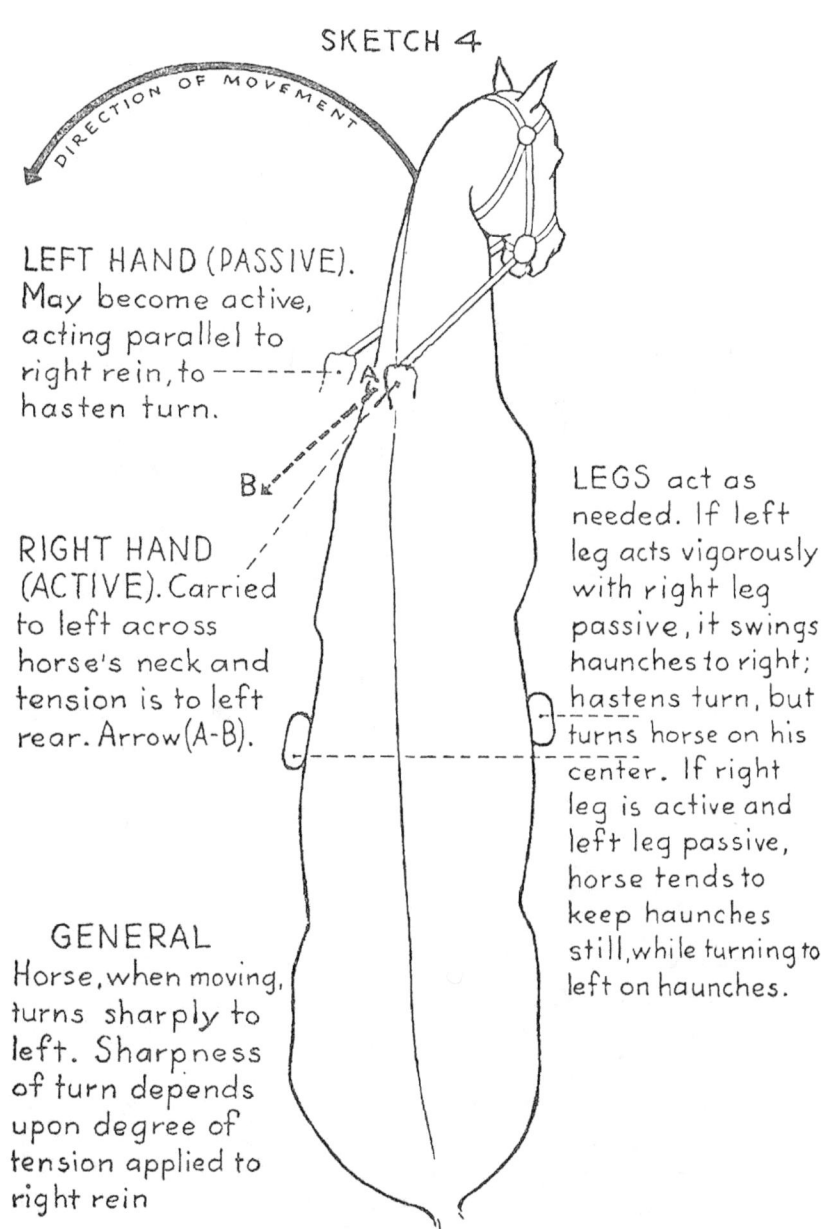

SKETCH 4

DIRECTION OF MOVEMENT

**LEFT HAND (PASSIVE).** May become active, acting parallel to right rein, to hasten turn.

**RIGHT HAND (ACTIVE).** Carried to left across horse's neck and tension is to left rear. Arrow (A-B).

**LEGS** act as needed. If left leg acts vigorously with right leg passive, it swings haunches to right; hastens turn, but turns horse on his center. If right leg is active and left leg passive, horse tends to keep haunches still, while turning to left on haunches.

**GENERAL** Horse, when moving, turns sharply to left. Sharpness of turn depends upon degree of tension applied to right rein

## 4th REIN EFFECT
Right Rein of indirect opposition (<u>in front</u> of the withers)

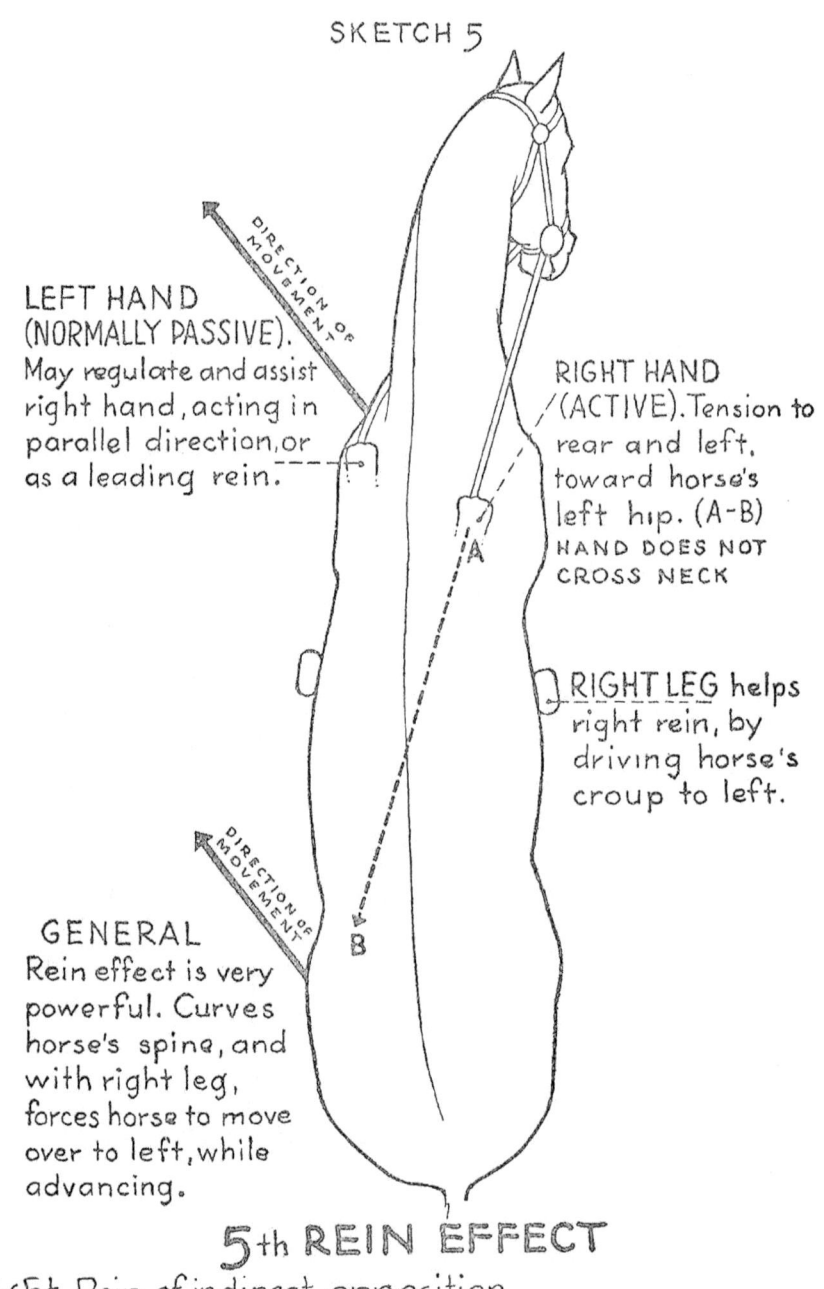

# Chapter 9

## The American Military Riding Style

### Photos of The Military Seat aka "The Chamberlin-Military Seat"
### 1942

*Figure 134.* Brig. General Chamberlin demonstrates the Military Seat as shown in FM 25-5 Animal Transport, Horsemanship and Horsemastership. A publication of the U.S. Cavalry School at Ft. Riley, 1942.

*Figure 135.* Chamberlin displays the Military Seat from a different perspective. Here Chamberlin uses a snaffle bridle. Photo reprinted with permission of the U.S. Cavalry and Armor Association.

*Figure 136.* Lt. Earl "Tommy" Thomson, displays the Military Seat. As a Chamberlin student, he wins the Olympic Individual Silver Medal for Eventing in 1932 and in 1936. U.S. Army photo.

*Figure 137.* Chamberlin with shorter stirrups for jumping rides in a Pariani Borsarelli model 320 saddle. Photo courtesy of Ms. Lydia Moore.

# The American Jumping Style
## According to Brig. General H. D. Chamberlin

*Figure 138.* Chamberlin up. He writes: "Engagement of the hocks. Neck and head beginning downward thrust. Note that rider is thrown out of the saddle by raising of forehand not by thrust of hind legs." Photo and quoted caption reprinted with permission of the U.S. Cavalry and Armor Association.

*Figure 139.* Chamberlin up. He writes: "Forelegs having cleared, head and neck raise, forcing shoulders down and croup up. Bascule begins. Rider remains out of saddle. Reins two inches too long." Photo and quoted caption reprinted with permission of the U.S. Cavalry and Armor Association.

*Figure 140.* Chamberlin up. He writes: "Fraction of second before landing. Note brace on stirrups and fixing of back muscles. Fingers relaxed." Photo and quoted caption reprinted with permission of the U.S. Cavalry and Armor Association.

*Photo 141.* Chamberlin up. He writes: "One foreleg grounded. Note great strain on horse. Rider tense, to remain out of saddle. All weight in stirrups and on knees. Martingale trifle too short." Photo and quoted caption reprinted with permission of the U.S. Cavalry and Armor Association.

***Photo 142.*** *Unknown rider up. Chamberlin writes: "Lower legs in correct position. Form perfect." Photo and caption reprinted with permission of the U.S. Cavalry and Armor Association.*

***Photo 143.*** *Major Chamberlin on Tanbark going over a 5'3" gate with hedge in front. Photo courtesy of Ms. Lydia Moore.*

*Figure 144.* Lt. John W. Wofford up. Chamberlin writes: "Beautiful balance. Rider's hands correctly following horse's mouth." Photo and quoted caption reproduced with permission of the U.S. Cavalry and Armor Association.

*Figure 145.* Major Chamberlin on Tanbark, his choice mount for the Olympic Prix des Nations *of 1932. Just before the competition, the horse went temporarily lame. Chamberlin won the silver individual medal on Show Girl, the team's backup mount. Photo courtesy of Ms. Lydia Moore.*

# The U.S. Cavalry's March Protocol

Until the mid-twentieth century, the U.S. Cavalry was a long-distance riding force equaled only by the Russian cavalry of World War II. Below you will find the long distance riding protocol prescribed by the U.S. Cavalry to enable its horses and troopers to travel 30 miles each day indefinitely. The protocol enables a cavalry unit to travel 100 miles in 24 hours (with extended rest periods at noon and early evening) and to be ready for combat the next day. It also enables an individual cavalry courier and a well-conditioned horse to travel, in an emergency, as far as 170 miles in 28 hours of hard riding.

—Warren C. Matha, Editor

## C. R. T. C. MARCH SCHEDULE

|  | One hour's march with an 8-minute halt | | | One hour's march with a 5-minute halt | | |
|---|---|---|---|---|---|---|
|  | I | II | III | IV | V | VI |
| Approximate rate of march in M.P.H. | 4½ | 5 | 5½ | 5 | 5½ | 6 |
| Walk | 7 | 5 | 4 | 6 | 4 | 3 |
| Trot | 3 | 5 | 6 | 4 | 6 | 7 |
| Walk | 7 | 5 | 4 | 6 | 4 | 3 |
| Trot | 3 | 5 | 6 | 4 | 6 | 7 |
| Walk | 7 | 5 | 4 | 6 | 4 | 3 |
| Trot | 3 | 5 | 6 | 4 | 6 | 7 |
| Walk | 7 | 5 | 4 | 6 | 4 | 3 |
| Trot | 3 | 5 | 6 | 4 | 6 | 7 |
| Walk | 7 | 5 | 4 | 6 | 4 | 3 |
| Trot | 3 | 5 | 6 | 4 | 6 | 7 |
| Walk | 0 | 0 | 0 | 3 | 3 | 3 |
| Lead | 2 | 2 | 2 | 2 | 2 | 2 |
| Halt | 8 | 8 | 8 | 5 | 5 | 5 |
| Total Minutes of Trot Per Hour | 15 | 25 | 30 | 20 | 30 | 35 |

### Rule For Rolling Terrain

If you cannot follow the trot periods given in the above tables due to hills, etc., use the following rule: The time-keeper knows the total minutes trotted since the last halt. Deduct from required minutes to know the number of minutes you must trot before the next halt.

### Rate Of Gaits:
Walk, 4 M.P.H. — Trot, 8 M.P.H. Gallop, 12 M.P.H.

*Figure 146. The CRTC Long Distance Riding Protocol. U.S. Army*

# How to Negotiate
## Steep Slides and Banks, Drop jumps, and Similar Obstacles.

For many riders, leaning forward from the hips while negotiating down a steep slide or bank or while jumping off of a cliff seems counter intuitive. According to Chamberlin, nothing can be further from the truth. As Chamberlin writes: "There is no exception to the rule that the body must be inclined forward *at all times...*"[13] By inclining even a trifle forward from the hips, the rider frees up the horse's hindquarters to come well under, regulates the rate of descent, and prevents the hind end from collapsing under the strain. Leaning forward also puts the rider's weight over the forehand where it belongs. Leaning forward also pushes the horse's hooves deeper into the soil to aid stability as horse and rider descend. The rider must always remember to negotiate the downward movement straight and never at an angle. This minimizes the chance that the horse might stumble sideways and thereby cause a disastrous fall.

—Warren C. Matha, Editor

---

13  Chamberlin, Harry, *Riding and Schooling Horses*, Xenophon Press 2020.

*Figure 147.* Officers descend a slide in "Break Neck Canyon" at Ft. Riley. Notice the body forward with buttocks pushed well to the rear. Riders brace against the stirrups. Riders must descend the slide straight down and not at an angle. Photo reprinted with permission of the U.S. Cavalry and Armor Association.

*Figure 148.* The proper seat for negotiating slides and drop jumps frees the horse's hind quarters, helps control the rate of descent, places the rider's weight over the horse's forehand and thereby pushes the forelegs deep into the soil also to help control the rate of descent. 1942 Ft. Riley. U.S. Army photo.

*Figure 149.* The Cavalry Replacement Training Center graduate and Olympic Gold Medalist William Steinkraus at Hickstead displays Chamberlin's theory regarding how to descend a steep bank or slide in proper form. Photo reprinted with permission of L'Année Hippique/Jean Bridel.

# Chapter 10

## End of the Trail

**By Warren C. Matha, Editor**

Brigadier General Harry Dwight Chamberlin's career in Olympic and other international competition ends in 1932. He is 45. The requirements of his military career demand that he move on. In spite of the day to day demands of his military responsibilities, he continues to think about horsemanship. In his free time, he writes two books, both critically acclaimed:

*Riding and Schooling Horses* [Xenophon Press 2020]

"…the perfect handbook to horsemanship amply illustrated and scrupulously simple in language."—*The Washington Post.* [14]

"If you read only one book on riding, then it should be *Riding and Schooling Horses.*"[15]—Captain Paul Kendall, Instructor of Horsemanship, The Advanced Equitation Course, The Cavalry School, Ft. Riley.

*Training, Hunters, Jumpers, and Hacks.* [Xenophon Press 2019]

"…it is, in its field, the greatest book of the century. I know of nothing comparable produced abroad." [16]—Vladimir Littauer.

---

14  See *Washington Post* review 1935.
15  See Captain Paul Kendall, "Horseman's Primer," *Horse and Horseman Magazine*, November 1938.
16  Littauer, Vladimir S., *The Development of Modern Riding: The Story of Modern Riding from Renaissance Times to The Present.* Howell, 1991

The balance of his writings, this volume presents. After the attack on Pearl Harbor, he commands a unified task force in the South Pacific during the early days of World War II. His mission: to secure, fortify, and defend a chain of islands vital to keeping the lines of communication and supply open between Australia and the United States. He completes his mission in spectacular fashion. At the height of his military career and on the threshold of even greater military command responsibilities, he falls ill—a victim of colorectal cancer. It derails a brilliant career. Nonetheless, Army Chief of Staff General George C. Marshall holds Chamberlin in such high esteem that he keeps Chamberlin on active duty until the very end. On September 29, 1944, Brigadier General Harry D. Chamberlin passes away from the cancer at the early age of 57.

From the day in 1910 that he takes the oath on the plain at West Point, from the rank of Second Lieutenant to the rank of Brigadier General, Chamberlin remains one of the most competent, accomplished, respected, and well-liked military officers of his generation.

As solder, horseman, and military historian, Lt. Colonel Louis DiMarco (*ret.*) PhD writes:

> "… in an era that produced the greatest crop of outstanding soldiers in America's history, Harry Chamberlin was a soldier's soldier. His peers—men whose names will forever be associated with the great American military that won World War II—Marshall, MacArthur, Eisenhower, Bradley, Patton and Truscott among many others, respected him, admired him, and valued him as a colleague and friend."[17]

As an equestrian theorist, General Chamberlin ranks second to none in influence in America and second only to Federico Caprilli in influence internationally. As a military officer, horseman, horse trainer, instructor, Olympic competitor, and author, Chamberlin leaves a legacy of learning and original thinking equaled by few others in the field of equestrian sport. Horsemen and authors such as Vladimir Littauer, James Wofford, George H. Morris, and William Steinkraus all agree.

Chamberlin writes: "Nothing, aside from the dearest human relationships, can give the pleasure found in working and playing with a horse."[18] Hopefully, this volume has contributed to your knowledge of America's

---

17  Louis DiMarco, Lt. Col. Introduction to *General Chamberlin: America's Equestrian Genius*, Warren Matha, Xenophon Press, 2020.
18  Chamberlin, Harry D. Lt. Col., *Riding and Schooling Horses*, Xenophon Press, 2020.

equestrian genius—Harry Dwight Chamberlin; to your understanding of his riding and training concepts; to your knowledge of how the American way of riding evolved; and most of all, to the pleasure that you find "in working and playing with a horse."

*Figure 150.* Brigadier General Harry D. Chamberlin
May 19, 1887–September 29, 1944

# Bibliography

Ashton, John. "A Visit to Saumur," *The Cavalry Journal*, November-December 1925.

Augur, Lt. Col. Wayland and Jones, Jr. Lt. William P., "C.R.T.C At End of First Cycle," *The Cavalry Journal*, p. 42-47, July-August, 1941.

Beudant, Captain Etienne, *Horse Training Out-Door and High School.* Translated by Lt. Col. John A. Barry, U.S.Cavalry, Charles Scribner's Sons, 1931. [Xenophon Press 2014]

Burnett, Lt. Col. E. M. and Zeller, Major M. *"Horsemanship Training at our CRTC,"* The Cavalry Journal, p.53, January-February, 1942.

Cameron, Major George H., Fourteenth U.S. Cavalry, Assistant Commandant, *Notes on Equitation and Horse Training, translated from the French*, The Mounted Service School, Ft. Riley, Kansas 1910.

Cameron, Captain George H., Assistant Commandant, *Saumur Notes, Notes on Equitation and Horse Training, In Answer to the Examination Questions at the School of Application For Cavalry at Saumur, France,* Translated from the French, The Mounted Service School, Ft. Riley, Kansas 1909.

Carter, William H., General, United States Army, *Horses Saddles and Bridles*, The Lord Baltimore Press, The Friedenwald Company, 1906.

*Cavalry Drill Regulations*, United States Army, Adopted Oct. 3, 1891, D. Appleton and Company, New York, 1892.

Chamberlin, Brig. General Harry D., "Horsemastership, Four Exercises to Train Remounts and Reclaim Spoiled Horses," *The Cavalry Journal*, November-December, 1941.

Chamberlin, Brig. General Harry D. *Breaking, Training and Reclaiming Cavalry Horses,* Monograph published by the US Army, 2$^{nd}$ Cavalry Division, November 1941.

Chamberlin, Colonel Harry D., "Cavalry Training," *The Cavalry Journal*, September–October 1940.

Chamberlin, Colonel Harry D., "Crossing Rivers" *The Cavalry Journal*, January-February 1941.

Chamberlin, Harry D. Lt. Col., *Riding and Schooling Horses*, Derrydale Press, 1934.[Xenophon Press 2020]

Chamberlin, Harry D., Lt. Col. *Training Hunters, Jumpers, and Hacks*, Derrydale Press, 1937. [Xenophon Press 2019]

Chamberlin, Lt. Colonel Harry D., "The Conformation of Three-Day Horses," *The Cavalry Journal*, May-June 1937.

Chamberlin, Col. Harry D. The World's Best Rider Demonstrates Correct Technique I, *The Chicago Tribune, May 11,1936*.

Chamberlin, Col. Harry D. The World's Best Rider Demonstrates Correct Technique II, *The Chicago Tribune, June 7, 1936*.

Chamberlin, Major Harry D. "The Modern Seat," *The Cavalry Journal*, May-June, 1934.

Chamberlin, Major Harry D., "The Italian Cavalry School at Tor di Quinto" *The Cavalry Journal*, 1924.

Chamberlin, Major Harry D., "Observations on Riding and Training Jumpers," *The Rasp*, The Cavalry School, Ft. Riley, Kansas,1922.

Cavalry Board, "Report of the Cavalry Board on the Adoption of the Military Seat" *The Cavalry Journal*, 1929.

Cole, General John Tupper, *Introduction to Chamberlin Training Hunters, Jumpers, and Hacks*, Arco, Second Edition, 1973.

De Kerbrech, General François Faverot, *Methodical Dressage of the Riding Horse, From The last teachings of François Baucher As recalled by one of his students: General François Faverot de Kerbrech*. Translation by Michael L. M. Fletcher, Edited by Richard and Frances Williams, Xenophon Press LLC 2010.

DiMarco, Louis A., Major USA, *Brigadier General Harry D. Chamberlin, The Cavalry's Greatest Horseman 1887-1944*, unpublished manuscript.

Fillis, James, *Breaking and Riding with Military Commentaries. Aka Principles of Dressage and Equitation*, Xenophon Press, 2017.

Fort Riley, Kansas of The United States Army, *Historical and Pictorial Review, 1st Training Regiment, Cavalry Replacement Training Center*, The Army and Navy Publishing Company 1941.

French Department of War, *École d'Application de Cavalerie, Saumur, France*, 1923

International Olympic Committee, *The Official Report of the Games of the Xth Olympiad Los Angeles* 1932.

Kendall Captain Paul, "Horseman's Primer," *Horse and Horseman Magazine*, November 1938.

Littauer, Vladimir S. *Common Sense Horsemanship*, Second Edition, D.Van Nostrand Company, 1963.

Littauer, Vladimir S., *The Development of Modern Riding: The Story of Modern Riding From Renaissance Times to The Present.* Howell, 1991.

*Manuel of Equitation of the French Army*, 1912 translated by Lt. A. Chaffee, Jr., U.S. Cavalry, Mounted Service School, Ft. Riley. 1913.

Marshall, F.C., *Elements of Hippology*, U.S. Military Press at West Point, 1906.

Matha, Warren, *General Chamberlin: America's Equestrian Genius*, Xenophon Press, 2020.

Morris, George H., *Four Show Jumping Masters—Part 4:* Gordon Wright https://www.horsemagazine.com/thm/2010/07/four-showjumping-masters-part-4-gordon-wright/

Mott, Lt. Co. T. Bentley, Second Field Artillery, "Mounted Service School Rejects Caprilli...." *The Rasp*, Mounted Service School, 1912.

Ottevaere, James A., *American Military Horsemanship, The Military Riding Seat of the United States Cavalry*, Author House 2005.

Racinet, Jean-Claude, *Another Horsemanship: A Manual of Riding in the French Classical Tradition.* Xenophon Press, 1994.

Racinet, Jean-Claude, *Racinet Explains Baucher*, Xenophon Press, 1997.

Randolph, Captain Thomas J., The Cavalry School Library, The Cavalry Journal, November-December, 1936.

Robinson, Brig. General Donald A., The Cavalry Replacement Training Center, The Cavalry Journal, March-April 1942.

Santini, Captain Piero, *Riding Reflections*, Huntington Press, 1933.

Santini, Captain Piero, *The Forward Impulse*, Huntington Press, 1936. [Xenophon Press 2016]

The Cavalry School, *Horsemanship and Horsemastership, Volume 1 Education of the Rider, Education of the Horse,* Academic Division, Fort Riley, Kansas 1942 (FM-25-5).

The Xth Olympiad Committee of the Games of Los Angeles, *The Games of the Xth Olympiad, Los Angeles 1932*, Official Report, U.S.S. 1932, LTD, 1933.

The United States Department of War, *Drill Regulations, Cavalry 1891*, U.S Cavalry, adopted October 3, 1891.

Wythe, Major George, Infantry, United States Army, *Report of the Games Committee*, United States Army, 1919.

Wythe, Major George, "*The Inter-Allied Games,*" Published by the Games Committee July, 1919. https://ia800201.us.archive.org/18/items/cu31924014114353/cu31924014114353.pdf.

Yale, Major Wesley W., "Cavalry Instructional Methods," *The Cavalry Journal*, November-December 1940.

# Xenophon Press Library

www.XenophonPress.com
Xenophon Press is dedicated to the preservation
of classical equestrian literature.
We bring both new and old works to English-speaking riders.

*30 Years with Master Nuno Oliveira,* Henriquet 2011
*A Rider's Survival from Tyranny,* de Kunffy 2012
*Another Horsemanship,* Racinet 1994
*Austrian Art of Riding,* Poscharnigg 2015
*Broken or Beautiful: The Struggle of Modern Dressage,* Barbier 2020
*Classic Show Jumping: the de Nemethy Method,* de Nemethy 2016
*Divide and Conquer Book 1,* Lemaire de Ruffieu 2016
*Divide and Conquer Book 2,* Lemaire de Ruffieu 2017
*Dressage for the 21st Century,* Belasik 2001
*Dressage in the French Tradition,* Diogo de Bragança 2011
*Dressage Principles and Techniques: A Blueprint for the Serious Rider,* Tavora 2018
*Dressage Principles Illuminated, Expanded Edition,* de Kunffy 2020
*Dressage Sabbatical: A Year of Riding with Classical Master Paul Belasik,* Caslar 2016
*École de Cavalerie Part II,* Robichon de la Guérinière 1992, 2015
*Equine Osteopathy: What the Horses Have Told Me,* Giniaux 2014
*Fragments from the Writings of Max Ritter von Weyrother,* Fane 2017
*François Baucher: The Man and His Method,* Baucher/Nelson 2013
*General Chamberlin: America's Equestrian Genius,* Matha 2020
*Great Horsewomen of the 19th Century in the Circus,* Nelson 2015
*Gymnastic Exercises for Horses Volume II,* Eleanor Russell 2013
*H. Dv. 12 German Cavalry Manual of Horsemanship,* Reinhold 2014
*Handbook of Jumping Essentials,* Lemaire de Ruffieu 2015
*Handbook of Riding Essentials,* Lemaire de Ruffieu 2015

*Healing Hands,* Giniaux, DVM 1998
*Horse Training: Outdoors and High School,* Beudant 2014
*I, Siglavy,* Asay 2018
*Learning to Ride,* Santini 2016
*Legacy of Master Nuno Oliveira,* Millham 2013
*Lessons in Lightness: Expanded Edition,* Mark Russell 2019
*Methodical Dressage of the Riding Horse,* Faverot de Kerbrech 2010
*Military Equitation or, A Method of Breaking Horses, and Teaching Soldiers to Ride,* Pembroke, and *A Treatise on Military Equitation,* Tyndale 2018
*Principles of Dressage and Equitation, a.k.a. Breaking and Riding,* Fillis 2017
*Racinet Explains Baucher,* Racinet 1997
*Riding and Schooling Horses,* Chamberlin 2020
*Riding by Torchlight,* Cord 2019
*Science and Art of Riding in Lightness,* Stodulka 2015
*The Art of Riding a Horse,* D'Eisenberg 2015
*The Art of Traditional Dressage, Volume I DVD,* de Kunffy 2013
*The Chamberlin Reader,* Chamberlin/Matha, 2020
*The de Nemethy Method: A training seminar,* 8 DVD set, de Nemethy 2019
*The Ethics and Passions of Dressage Expanded Edition,* de Kunffy 2013
*The Forward Impulse,* Santini 2016
*The Gymnasium of the Horse,* Steinbrecht 2018
*The Horses, a novel,* Elaine Walker 2015
*The Italian Tradition of Equestrian Art,* Tomassini 2014
*The Maneige Royal,* de Pluvinel 2010, 2015
*The New Method of Dressing Horses,* Cavendish 2020
*The Portuguese School of Equestrian Art,* de Oliveira/da Costa 2012
*The Spanish Riding School & Piaffe and Passage,* Decarpentry 2013
*To Amaze the People with Pleasure and Delight,* Walker 2015
*Total Horsemanship,* Racinet 1999
*Training Hunters, Jumpers, and Hacks,* Chamberlin 2019
*Training with Master Nuno Oliveira,* 2 DVD set, Eleanor Russell 2016
*Truth in the Teaching of Master Nuno Oliveira,* Eleanor Russell 2015
*Wisdom of Master Nuno Oliveira,* de Coux 2012

www.ingramcontent.com/pod-product-compliance
Lightning Source LLC
Chambersburg PA
CBHW060500240426
43661CB00006B/860